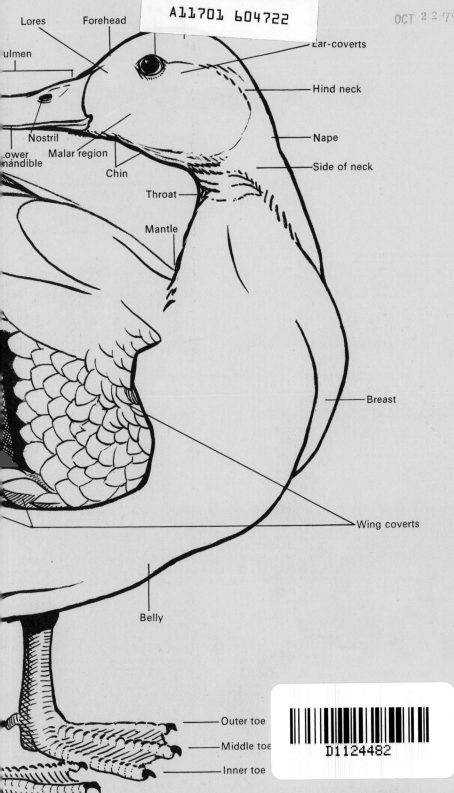

Lores

Forehead

Ear-coverts

ulmen

Hind neck

Nape

Nostril

Side of neck

Lower
mandible

Malar region

Chin

Throat

Mantle

Breast

Wing coverts

Belly

Outer toe

Middle toe

Inner toe

Webbing

WILDFOWL
of the World

ERIC SOOTHILL
and
PETER WHITEHEAD

Photographs by
Ardea Photographics, with Eric Soothill and
Joe Blossom

BLANDFORD PRESS
Poole   Dorset

First published 1978

Copyright © 1978 Blandford Press Ltd.
Link House, West Street
Poole, Dorset BH15 1LL

ISBN 0 7137 0863 8

British Library Cataloguing in Publication Data

Soothill, Eric
  Wildfowl of the world.
  1. Waterfowl
  I. Title II. Whitehead, Peter
  598.4'1   QL696.A52

  ISBN 0–7137–0863–8

Set in 9 on 10 pt Baskerville
Printed and bound in Great Britain by
Cox & Wyman Ltd.,
London, Fakenham and Reading

Contents

Acknowledgements

Most of the colour photographs in this book were supplied by Ardea Photographics. Full illustration credits are as follows:

Ardea/Kenneth Fink 31, 35, 41, 43, 47, 49, 53, 57, 63, 71, 75, 77, 79, 83, 85, 91, 101, 103, 105, 107, 109, 113, 119, 125, 131, 133, 135, 141, 143, 145, 147, 149, 151, 155, 157, 159, 161, 163, 165, 167, 169, 173, 175, 177, 181, 183, 185, 191, 193, 203, 207, 209, 213, 215, 219, 223, 227, 231, 233, 235, 237, 241, 245, 249, 253, 257, 259, 261, 263, 265, 267, 271, 273, 275; Ardea/Peter Stein 45, 111, 171, 239; Ardea/Ian Beames 55, 93, 225; Ardea/Peter Laub 59, 89, 117; Ardea/F. Collet 51, 279; Ardea/Clen Haagner 29, 281; Ardea/J. A. Bailey 277; Ardea/Graeme Chapman 137; Ardea/M. D. England 81; Ardea/Don Hadden 197; Ardea/Gary Jones 211; Ardea/C. Mylne 81; Ardea/Syd Roberts 247; Ardea/Richard Vaughan 199; Ardea 221.

Joe Blossom 27, 33, 61, 73, 115, 123, 127, 139, 153, 179, 187, 189, 195, 201, 217, 243, 251, 269; Eric Soothill 39, 65, 67, 69, 95, 97, 99, 121, 129, 229; Roy Rhodes 205; B. A. Crosby 255.

Joe Blossom also provided the line illustrations for the book.

The distribution maps were drawn by Peter Sarson and Tony Bryan.

Dedication

*To the memory
of our parents*

Foreword

Out of our dim and distant unknown past, and throughout human history, the wildfowl of the world have been a part of the intimate furnishings of our environment: objects of fascination and fancy, of ritual and legend, of meaning far beyond mere provender for the family table. Those splendid skeins of geese we see streaming across a springtime evening sky draw a response from us so deep we cannot fathom it. Could it be, we ask something in our own genetic memory that responds to sights and sounds aeons older than any of us? Is this not an ancient marvel, born anew in us today?

We know the recent history, recognizing these same threshing wings, this same fluid grace, in the jade carvings of ancient China; we see how the nameless artists of the Nile painted parades of geese across the walls of tombs and temples; we know how artisans of many lands and cultures have fashioned gold and silver into precious wildfowl ornaments for kings and princes. And we remember that Zeus, king of all the gods, became a swan for Leda.

A few species of ducks and geese have been domesticated for thousands of years, but the species that live free far outnumber those few; it is the wild legions that stir our imagination and excite our aesthetic sensitivity. Yet today it is not only the hunter and provider who thrills to the dawn flight of the wigeon along the rivercourse, or the plunge of the teal into the marsh. Millions who have never owned or fired a weapon now share the marvels of the wildfowl quest. Hunting with camera, binoculars or simply with eyes and ears, they experience the bugling of swans high overhead above a dawn mist, the helter-skelter of a flock of pintail rocketing in to a woodland pool, an arrow of scaup skudding low over a wintry sea. Each of us, as enthusiasts, have our own gallery of images that will never fade. For me, perhaps, a field on the edge of the Senegal River with the sky a deepening purple, as tens of thousands of Garganey sweep overhead in a rush of wings like endless surf, almost invisible; of Snow Geese overhead in New Jersey, of eiders drifting across a grey North Sea, or of a lake in California with a raft of 17,000 Northern Shovelers. These are messages the world is sending us: life is abundant, life is good!

This book is a rarity. It is not merely filled with the beauty and poetry of wildfowl, it is filled with knowledge. It is a useful book, authentic, accurate, comprehensive and it presents concise, yet precise accounts of almost every species of goose, swan, screamer, and duck found anywhere in the world, and tells where to look for them. And the gallery of colour portraits is unsurpassed.

While we turn the pages, to marvel at the images of the birds themselves and find the answers to our questions, let us not forget that these magnificent creatures are here today by our grace and at our mercy. Whether we like it or not, we now possess, as never before, the weapons of their destruction. No longer are they the feeble bows and arrows or the fowling pieces of yesterday. Today's weapons are far more insidious and difficult to control. They are the oil spill, the destruction of marsh and estuary and swamp and shore, the chemical (and atomic) pollution of air and water.

It would be preposterous to suggest that we must save the environment solely to ensure the future of our wildfowl, but in a world in which they cannot survive, the human race cannot live.

The cause of the environment is everyone's concern. There is no more vital, or urgent cause than the health of the world we share – with the wonderful wildfowl and with all living things.

Robert Arbib
National Audubon Society
New York, June 1978

Using the Book

The book has been planned so that it can be used on a world-wide basis by all those who are interested in wildfowl.

The classification and main characteristics of the wildfowl families are explained in the 'Introduction' and there then follow chapters giving details of places where wildfowl can be seen and studied – both in the wild and in public and private collections.

The main part of the book is the detailed descriptions, photographs and distribution maps for 128 species, together with additional notes on sub-species and related minor species. These additional notes are located with the descriptive notes for the main species. The colour photograph is always that of the main species described.

The common and Latin names are given for each species and alternative common names appear in parentheses. The species illustrated and described can be found by use of the indexes of both English and Latin names of all the birds covered by the book.

The Distribution Maps

Area where a species is known to breed. It may be sedentary or make local movement within this breeding area. Birds of the Northern Hemisphere tend to migrate to the southern part of their breeding area, whilst birds of the Southern Hemisphere can be expected to make a similar migration to the northern part of their breeding area.

Area where a species occurs during winter or on migration, but where it is not known to breed.

Some species, although having wintering quarters, will still remain within their breeding areas. This is a rather complex situation and is not indicated on the maps.

Wherever possible, the distribution of sub-species has been included on the map *incorporated* with that of the main species. However, this has only been done in cases where no possible confusion could arise. The maps should *always* be read in conjunction with the 'Distribution' section for any bird.

Introduction

The natural order Anseriformes comprises the world's ducks, geese, swans
and screamers. There are over a
hundred and forty species in all, the
· exact number depending on how many
of the more controversial forms are considered to be full species. The order is
divided into three families:

ANHIMIDAE

Contains the three
species of Screamer,
restricted to tropical
and sub-tropical
South America.

PARANYROCIDAE

An extinct family
represented by a
single species
known only as a
fossil from the
Lower Miocene
period.

ANATIDAE

A large family with world-wide
distribution and containing all
the species generally termed
'wildfowl' in Britain, or
'waterfowl' in North America; in
other words the 'ducks, geese and
swans'.

The Anatidae are further divided
into three sub-families.

ANSERANATINAE

A sub-family with only
one genus containing a
single species, the rather
primitive Magpie Goose
of the Australasian
region which has toes
only slightly webbed
and which moults its
flight feathers
progressively, so that it
is never totally flightless.

ANSERINAE

Contains six genera
which include the whist-
ling ducks or tree ducks,
the swans, and the true
geese.

ANATINAE

The largest sub-family
containing all the
sheldgeese, shelducks,
dabbling ducks, diving
ducks, sea ducks,
perching ducks,
saw-billed ducks,
stifftails, and steamer
ducks.

These sub-families are divided again into tribes consisting of one or more genera, and
each genus contains at least one, usually a number of different species.

General Characteristics

All wildfowl possess certain characteristics which set them apart from other groups of birds. Basically, they are equipped for an aquatic or semi-aquatic existence, having the front three toes connected by webbing, with the hind two placed a little higher. Only the Magpie Goose and Hawaiian Goose have partially webbed feet. All species lay white or pale coloured, unspotted eggs and have nidifugous young covered in thick down. With the exception of the Magpie Goose, and possibly some of the South American Sheldgeese, they have the notable characteristic of shedding the flight feathers of the wings in a post-breeding moult. This leaves them in a flightless condition for a period of 3 or 4 weeks and is usually timed to coincide with the fledging period of the young.

The bills of wildfowl are alone sufficiently distinctive to avoid confusion with other bird families. They are usually blunt, somewhat spatulate in shape, covered with a thin, soft membrane, with a harder tip or 'nail' on the upper mandible. The bill and tongue have special characteristics developed to suit particular methods of feeding. The edges of the tongue have small spiny processes and the edges of the bill have rows of horny lamellae – fine plates or tooth-like serrations. In geese these provide serrated cutting edges suitable for grazing, in some of the ducks they are used to filter fine particles of food from water or mud, being twice as numerous in dabbling ducks than in diving ducks. In the Mergansers, which have a much harder bill, they are of saw-tooth formation, ideal for gripping fish.

Another common feature is the thick, waterproof plumage, with a dense coat of insulating down underneath. The preen gland is large and tufted.

In addition to the characteristics which are common to all the species, thus uniting them into one family, there are often features peculiar to only some of the family. These features are sufficiently distinctive to necessitate the division of the family into sub-families.

Swans and Geese

Both belong to the same sub-family Anserinae. There is no dimorphism in the plumage, which is usually of fairly uniform colouring. All but two of the swans have completely white adult plumage, the exceptions being the Black Swan of Australia and the Black-necked Swan of South America. Juvenile swans are normally brown or grey. Most of the true geese are sombrely coloured in blacks, whites, greys and browns, and again the sexes are very similar in appearance. Most are fairly large birds, with the exception of the Whistling Ducks which are also included in this sub-family. There is only one moult per year, so no 'eclipse' plumage as in most ducks after the breeding season. The swans of the Northern Hemisphere, belonging to the genus *Cygnus*, includes the heaviest of all flying birds. Maximum weight recorded for the Mute Swan is over 22 kg, and the heaviest known Trumpeter Swan weighed 17 kg. Long tapering bodies and long necks are a common feature, some of the swans having necks equal in length to the body and sometimes even longer.

Geese are mainly terrestrial in their feeding behaviour, their strong bill with 'toothed' edges to the upper mandible being well adapted for grazing. They are divided into two fairly well-defined genera – the 'grey geese' of the genus *Anser*, and the 'black geese' of the genus *Branta*.

Whistling Ducks

Very similar to swans and geese in general behaviour and in anatomical structure, but are much smaller birds. They have long necks, usually held erect, and broad rounded wings with notched or emarginated primaries which produce a 'whirring' sound in flight. Two of the species have wavy furrows on the neck, similar to those of geese in the genus *Anser*. The males share in the incubation, as does the Black Swan, in addition to helping care for the brood, and pairs usually mate for life, as do the swans and geese.

Ducks

The sub-family Anatinae, besides being the largest is also the most diverse, containing a number of tribes with their own distinct differences, but all possessing to a greater or lesser degree a number of common features which qualify them as 'ducks'. They are usually smaller than swans and geese, with shorter necks and narrower, more pointed wings, and rapid wing beats. There is often a conspicuous sexual dimorphism in plumage, with the males being much more brightly coloured, or having striking feather modifications. There are two body moults per cycle, the most noticeable feature of which is the 'eclipse' plumage. This is the plumage assumed by the drakes during the breeding season, and closely resembles the normal drab plumage of the females and immatures. Another plumage feature is the speculum or wing mirror resulting from the bright metallic colouring of the secondary feathers.

Ducks also exhibit sexual dimorphism in voice; this is due to the presence, in males only, of a *traceal bulla* – an asymmetrical enlargement of the windpipe causing the distinct difference in the calls of male and female.

The elaborate courtship displays of ducks are not shared by the swans and geese, which have more simple rituals, and the pair bond between ducks is

much more temporary and seldom extends beyond one breeding season. The males of this sub-family do not share in incubating the eggs, nor do they normally assist in rearing the young.

The various tribes of ducks each have their own peculiarities which set them apart from the rest. A few of the most important features are summarized below.

Sheldgeese and Shelducks

Somewhat intermediate between geese and ducks. The genus *Chloephaga* consists of five species of goose-like grazing birds found only in South America. Some Shelduck will also graze in addition to dabbling and up-ending. Both males and females in this tribe are usually brightly coloured and in some species they are very much alike. Voices however, are dissimilar, the males whistling and the females cackling. There is a metallic green speculum, but usually no eclipse plumage. The downy young are all very similar to each other with the same basic pattern of black and white plumage.

Dabbling ducks

The majority of dabbling ducks are placed in the large genus *Anas*, which includes Mallards, Teal, Pintails, Wigeon and Shovelers; they are also known as River Ducks, Surface-feeding Ducks, or Puddle Ducks. They are mostly small-to-medium sized with short legs set well back on the body and so they are not such capable walkers as the Sheldgeese and Shelducks. They have a horizontal stance and progress with a definite waddle. Feeding is mainly from the surface of the water, or by up-ending, while some species are regular grazers. Although capable of diving, they rarely do so, except to escape danger. They frequent mainly fresh or brackish water but occur on the seas during migration. Sexual dimorphism in plumage is most marked in the

[3]

Holarctic Region and particularly in those species which make long migrations. In the Southern Hemisphere most males have lost their bright colouring and closely resemble females at all times of the year. Most have fairly long pointed wings and are able to take off from land or water at a very steep angle, unlike the diving ducks with their heavier wing loading. They also have a slower wing beat than the diving ducks.

Courtship displays are highly developed, often commencing in the winter flocks, and breeding takes place in the first year. Nests are usually located on the ground, well concealed, but sometimes at a considerable distance from water. The downy young are generally similar and much like Mallard ducklings, with dark stripes on the head, and light spots on wing and rump. Voices of male and female are different, the males making 'whistling' or 'grunting' sounds, the female having a harsh 'quack'. Only the Mallard in this tribe has been domesticated.

Diving ducks

Medium-sized ducks of chiefly freshwater habitats, with rotund, heavy bodies. The wings are less pointed than the dabbling ducks with faster, whistling wing beats, and a long take-off run is required to become airborne. The legs are short, the feet large and positioned towards the rear of the body; adaptations to a highly aquatic way of life. Consequently diving ducks walk awkwardly and with an upright stance. There are two families, *Aythya* and *Netta*, the latter being somewhat intermediate between dabbling and diving ducks, obtaining some of their food on the surface. The family *Aythya* are all expert divers and obtain practically all their food underwater.

Members of the tribe are less brightly coloured than most dabbling ducks and do not have a metallic speculum. Voices are dissimilar, the males having various 'whistling' notes used mainly during courtship, the females do not quack but make various harsh 'croaking' noises.

Gregarious at most times of the year, in winter the flocks are sometimes predominantly of one sex only. Scaup are almost exclusively salt-water birds in winter. Nests are usually over shallow water or very close to the edge.

Downy young are rather similar to those of dabbling ducks but lack the stripes.

Sea ducks

Included under this heading are the Eiders, Scoters, Goldeneyes and Mergansers. They occur in both fresh water and salt water – although the Eiders and Scoters are more or less confined to marine habitats, except during the breeding season. Apart from the rare Brazilian Merganser, the tribe is restricted to the Northern Hemisphere. They are mostly medium-sized ducks and all are very proficient divers. The body is similar in shape to other diving ducks but slightly more elongated, most noticeably in the Mergansers. The wings are somewhat shorter and produce a 'whistling' sound in flight, more pronounced in some species than others. Take-off is rather laborious for most species, flight heavy and usually low over the water but not slow. The Long-tailed Duck is reputedly one of the fastest fliers of all ducks. The wings are also used in diving and propulsion underwater by Eiders, Scoters, Long-tailed Duck and Harlequin.

All feed almost entirely on animal matter in the form of molluscs, crustaceans and fish. Feeding in flocks is normal and most species are highly gregarious for much of the year.

Migrations are not as lengthy as in most holarctic species, the major winter requirement being little more than ice-free water for feeding. Moult migrations are also a well-developed feature. Plumage of the drakes is very variable, from the mainly black Scoters to the impressive-looking Harlequins. The

Long-tailed Duck (Oldsquaw) is noteworthy for having three distinct plumages during the year. There is no metallic speculum except in the Harlequin.

The bills exhibit a wide range of different shapes, the deep bills of Eiders and Scoters swollen at the base to accommodate the large salt glands and the long, narrow, serrated bills of the Merganser well adapted for catching and gripping fish.

Nests occur in a wide variety of situations; on the ground, or in holes on the ground, or trees, near to water but sometimes a considerable distance away.

There is no marked uniformity of appearance in the downy young as with dabbling ducks. Two or three years are required to reach maturity.

Perching ducks

The perching ducks of the tribe *Cairinini* are a very diverse group exhibiting a wide range of sizes from the Spur-winged Goose, specimens of which may weigh almost 10 kg, to the Pygmy Geese or Cotton Teal of the tropical genus *Nettapus*, some of which weigh less than 200 g. These are the smallest of the wildfowl. Most species of the tribe inhabit well wooded areas for at least part of the year and their distribution is tropical and sub-tropical. One species, the Mandarin, has been introduced to Europe, whilst the Muscovy Duck has been widely domesticated.

All species perch in trees or on fallen logs, some more readily than others, and nests are usually in holes in trees, even those of the largest species if suitable holes are available. There is a spur-like projection on the bend of the wing and the feet are equipped with strong claws.

Bills are goose-like, a number of species being termed 'goose' in the common names. Males of the family *Aix* (Wood duck and Mandarin) have splendid breeding plumages.

Downy young generally resembles those of dabbling ducks, but are very agile climbers.

Stifftails

This tribe consists of the Black-headed Duck of South America, the Musk Duck of Australia, and six typical Stifftails of the genus *Oxyura*. They are fresh-water species distributed mainly in the Southern Hemisphere but with representatives on all continents. They are expert divers with short, rounded bodies and long stiff tail feathers which provide directional stability for underwater movement. The feet are large and placed well to the rear of the body, so most walk with some difficulty and are seldom seen on land.

Flight is not strong, usually low down and with rapid beating of short rounded wings. Frequently nocturnal in habits.

Males of *Oxyura* in breeding plumage are more or less chestnut, with brilliant blue bills. Displays are elaborate.

The Black-headed Duck is the only member of the *Anatidae* known to be invariably brood parasitic, although some of the *Oxyura* occasionally deposit eggs in nests other than their own. Nests of all species are usually in thick aquatic vegetation, sometimes old nests of other species are used. Eggs are very large in relation to the size of the birds.

Steamer ducks

An aberrant tribe inhabiting the southern parts of South America and sharing certain characteristics with the South American Sheldgeese. There are three species, two of which are flightless, but which are able to propel themselves very rapidly over the water by paddling with both wings and feet. They are excellent divers and feed mainly on marine molluscs and crustaceans.

Important Wetlands for Wildfowl*

Afghanistan

Lake Ab-i-Istada

Over 50,000 ducks use the lakes on passage. It is also used by large numbers of Cranes. In March 1970 these included seventy-six Siberian Cranes *Grus leucogeranus*, which represents a large proportion of the remaining world population.

Alaska

The north-west coast is the only breeding ground for the Emperor Goose *Anser canagicus* in the whole of the North American continent, with the Outer Aleutian Islands providing the primary North American wintering grounds. Other breeding geese include the Black Brent Goose *Brenta nigricans*, and in the northern half of Alaska the White-fronted Goose *Anser albifrons*.

Several species of Canada Geese are also found breeding:

Aleutian Canada Goose *Branta canadensis leucopareia*.

Taverner's Canada Goose *B. c. tavernerii*.

Lesser Canada Goose *B. c. parvipes* in eastern Alaska.

Vancouver Canada Goose *B. c. fulva* in coastal areas of south-east Alaska.

Dusky Canada Goose *B. c. occidentalis* in the Copper River delta, south-central Alaska coast.

Cackling Canada Goose *B. c. minima* which nests in a small goose district along the Bering Sea between the Yukon and Kuskokwim Rivers.

The Trumpeter Swan *Cygnus buc-*

*Dimensions, etc. given in 'local' units.

cinator is also a breeding species and the Whistling Swan *Cygnus columbianus* breeds in remote tundra.

The Scaup *Aythya marila* breeds on the Bering Sea coast of Alaska and the Lesser Scaup *Aythya affinis* in eastern Alaska.

Two other ducks which breed, but in forested regions of Alaska are the Canvasback *Aythya valisheria* and the Goldeneye *Bucephala clangula*.

Albania

At the mouth of the Drini there is the Kune Reserve which comprises the Kune lagoon, the mouth of the Drini and the surrounding land. Many species of duck breed there and large flocks congregate to winter in the area.

Australia

Cobourg Peninsula

Situated north-west of Darwin on the Northern Territory coastline. In 1961 some 1920 km² of the peninsula were classified as a flora and fauna reserve, and as a wildlife sanctuary in 1962. Its numerous mangrove swamps play an important role as breeding and wintering sites for many indigenous species of waterfowl, including the endemic Magpie Goose *Anseranas semipalmata*.

Austria

Neusiedler See and Seewinkel

A lake area of 32,000 ha (47° 40'–58' N, 16° 40'–17° 00' E), open water 18,000 ha.

Seewinkel comprises eighty alkaline ponds.

The Neusiedler See is a shallow fresh-water lake with a broad belt of

Phragmites (up to 6 km wide in places). It is considered to be one of the most important Central European wetlands.

Around the lake and in the vicinity of the alkaline ponds are important breeding grounds for Grey Lag Goose *Anser anser*, Mallard *Anas platyrhynchos*, Garganey *A. querquedula*, Gadwall *A. strepera* and Ferruginous Duck *Aythya nyroca*.

It is also used as a moulting area by Pintail *Anas acuta*, Gadwall *Anas strepera*, Shoveler *Anas clypeata*, Grey Lag Goose *Anser anser* and others. Sometimes over 100,000 geese use it as autumn and wintering quarters, with average peak populations of White-fronted Goose *Anser albifrons* (30,000), Bean Goose *Anser fabilis* (10,000) and Grey Lag Goose *Anser anser* (6,000). Average peaks for ducks wintering there are Mallard *Anas platyrynchos* (10,000), and (1,250 each of the following species), Gadwall *A. strepera*, Pintail *A. acuta* and Shoveler *A. clypeata*.

Rheindelta in the Bodensee

An area of 7,500 ha at the eastern end of the Bodensee and Rheindelta. Consisting of open water and large reedbeds and marshes. It is of particular importance as a breeding area for Anatidae such as Gadwall *Anas strepera*, Shoveler *A. clypeata*, Garganey *A. querquedula* and Red-crested Pochard *Netta rufina*.

Bangladesh

About 80 per cent of Bangladesh is criss-crossed by the Ganges, the Brahmaputra and the Meghna. It is in fact one of the world's largest river deltas, most of which is flat and riverine with countless marshy areas and lakes called 'bils', 'haors' or 'baors'. The Bay of Bengal washes some 480 km of its coastline and there are many offshore islands both large and small. Situated in the south-eastern corner are the largest mangrove forests in the world – the Sunderbans with an area of 5,771 km^2.

Expeditions in 1966 and 1967, under the leadership of Guy Mountfort, noted the following wildfowl.

Hakaluki Haor

Indian Tree Duck *Dendrocygna javanica*, Grey Lag Goose *Anser anser*, Pintail *Anas acuta*, European Teal *A. crecca*, Spot-bill Duck *A. poecilorhyncha*, Gadwall *A. strepera*, Garganey *A. querquedula*, Shoveler *A. clypeata*, Pochard *Aythya ferina*, Tufted Duck *A. fuligula* and Indian Pygmy Goose *Nettapus coromandelianus*.

Hail Haor

Indian Tree Duck *Dendrocygna javanica*, Fulvous Tree Duck *D. bicolor*, Bar-headed Goose *Anser indicus*, *Anas acuta*, *A. crecca*, *A. strepera*, *A. querquedula*, *Aythya fuligula* and *Nettapus coromandelianus*.

Belgium

There are four wetland areas of international importance for some European or Eurasian populations of waterfowl but the Belgian wetlands cannot be compared with the famous sites to be found in neighbouring countries.

These four areas are:

1 The coastal region, including the Zwin and the esturay of the IJzer, etc.
2 Damme and the surrounding polder north of Bruges – wintering grounds for wild geese.
3 The flood plain of the IJzer which includes the Blankaart Lake.
4 The Kalmthout heath.

There are many smaller sites, important only at a national level, that also have populations of Anatidae.

[7]

Bulgaria

Lake Sreberna

Breeding species include: Mute Swan *Cygnus olor*, Grey Lag Goose *Anser anser*, Red-crested Pochard *Netta rufina*, Mallard *Anas platyrhynchos*, Gadwall *A. strepera* and Ferruginous Duck *Aythya nyroca*. The Sreberna–See Reserve has the only breeding colony of Dalmatian Pelican *Pelecanus crispus*, in Bulgaria.

The marshes of Arkutino, Djavolsko and Alepu, situated near the Black Sea coast also provide nesting sites for a variety of wildfowl.

Canada

The Delta Waterfowl Research Station

Situated at the south end of Lake Manitoba at the edge of the famous Delta Marsh, one of the largest pristine marshes in the Canadian Wheat Belt and 75 miles north-west of Winnipeg. It was in 1931 that James Bell Ford started the Delta Station, the marsh covers about 95 sq. miles and is one of the finest waterfowl breeding areas in Canada. Ten species of duck breed there regularly: Mallard *Anas platyrhynchos*, Gadwall *A. strepera*, Blue-winged Teal *A. discors*, Shoveler *A. clypeata*, Pintail *A. acuta*, Redhead *Aythya americana*, Canvasback *A. valisheria*, Lesser Scaup *A. affinis*, White-winged Scoter *Melanitta fusca deglandi*, and Ruddy Duck *Oxyura jamaicensis*. Also breeding are a few American wigeon *Anas americana*, Green-winged Teal *A. crecca* and Goldeneye *Bucephala clangula*.

Waterfowl damage to Canadian grain, based on a report by the Canadian Wildlife Services, seems to have existed ever since the early settlers first cropped the land. Waterfowl fed on upland grain fields and severe damage became prevalent in the mid-1940s. In all probability the two main causes were that grain was allowed to ripen in the swath before threshing and there was an increased acreage of durum, wheats and barley, much preferred by ducks.

Crop damage is caused mainly by Mallards and Pintails, with the Mallards doing most damage, being more of them and the fact that they remain later in autumn and have a greater tendency to field feed. Ducks, generally waste more than they eat by trampling and fouling. During 1959 the damage caused in the three prairie provinces was estimated at 12·6 million Canadian dollars. Therefore, a small reduction in crop damage of 5 per cent could save a million dollars annually.

Breeding species found in areas of Arctic Canada are listed below.

Southampton Island

Whistling Swan *Cygnus columbianus*, Canada Goose *Branta canadensis hutchinsi*, Brent Goose *Branta bernicla*, Snow Goose and Blue Goose *Anser caerulescens*, Ross's Goose *Anser rossi*, Long-tailed Duck (Old Squaw) *Clangula hyemalis*, Common Eider *Somateria mollissima v-nigra*, King Eider *Somateria spectabilis*.

Mackenzie Delta

Whistling Swan *Cygnus columbianus*, Canada Goose *Branta canadensis leucoparia*, Black Brent Goose *Branta nigricans*, White-fronted Goose *Anser albifrons*, Snow Goose and Blue Goose *Anser caerulescens*, Pintail *Anas acuta*, Long-tailed Duck (Old Squaw) *Clangula hyemalis*, Red-breasted Merganser *Mergus serrator*.

Perry River

Whistling Swan *Cygnus columbianus*, Canada Goose *Branta canadensis parvipes*, Brent Goose *Branta bernicla*, Black Brent Goose *Branta nigricans*, White-fronted Goose *Anser albifrons*, Snow Goose and Blue Goose *Anser caerulescens*, Ross's Goose *Anser rossi*, Long-tailed Duck (Old Squaw) *Clangula hyemalis*, Common Eider *Somateria mollissima borealis*, King Eider *Somateria spectabilis*.

Czechoslovakia

Velký a Malý Tisý State Nature Reserve

Established in 1957 and is part of the extensive pond complex in the Třeboň basin of southern Bohemia, covering an area of 706 ha, of which there is a water surface of 342 ha. The reserve is made up of nine ponds both large and small plus a multitude of islets, creeks, peninsulas, waterlogged willow undergrowth, reeds and small woods.

Apart from providing nesting sites for a variety of species it also offers refuge to ducks and geese during the autumn hunting season and the spring migration.

Lednické Rybniky State Nature Reserve

Established in 1953 near Lednice in the Dyje valley of southern Movaria. It covers an area of 552 ha comprising five large ponds with the surrounding woodland providing 300 ha. As it lies on the main migration route from northern Europe to the south, the reserve is a very important refuge for migrants. In autumn, some 5,000 to 10,000 geese (mainly Bean Geese *Anser fabilis* and White-fronted Geese *A. albifrons*) gather, as well as tens of thousands of ducks.

Denmark

Ulvedybet

A wetland site (57° 04′ N, 9° 34′ E) of 900 ha on the bank of Limfjord in Northern Jutland. The wildfowl reserve is mainly shallow water and marshland and is an important habitat for migrating ducks and geese. Numbers of up to 30,000 to 40,000 birds gather at one time, being chiefly Mallard *Anas platyrhynchos*, European Teal *A. crecca*, European wigeon *A. penelope*, Grey Lag Goose *Anser anser* and Bean Goose *A. fabilis*.

Vejlerne

Separated from Ulvedybet by 25 km of less-favourable habitat is this other reserve (57° 04′ N, 9° oo′ E), with an area of 6,000 ha. It comprises large, wet grazed meadows, lagoons and marshland and is important during migration for many thousands of ducks such as *Anas platyrhyncos*, *A. crecca*, and *A. penelope*. Grey Lag Goose *Anser anser* and many ducks use it as a moulting area.

Nissum Fjord

Including the Felsted Kog Reserve (56° 20′ N, 8° 10′ E), a shallow fjord containing extensive reedbeds and surrounded by meadows. It provides a breeding area for Mallard *Anas platyrynchos*, Pintail *A. acuta*, Gargany *A. querquedula* and Shoveler *A. clypeata*. The large numbers of Brent Geese *Branta bernicla hrota* (up to 4,000 individuals) make it Denmark's main resting place for that species and important as a resting place for the Pink-footed Goose *Anser brachyrhyncus*.

Ethiopia

Large numbers of waterfowl are known to be supported by the lakes at Akaki, Alemeya, Awasa, Basaaka, Debra Zeit, Koka and Tendaho, but it is not known which water is utilized by the numbers of palearctic ducks that occur in the Langano–Zwai area.

Unmarked on any map and at over 3,000 m is the small shallow and permanent Lake Arakit, where in the northern winters of 1971/2 and 1972/3 concentrations of over 10,000 ducks have been seen.

Finland

Aspskär Nature Reserve

A rich waterfowl area in the outer archipelago with a land area of 27 ha, and a water area of 342 ha.

Söderskär–Långorën Nature Reserve

A land area of 52 ha, and a water area of 1,330 ha is one of the first places to lose its snow cover during early spring. Consequently, it holds large concentrations of birds over short periods. Breeding species include. Eider Duck *Somateria mollissima*, Tufted Duck *Aythya fuligula*, Velvet Scoter *Melanitta fusca* and Red-breasted Merganser *Mergus serrator*.

Valassaaret–Björkögrunde

A bird sanctuary with a land area of 600 ha, and a water area of 17,000 ha. Both are focal points on the migration route through the Gulf of Bothnia. There are large breeding populations on Valassaaret, where in 1962 the following pairs of birds were known to breed: Tufted Duck *Aythya fuligula* (187 pairs), Scaup *A. marila* (115 pairs), Velvet Scoter *Melanitta fusca* (294 pairs) and Red-breasted Merganser *Mergus serrator* (135 pairs).

France

Gulf of Morbihan

The presence of *Zostera* meadows in the shallows of the Gulf is presumably the attraction for the wintering Anatidae. These are grazed not only by the Brent Goose *Branta bernicla* (which in any normal winter can number 5,000 to 6,000) but also by some 20,000 to 30,000 European Wigeon *A. penelope*. Thus the Gulf of Morbihan winters almost half the population of these two species for the whole of France. The development of oyster culture has very much reduced the surface area of *Zostera* meadows, which once virtually covered the entire Gulf.

The attraction of this region for Mallard *Anas platyrynchos* and European Teal *A. crecca* is undoubtedly the abundance of coastal marshes, where at night-time they come to feed. For example, the marshes of Succinio peninsula. Numerous projects for tourism are a serious threat to these marshes.

Aiguillon Bay and Poitevin Marshes

In 1973 hunting was prohibited in half of Aiguillon Bay and this has proved very beneficial to the bird populations. On the other hand, the Poitvin Marshes have become less favourable for waterfowl since the extension of maize growing in that area. However, in 1973, a reserve of 200 ha was established on the communal marsh of Saint-Denisdu-Payré and since October of that year, winter and spring populations of European Teal *A. crecca* (3,000) and Shoveler *A. clypeata* (2,000), have been recorded.

German Federal Republic

Selenter See

Not only one of the largest eutrophic inland lakes of Schleswig-Holstein but also Europe's largest moulting area of Tufted Duck *Aythya fuligula*, with a moulting population of 6,000 to 8,000 birds; the Red-crested Pochard *Netta rufina* also chooses to moult there. Breeding species at the lake include Grey Lag Goose *Anser anser*, Pochard *Aythya ferina*, Gadwall *Anas strepera*, Goldeneye *Bucephala clangula* and Goosander *Mergus merganser*.

Grüne Insel

On the Eider estuary on the west coast of Schleswig-Holstein, and a very important resting area for the Barnacle Goose *Branta leucopsis*, when at times there are 12,000 birds.

Other important areas of the west coast, with maximum numbers given, are Rodenäs near the Hindenburgdamm, where 7,500 Pink-footed Geese *Anser brachyrhynchus* have been recorded, and Sylt–Hörnum on the southern tip of the island, where as many as 20,000 Eider Ducks *Somateria mollissima* have been counted.

Mellum

Thirty-five sq. km of shallows with channels, sandbanks and deserted meadows. The area is a National Nature Reserve and lies between Aussenweser and Aussenjade in Lower Saxony. The island, which is completely free from hunting, is wardened from the end of April until the beginning of October. Maximum numbers of migrating and wintering wildfowl are given as: European Wigeon *Anas penelope* (3,000); Shelduck *Tadorna tadorna* (3,500); Brent Goose *Branta bernicla* (1,000).

Asseler Sand

On the west bank of the Lower Elbe in Lower Saxony. The outer marshes have an area of 6,000 ha, there is pasture land with reeds and scattered bushes. The area is of importance for its swans and the following have already been counted there: Whooper Swan *Cygnus cygnus* (100) and Bewick's Swan *C. bewickii* (700).

Öpfinger Reservoir

At this reservoir in Baden–Württemburg, some maximum numbers are Mallard *Anas platyryhnchos* (11,600), European Teal *A. crecca* (2,000) and Pochard *Aythya ferina* (6,600).

The Rhine between Burkheim and Ottenheim

An area of some 37 sq. km includes extensive river forest and meadows east of the river which are intersected by a great many branched water courses.

Some maximum numbers of migrating waterfowl in the area are: European Teal *Anas crecca* (950), Mallard *A. platyrhynchos* (17,400), Pochard *Aythya ferina* (8,800), Tufted Duck *A. fuligula* (5,700) and Goldeneye *Bucephala clangula* (500).

An important wintering ground for Bean Goose *Anser fabilis* lies between Weiswil, Forchheim and Sasbach, where up to 550 individuals have been seen.

Ismaninger Teichgebeit

Since the late 1960s the breeding population of Gadwall *Anas strepera* and Tufted Duck *Aythya fuligula* has greatly increased and the moulting flocks of ducks has reached the numbers: Pochard *Aythya ferina* (20,000), Tufted Duck *A. fuligula* (5,000 plus – drakes) with Red-crested Pochard *Netta rufina* (between 500 and 800).

Great Britain

Loch Leven, Kinross

An area of 1,400 ha (56° 11′–13′ N, 3° 20′–25′ W). Considered to be Scotland's most important inland water area for breeding and wintering wildfowl. In the wintering and resting area maximum figures are as follows: Whooper Swan *Cygnus cygnus* (600), Pink-footed Goose *Anser brachychynchus* (12,000), Grey Lag Goose *A. anser* (3,000) and (1,000) each of the species that follow: Mallard *Anas platyrhynchos*, European Teal *A. crecca*; Wigeon *A. penelope*, Pochard *Aythya ferina* and Tufted Duck *A. fuligula*.

The Coastal Broads, Suffolk and Essex marshes

An area of 22,000 ha (51° 32′–52° 24′ N, 0° 50′–1° 43′ E), with extensive mudflats and sand; salt, brackish and fresh-water marshes; lagoons and large widely spread reedbeds. It provides a wintering and migrating area for several species when, on the odd occasion, up to 15,000 ducks have been recorded in the Havergate area alone. The Essex coast is known for the concentrations of wintering Brent Geese *Branta b. bernicla* with maximum populations of 10,300 in 1960–1 and 8,800 in 1963–4.

North Nofolk marshes

An area of 1,000 ha (52° 58′–59′ N, 0° 41′–1° 05′ E). A most valuable breeding area for Mallard *Anas platyrhynchos* (300 pairs), Shoveler *A. clypeata*, Teal *A. crecca*, Garganey *A. querquedula* and Shelduck *Tadorna tadorna*.

It is also a wintering and migration area for Wigeon *Anas penelope*, Brent Goose *Branta bernicla* and Shelduck *Tadorna tadorna*.

The Solway Firth

An area of 12,750 ha (54° 40′–55° 08′ N, 3° 03′–4° 59′ W) and an important wintering area for many species. Maximum figures quoted are: Grey Lag Goose *Anser anser* (10,000), Pink-footed Goose *A. brachyrhynchus* (15,000), White-fronted Goose *A. albifrons flavirostris* (500), Barnacle Goose *Branta leucopsis* (2,800), Wigeon *Anas penelope* (5,000 to 10,000), Pintail *A. acuta* (1,000) and several thousand Common Scoter *Melanitta n. nigra* and Scaup *Aythya marila*.

Abberton Reservoir, Essex

An area of 500 ha (51° 49′–51′ N, 0° 49′–54′ E) and one of the most important wetland areas for Anatidae in England. It is a permanent, lowland artificial reservoir and rich with aquatic and marsh plants. Maximum autumn passage figures are quoted as: Teal *Anas crecca* (12,000), Wigeon *A penelope* (5,300), Mallard *A. platyrhynchos* (4,000), Shoveler *A. clypeata* (1,400), Pintail *A. acuta* (450), and Pochard *Aythya ferina* (3,870). Also no fewer than 300 Mute

Swans *Cygnus olor* during most autumn and summer moults is usual.

The Wash and East Anglian Fens

An area of 5,322 ha, plus 75 km of coast (52° 19′–53° 10′ N, 0° 15′ W–0° 30′ E). This is an extensive area of salt-marsh with intertidal sands, fens and many regularly flooded river meadows.

It is a breeding area for many species of Anatidae as well as a very important wintering area. In the Wash area there are 20,000 ducks and between 5,000 and 6,000 geese. With the Ouse and Nene Washes, wintering figures are: Bewick's Swan *Cygnus bewickii* (700 plus), Mallard *Anas platyrhynchos* (3,400), Teal *A. crecca* (3,300), Wigeon *A. penelope* (19,000), Shoveler *A. clypeata* (500) Pintail *A. acuta* (5,000) and Pochard *Aythya ferina* (2,000).

Greece

Several hundred thousand waterfowl are known to winter in the wetlands of Greece, or to use them as feeding and resting areas during migration.

Gulf of Arta

A vast area of water connected, by a narrow inlet, to the Ionian Sea near Prevesa (38° 52′–39° 06′ N, 20° 44′–21° 09′ E). In winter 20–30 per cent of the country's wetland wildfowl population may be found there. The maximum concentrations in recent years are quoted as: Pintail *Anas acuta* (48,000), Teal *A. crecca* (45,000), Wigeon *A. penelope* (55,000), Shoveler *A. clypeata* (18,000) and Pochard *Aythya ferina* (31,500).

Evros Delta

The Evros/Meric Delta is situated on the Greek–Turkish border (40° 43′–51′ N, 26° 05′–20′ E). Many species of Anatidae are present with the following maximum concentrations: Mute Swan

Cygnus olor (270), Whooper Swan *C. c. cygnus* (400), Shelduck *Tadorna tadorna* (316), Pintail *Anas acuta* (36,000), Teal *A. crecca* (28,500), Mallard *A. platyrhynchos* (26,000), Gadwell *A. strepera* (1,060), Wigeon *A. penelope* (63,000) and Shoveler *A. clypeata* (1,285).

The White-fronted Goose *Anser albifrons* had a peak year in 1969 when 35,000 individuals were observed, but since then the numbers have not risen above 1,000.

Gulf of Mesolonghion

Suitable waterfowl habitat is to be found outside the dunes, where several thousand ducks winter. These include Shelduck *Tadorna tadorna*, Teal *Anas crecca*, Wigeon *A. penelope* and Pochard *Aythya ferina*.

Lagoon of Kotchi

This lagoon in southern Greece is without doubt the most important site on the Peloponnesus. In January 1973 counts totalled 34,000 ducks, including Pintail *Anas acuta* (12,000), Mallard *A. platyrhynchos* (2,000), Wigeon *A. penelope* (6,000) and Shoveler *A. clypeata* (12,000).

Hungary

Lake Balaton including Kisbalaton

Kisbalaton was once a bay of Lake Balaton (46° 40' N, 17° 15' E), now it is separated and forms an extensive *Phragmites* bed of some 1,400 ha, the major part of which is now a nature reserve, with such breeding species as Mallard *Anas platyrhynchos*, Gadwall *A. strepera*, Garganey *A. querquedula*, Shoveler *A. clypeata*, Pintail *A. acuta*, Pochard *Aythya ferina* and Ferruginous Duck *A. nyroca*.

During migration, large numbers of duck are to be seen on the lake, especially Goldeneye *Bucephala clangula* and Tufted Duck *Aythya fuligula*.

Flood plains, lakes and marshes of Puszta Hortobagy

An area of 450,000 ha (47° 15'–48° 00' N, 20° 45'–21° 45' E) with steppes, some marshes and ponds, although much of it is now broken up. It is an important breeding area for Grey Lag Goose *Anser anser*, Mallard *Anas platyrhynchos*, Garganey *A. querquedula* and Gadwall *A. strepera*. It is also of note for migrating and wintering Anatidae.

Iceland

The importance of Icelandic wetlands to waterfowl are threefold. They are used as breeding grounds; as resting places between Western Europe, Greenland and Arctic Canada by migrating geese and as wintering areas by sea ducks.

Ferjubakkaflói–Nordura

An area of 1,500 ha (64° 38' N, 21° 44' W) consisting of peat swamps, flood plains and rivers. Important concentrations of wildfowl occur, especially Whooper Swan *Cygnus c. cygnus* (up to 1,800) and White-fronted Goose *Anser albifrons flavisrostris* (1,200).

Borgarfjördur

Moulting flocks of up to 100,000 Eider Ducks *Somateria mollissima* are supported by the dense mussel banks that occur in the outerparts of this large estuary of some 7,000 ha (64° 30' N, 22° 00' W).

Breidafjördur

An area of 270,000 ha (65° 20' N, 23° 00' W).

On the spring migration, the *Zostera* flats along the southern shores hold up to 4,000 Brent Geese *Branta bernicla hrota*. Between 80,000 and 100,000 Eider Duck *Somateria mollissima* are known to breed there annually.

Mývatn–Laxá

The area of 20,000 ha (65° 40' N, 17° 00' W), comprises many types of wetland, including the shallow Lake Mývatn with an area of 4,000 ha and its effluent river, the Laxá. It is estimated that between 10,000 and 20,000 pairs of ducks nest in the region of Mývatn. At one time the most numerous duck the Scaup *Aythya marila*, has decreased steadily in recent years and now the Tufted Duck *A. fuligula* is undoubtedly the most abundant.

In this area sixteen species of duck are regular breeders and of these fourteen of them nest at Mývatn. Europe's entire population of Barrow's Goldeneye *Bucephala islandica* (about 1,000 pairs) nests and for the most part winters in the area. Mývatn is also Iceland's stronghold for Gadwall *Anas strepera*, Pochard *Aythya ferina* and Common Scoter *Melanitta nigra*. In fact, they are either absent or very rare elsewhere in Iceland. Breeding along the River Laxá are about 100 pairs of Harlequin Duck *Histrionicus histrionicus*. Mývatn is also of importance as a moulting area and birds from a wide area gather there, including about 6,000 Whooper Swans *Cygnus c. cygnus* and many ducks, especially male Wigeon *Anas penelope*.

Thjórsárver

This is a semi-tundra area of 15,000 ha (64° 35′ N, 19° 15′ W) in the uninhabited central 'desert' of Iceland, it has numerous rivers and lakes and is located at the headwaters of the River Thjórsá.

It is the main breeding ground for the Pink-footed Goose *Anser brachyrhynchus* providing approximately two-thirds of the production of the Iceland–Greenland population. Breeding numbers in 1970 and 1971 were in the region of 11,000 pairs but decreasing in 1974 to about 8,000 pairs.

Iran

Lake Rezaiyeh

An area of 483,000 ha (37° 30′ N, 45° 30′ E).

In August of 1970 the whole of Lake Rezaiyeh and its islands was declared a Protected Region. At that time it was estimated that breeding populations of Greater Flamingoes and White Pelicans on this lake totalled 50,000 and 2,800 respectively. It is also an important breeding area for Ruddy Shelduck *Tadorna ferruginea* and Shelduck *T. tadorna*.

Pahlavi Mordab

This area of 225 ha (37° 25′ N, 49° 30′ E) at Selke on the south side of the main Mordab was declared a Protected Region in September 1970. It consists of flooded meadows and shallow freshwater marshes. These marshes (*adbandans*) provide excellent winter feeding habitat for between 50,000 and 80,000 wildfowl and is one of Iran's most important wetlands.

Amirkelayeh

An area of 2,400 ha (37° 17′ N, 50° 12′ E).

Extensive *Phragmites* reedbeds surround this permanent shallow freshwater lake. The entire lake and its surrounding marshes were declared a Protected Region in 1971. It is an important wintering area for wildfowl, especially Red-crested Pochard *Netta rufina*.

Seyed Mahalleh

This important wintering area for wildfowl (36° 45′ N, 53° 00′ E) comprises a 350 ha complex of shallow, fresh-water irrigation ponds and trapping reserves, surrounded by rice-paddies.

Iraq

The Iraqi Government now supports the Natural History Centre which is the main organization studying the vast numbers of waterfowl that migrate to Iraq, particularly to winter.

Swans are uncommon winter visitors,

but geese are seen in large concentrations from late November to early February.

They arrive in October but most have left by March. Their regular haunts are the *khors* or *haurs* (temporary or permanent marshes) east of a line from Khanaqin to Amara via Baghdad and Kut. The Grey Lag Goose *Anser anser* is the most numerous species followed by the White-fronted Goose *A. albifrons*.

As for ducks, the Marbled Teal *Anas angustirostris* is a summer visitors while Pintail *Anas acuta* and European Teal *A. crecca* are the most common winter visitors.

Ireland

Lough Neagh

An area of 47,562 ha and the entire area of the lough and the margin is protected as an Area of Scientific Interest. Two Wildfowl Refuges have been set up along the shore, one in Antrim Bay in the north-east corner, the other in Doss Bay at the north-west corner. Extremely important as a wintering area for ducks and swans with maximum estimates of Tufted Duck *Aythya fuligula* (21,800) and Goldeneye *Bucephala clangula* (2,800). In most winters there are up to the following numbers of swans: Whooper Swan *Cygnus c. cygnus* (500) and Bewick's Swan *Cygnus bewickii* (300).

North and South Slobs and Harbour

An area of 3,035 ha (52° 15′–30′ N, 6° 15′–35′ W).

The first National Wildfowl Refuge (200 ha) was acquired on North Slob in County Wexford by the Forest and Wildlife Service of the Department of Lands in conjunction with a voluntary conservation body, the Irish Wildbird Conservancy, and with the assistance of the World Wildlife Fund. Two local nature reserves have been set up by the

IWC, Rosslare Point by agreement with the landowner and Tern Island by acquisition. Shooting on both Slobs is strictly controlled. The Slobs are important wintering grounds for Anatidae with White-fronted Goose *Anser albifrons flavirostris* (4,500), Brent Goose *Branta bernicla* (1,000) and Scaup *Aythya marila* (3,000) – January peaks. Also Barnacle Goose *Branta leucopsis*, Mute Swan *Cygnus olor*, Whooper Swan *C. c. cygnus*, Wigeon *Anas penelope*, Teal *A. crecca*, Mallard *A. platyrhynchos* and Tufted Duck *Aythya fuligula*.

Inishkea Islands

An area of 380 ha plus (54° 08′ N, 10° 11′ W), two islands (380 ha) and eleven smaller islands in County Mayo. The north island, which has a small brackish lake, is almost entirely covered with *Plantago* sward. The south island has about one-third *Plantago* cover.

These islands, for which *Plantago* sward provides grass grazing, are the main wintering localities of the Barnacle Goose *Branta leucopsis* in Ireland. In March of 1962, some 2,500 individuals were counted, this represents over 50 per cent of the Irish population. Small numbers of White-fronted Geese *Anser albifrons flavirostris* also occur.

Tralee Bay and Castlemaine Harbour

In County Kerry (52° 05′–18′ N, 9° 45′–10° 00′ W) an area of 1,500 ha with coastal waters and marshes. It is the principal wintering area in Ireland for the Brent Goose *Branta bernicla hrota*; up to 4,000 have been counted. Also an important area for Wigeon *Anas penelope*.

Israel

The Huleh Swamp Nature Reserve, which was established in 1956, is the only wetland reserve. In Israel only the Marbled Teal *Anas angustirostris*,

Mallard *A. platyrhynchos* and Ferruginous Duck *Aythya nyroca* breed and these in small numbers. Almost all waterfowl observed are either wintering or passing through on migration.

Italy

Lago di Mezzola, Sondrio
An area of 1,098 ha (46° 13′ N, 09° 27′ E) formed by the River Mera. This lake is very deep in the middle but with swamps along its edges that are used as resting places by migrating wildfowl from nearby Lake Como.

Laguna di Orbetello, Grosseto
The lagoon has an area of 887 ha (42° 27′ N, 11° 13′ E) is connected to the sea on each side of the Argentario Promentary, whose tip forms a protective barrier while the River Albegna reduces its salinity. It provides good wintering conditions and is consequently the Italian wetland most frequented by waterfowl. In recent years it has been made a protected area.

Sardinia
Stagno di Molentargius, Stagno di Cagliari, Stagno di Cabras and Stagno di s'Ena arruba e canale di Sassu are four wetlands of international importance as resting places for waterfowl including: Pintail *Anas acuta*, Teal *A. crecca*, Shoveler *A. clypeata*, Pochard *Aythya ferina* and Ferruginous Duck *A. nyroca*, with the White-headed Duck *Oxyura leucocephala* being a regular breeding species.

Jordan

Al-Azraq is Jordan's most important region for winter gatherings of wildfowl in general and ducks in particular. A count made on 25 February 1974, after the heaviest recorded rain for 30–40 years, gave the following estimates: Geese 100, Shelduck *Tadorna tadorna* (14,000), Pintail *Anas acuta* (17,000), Teal *A. crecca* (24,000), Mallard *A. platyrhynchos* (3,000) Wigeon *A. penelope* (8,000) Garganey *A. querquedula* (8,000) and Shoveler *A. clypeata* (10,000).

Madagascar

The large number and vast extent of marshes and pools adjacent to such permanent lakes as Alaotra (the largest in Madagascar), Itasy, Andranomena and Masianaka, are extremely important for waterfowl.

Mali

Birds on migration from Europe and Asia find ideal wintering zones in the wetlands of Mali and particularly in the central delta of the Niger River.

Morocco

Merja zerga
An area of 3,000 ha of shallow salt-water lagoons separated from the sea by sand dunes (34° 50′ N, 6° 20′ W). Some 30,000 to 50,000 ducks winter there including Teal *Anas crecca*, Shoveler *A. clypeata*, Wigeon *A. penelope*, Marbled Teal *A. angustirostris*, Mallard *A. platyrhynchos* and Shelduck *Tadorna tadorna*.

Netherlands

The wetlands and grasslands along the shores of Haringvliet and Hollansch Diep comprise an area of about 3,000 ha. They are of great importance for the

Barnacle Goose *Branta leucopsis*, Grey Lag Goose *Anser anser*, White-fronted Goose *A. albifrons*, Shelduck *Tadorna tadorna*, Mallard *Anas platyrhynchos*, Wigeon *A. penelope* and Teal *A. crecca*.

IJsselmeer and its border lakes

Flevoland at the north-eastern portion of this new polder is now one of western Europe's major wintering areas for the Bean Goose *Anser fabilis*. Also, in recent years, an average of 60 per cent of the entire wintering population of White-fronted Geese *A. albifrons* in north-west Europe occurred at Flevoland, making it the principal wintering area for that species in this part of Europe. On occasions in excess of 100,000 individuals have been counted.

Up to 100 pairs of Grey Lag Geese *Anser anser* breed here and it is used as a moulting area for over 1,000 geese.

Markerwaard – up to 9,000 Smew *Mergus albellus* winter in this area. This represents over 90 per cent of the wintering population for north-west Europe or almost one-third of the entire world population. Other species wintering in the area are Wigeon *Anas penelope*, Pochard *Aythya ferina*, Tufted Duck *A. fuligula*, Scaup *A. marila*, Goldeneye *Bucephala clangula* and Goosander *Mergus merganser*.

USA

Even though the numbers of migratory waterfowl cannot really be compared today with those of a century ago, they still occur in enormous flocks. The lands and waters of Canada, Mexico and the USA sustain forty-eight species of ducks, geese and swans; a great natural asset that must be perpetuated.

The National Audubon Society has sanctuaries, with warden protection, that extend over more than a million acres of land and water, many of these are sanctuaries for waterfowl.

The Society's Richardson's Bay Sanctuary in Marin County and sanctuaries near Redwood City and Newark in the San Francisco Bay of California provide food and refuge for thousands of ducks and geese each year.

Lying in the heart of a major wintering ground for many species of ducks and geese is the Rainey Refuge near Abbeville in Louisiana with an area of 26,000 acres.

The National Wildlife Refuge System has over 370 Refuges, far too numerous to list. It was started in 1903 by President Theodore Roosevelt and is administered by United States Department of the Interior, Fish and Wildlife Service.

Lake Texoma

143,000 acres in Texas and Oklahoma and is one of the largest reservoirs in the USA. It was created by the Army Corps of Engineers in 1943 when building Dennison Dam on the Red River.

The Tishomingo National Wildlife Refuge

Established in 1946. It has 13,450 acres of water where, during autumn migration, 30,000 geese and 50,000 ducks gather to feed in the 600 acres of adjacent farmland. Included are Canada Geese, Snow Geese, White-fronted Geese, Mallards and Pintails.

Bear River National Wildlife Refuge

Sunbaked alkali flats on the Bear River delta in Utah have been flooded and converted into productive marshes. Here, peak populations of over one million waterfowl are supported.

Monte Vista Wildlife Refuge

Another such development located in southern Colorado. On greasewood flats more than 220 ponds, lakes and meadows have been fashioned since

[17]

1953. By 1961 the following species nested there: Mallard *Anas platyrhynchos*, Gadwall *A. strepera*, Pintail *A. acuta*, Blue-winged Teal *A. discors*, Green-winged Teal *A. crecca carolinensis*, Cinnamon Teal *A. cyanoptera* and Redhead *Aythya americana*. The wintering population is in the region of 70,000 individuals.

Norway

Munkfjord area in Finnmark
(66° 00′ N, 29° 20′ E.)

During migration the following maximums have been observed: Eider Duck *Somateria mollissima* (3,000), Long-tailed Duck *Clangula hyemalis* (3,000) and Goosander *Mergus merganser* (2,000).

Bavtajokka–Gorzzejokka–Anarjokka area
An area of 25,000 ha (68° 40′–69° 50′ N, 24° 20′–25° 30′ E) of extensive peatland areas in Kautokeino and Karasjok, Finnmark. A breeding area for Whooper Swan *Cygnus cygnus* and various species of ducks and geese.

Orrevatn (with surroundings on Jären, Rogaland)
An area of 1,500 ha (58° 44′–46′ N, 5° 31′–35′ E), comprising eutrophic to mesotrophic inland freshwaters and 5 km of coastline.

Important resting area for ducks on migration and a wintering area for ducks and swans.

Pakistan

In late August the arrival of migratory wildfowl often commences with the appearance of flocks of Teal *Anas crecca*, but more usually their arrival is the middle or late September. Then in quick succession come flocks of Pintail *Anas acuta*, Mallard *A. platyrhynchos*, Gadwall *A. strepera*, Shoveler *A. clypeata* and Pochard *Aythya ferina*. These are followed by Grey Lag Goose *Anser anser*, Bar-headed Goose *A. indicus*, Shelduck *Tadorna tadorna* and many others.

Although some waterfowl only stay in Pakistan for a short period before moving southwards, many thousands stay through its cool pleasant winter until March, or at latest early April, when their return northward begins.

Haleji Lake
This is a freshwater reservoir of 1,701 ha 96 km east of Karachi (24° 48′ N, 67° 47′ E) with abundant aquatic vegetation and food supply. Large concentrations of waterfowl stay in these relatively undisturbed waters from October through to February.

In summer it has breeding colonies of Spot-billed Duck *Anas poecilorhyncha* and Indian Pygmy Goose *Nettapus coromandelianus*.

Cheteji or Kinjir Lake
This is one of the largest fresh-water lakes, which is 115 km east of Karachi (24° 56′ N, 68° 03′ E) and covering an area of 13,445 ha. It provides both food and shelter for a number of waterfowl. Because of its large size and the depth of its water, it provides a suitable refuge for migrant diving ducks in winter, with perhaps the major population of Tufted Duck *Aythya fuligula*.

West Pakistan
The wetlands of Lal Suhanra are a sanctuary for waterfowl.

East Pakistan
The wetland areas available to wildfowl are restricted to the *haors* of Sylhet and a number of smaller areas in Mymensingh District. Together providing wintering quarters for between 100,000 and 150,000 ducks.

Poland

Fish ponds near Milicz

An area of 7,980 ha (51° 30′ N, 17° 05′ E), including 5,302 ha of reserves.

This is a complex of large fourteenth-century fish ponds, fourteen in number. It provides a breeding ground for many Anatidae including 200 pairs of Grey Lag Geese *Anser anser*, and a wintering and migration area for many thousands of ducks, a few Bean Geese *Anser fabilis* and many hundreds each of Grey Lag Geese *A. anser* and White-fronted Geese *A. albifrons*.

Leba and Gardno Lakes

An area of 4,000 ha (54° 45′ N, 17° 30′ E) where shallow overgrown lakes are separated from the Baltic by a narrow strip of land.

A breeding area for Grey Lag Goose *A. anser* and Mute Swan *Cygnus olor* also several other species of Anatidae.

It is an important area along the Baltic coast for birds resting on migration.

Portugal

Tejo Estuary and Valley

(38° 40′–55′ N, 8° 55′–9° 05′W.)

In winter many tens of thousands of the following species are to be seen: Mallard *Anas platyrhynchos*, Wigeon *A. penelope*, Shoveler *A. clypeata*, Teal *A. crecca* and Pochard *Aythya ferina*.

Rumania

Danube Delta and complex of lagoons at Razelm

At the beginning of winter there are enormous wildfowl concentrations in this area (44° 25′–45′ N, 28° 45′–29° 40′ E). In December of 1968 there were White-fronted Geese *Anser albifrons* (200,000) and Red-breasted Geese *Branta ruficolis* (25,000).

Tulcea and Lacul Tasaul

An area of about 88,000 ha. Estimated numbers in 1969–70 were: Whitefronted Goose *Anser albifrons* (30,000 upwards). Red-breasted Goose *Branta ruficolis* (4,100, but there were probably 5,000 in the whole area).

Senegal

Djoudj basin

An area of 12,000 ha (16° 20′ N, 16° 12′ W). Situated in the River Senegal delta, the basin was classified as a reserve in June 1963. From August to February it provides a refuge in Senegal for most palearctic migrants.

Numbers of birds observed in 1972 and 1973 include Fulvous Tree Duck *Dendrocygna bicolor* (1,500), White-faced Tree Duck *D. viduata* (50,000), Egyptian Goose *Alopochen aegyptiacus*, Pintail *Anas acuta* (50,000), Teal *A. crecca* (500), Garganey *A. querquedula* (100,000), Shoveler *A. clypeata* (7,000), Pochard *Aythya ferina* (500) and over 200 each of Ferruginous Duck *A. nyroca*, Comb Duck *Sarkidiornis melanotos* and Spur-winged Goose *Plectropterus gambensis*.

South Africa

The majority of South Africa's waterfowl can be referred to as residents or local migrants. True migrants from the north can only be described as rare vagrants.

There are sixteen species of Anatidae that occur regularly in South Africa, eight of which occur in large numbers and have quite a wide distribution, sufficiently so that they may be classed as huntable game.

The most common and probably the

[19]

best known is the Yellow-billed Duck *Anas undulata* and it has been referred to as the Mallard of the South. The Egyptian Goose *Alopochen aegptiacus* and the South African Shelduck *Tadorna cana* are gregarious and at times assemble in large flocks. In parts of the country, particularly in the immediate vicinity of large impoundments, they are often very destructive to young cereal crops. They may be found on almost all types of waters, even marshes, small dams and temporary pans.

The Red-billed Teal *Anas erythrorhyncha* is also quite common in some areas where it too occasionally causes damage to crops.

South Africa's largest waterfowl is the Spur-winged Goose *Plectropterus gambensis* and occurs throughout the country, mainly on the larger areas of water but is absent in the arid north-west.

Concentrations of these species, at the most, seldom exceed 5,000 birds.

According to estimates there are over 170,000 farm ponds, many of a seasonal nature; also 180 larger impoundments, with capacities of up to 5 million cubic metres, scattered throughout the country. In addition, there are four major impoundments and eighty-two large lakes have also been created.

The apparent trends of local migration are that the Yellow-billed Duck *Anas undulata* tends to keep to cooler areas although numbers intrude into south-eastern Botswana when the pans are full. The greatest wanderer is the Red-billed Teal *A. erythrorhyncha* occurring as far as Angola and Zambia with a wide ecological range from tropical coasts to true desert. The South African Shelduck *Tadorna cana* seems restricted largely to the central semi-arid areas, moving north-eastwards on the moult migration. The Egyptian Goose *Alopochen aegyptiacus* tends to cover the same area, while the Spur-winged Goose *Plectropterus gambensis* seems to visit the south-central mountainous

region but it may also tend towards a somewhat northerly movement.

A waterfowl breeding and research station has been established at Jonkershoek in Cape Province. In the Transvaal at Barberspan a reserve, ringing and research station is operational. In fact there are a large number of nature reserves throughout the country with others being developed continually in areas of importance.

Spain

The National Park of the Marismas of the Guadalquivir

This extends over 23,000 ha (36° 45′–37° 15′ N), or more and includes the Doñana Reserve (about 6,000 ha), Guadiamar and several private estates, most of which are marshy land. During winter, in the new area of the National Park, hundreds of thousands of ducks remain, as well as 12,000 to 20,000 Grey Lag Geese *Anser anser*. The latter come largely from the Baltic and Scandinavian countries.

Breeding species include the Marbled Teal *Anas angustirostris*, which is common and the White-headed Duck *Oxyura leucocephala* which is still present in the region.

Gigüela and Guadiana Land

Situated in the province of Ciudad Real, Central Spain. Breeding species include: Red-crested Pochard *Netta rufina* (3,000–6,000), Ferruginous Duck *Aythya nyroca*, Pochard *A. ferina*, Gadwall *A. strepera* and Marbled Teal *A. angustirostris*.

The Ebro Delta

An area of marshes, lakes, dunes and bays in Tarragona (40° 35′–50′ N, 0° 35′–55′ E) which occasionally during winter, shelters as many as 50,000 to

100,000 birds. It is also an exceptional breeding ground for Mallard *Anas platyrhynchos*.

The Albufera of Valencia

An area of 4,000 ha and a coastal lake of shallow brackish water in the east of Spain (39° 12'–25' N, 0° 14'–25' W). It is bordered by dense reedbeds and has a breeding population of 200–400 pairs of Red-crested Pochard *Netta rufina*. Other species that breed, but only in small numbers, are Pochard *Aythya ferina* and Ferruginous Duck *A. nyroca*.

Spitsbergen

There are many important bird sanctuaries in Svalbard, along the western coast from 76° 27' N, 16° 38' E to 79° 39' N, 10° 44' E. Four from a total of fifteen are Sörkapp, Isöyane, Forlandsöyane and Mosöya.

The sanctuaries are of special importance to the Barnacle Goose *Branta leucopsis*, Brent Goose *B. bernicla hrota* and Eider Duck *Somateria mollissima*.

Sweden

Falsterbo–Foteviken

An area of 5,550 ha (55° 25' N, 12° 55'E) which comprises shallow coastal water, lagoons, sandbanks, shore meadows and damp, treeless moors. From Måkläppen, in the south, it extends northwards to the small island of Dynan near Klagshamn. Few places in Europe can boast equal numbers of birds on passage – ducks, birds of prey and passerines. The coastal strip is used by large numbers of ducks as a resting place. The area is of importance as a moulting and wintering place, particularly for the Mute Swan *Cygnus olor*.

Helga å

An area of 5,145 ha (56° 00' N, 14° 13' E) covering the lower reaches of the Helga å, below Araslövssjön and including the Håslöv meadows (flat arable land along one of the largest water courses in Skåne). During the autumn and spring passage, thousands of ducks stay in the area, while thousands of Bean Geese *Anser fabilis* graze around Araslövssjon and Yngajö in March–April and October–November. Almost 1,000 Canada Geese *Branta canadensis* winter south of the lakes.

Rone Ytterholme–Laus holmar –Skenholmen

An area of 414 ha (57° 06'–57° 48' N to 18° 27'–19° 02' E) of very low-lying islands covered with short grass and practically void of trees and bushes. Tens of thousands of Barnacle Geese *Branta leucopsis* graze on these islands during April and May, with a much shorter stay from the end of September during autumn migration. The islands are also utilized by Brent Geese *Branta bernicla*, Grey Lag Geese *Anser anser* and a number of ducks during the course of migration.

Ånnsjön

An area of 2,900 ha (63° 16' N, 12° 33' E) of mire complexes and delta lands along with open and often very shallow shore. Breeding populations of eleven species of duck, all of which breed there regularly, include Pintail *Anas acuta*, Wigeon *A. penelope*, Common Scoter *Melanitta nigra*, Velvet Scoter *M. fusca* and Long-tailed Duck *Clangula hyemalis*.

Switzerland

Bodensee

From Luxburg (Egnach) to Uttwil/Kesswill there is an area of open water with reed swamps. Migrating and wintering waterfowl find it to be a good resting place. The high production of Zebra Mussel *Dreissena polymorpha* makes it of particular importance since over 10,000 birds occur there regularly between December and March. Among them are Gadwall *Anas strepera*, Pochard *Aythya ferina* and Tufted Duck *A. fuligula*.

Because of the current near the outlet of the River Rhine, the shallow bay of Konatanzer Bucht (400 ha) is usually ice-free throughout the winter months. It is one of the most famous wintering places for wildfowl in the northern foot-hills of the Alps. Here again, because of the mass production of Zebra Mussels, large concentrations of waterfowl (up to 38,000 birds) are attracted to the area; particularly Pochard *Aythya ferina* (20,000), Tufted Duck *A. fuligula* (7,000) and numbers of Gadwall *A. strepera*.

Untersee

At Ermatinger Becken west of Konstanz the Wollmatinger Ried (500 ha) is an area of open water 400 ha and reed swamps on the Swiss shore of 100 ha.

This shallow fresh-water lake is an important breeding area for Red-crested Pochard *Netta rufina* and provides a moulting area for *N. rufina* and Pochard *Aythya ferina* along with other species of ducks.

It is also used as a wintering area and a resting place on migration for between 15,000 and 20,000 birds, with maximums of Teal *Anas crecca* (4,000), Gadwall *A. strepera* (2,000), Red-crested Pochard *Netta rufina* (920) and Pochard *Aythya ferina* (11,700).

Stausee Niederried

An area of 54 ha comprising of 60-year-old storage reservoir with its large reed swamps and willow thickets provides wintering quarters for large numbers of wildfowl including Pochard *Aytheya ferina* (4,490), Tufted Duck *A. fuligula* (5,065) also Teal *Anas crecca* and Mallard *A. platyrhynchos*.

Thailand

During the rainy season much of Thailand is flooded for the purpose of rice growing. Together with the many permanent swamps, lakes, reservoirs, rivers and coastlines, this means that extensive areas are available for wildfowl.

The Indian Tree Duck *Dendrocygna javanica*, Indian Pygmy Goose *Nettapus coromandelianus*, Comb Duck *Sarkidiornis melanotos* and White-winged Wood Duck *Cairina scutulata* are the only resident species, although winter visitors include the Ruddy Shelduck *Tadorna ferruginea*, Pintail *Anas acuta*, Teal *A. crecca*, Spot-billed Duck *A. poecilorhynca*, Wigeon *A. penelope*, Garganey *A. querquedula*, Shoveler *A. clypeata*, Pochard *Aythya ferina*, Ferruginous Duck *A. nyroca*, Baer's Pochard *A. baeri* and Tufted Duck *A. fuligula*. Together these comprise the fifteen species of duck known in Thailand.

Bung Boraphet

A fresh-water lake in Nakorn Sawan Province, North-central Thailand. The area has both permanent swamps and temporary floods which attract some of the largest concentrations of waterfowl in the country.

Thale Noi

The largest body of fresh water in Thailand and is located in Songkla and Patalung provinces. It contains the largest selection of waterfowl.

Tunisia

Lac Kelbia

An area of 13,000 ha (35° 51' N, 10° 13' E), where breeding species include Shelduck *Tadorna tadorna* and White-headed Duck *Oxyura leucocephala*.

Turkey

In the lakes, lagoons and inundated areas of the Mediterranean and Aegean coastal regions there are eighteen wetlands of international importance. It is estimated that 4 million ducks and geese winter in Lake Amik and Seyhan–Ceyhan lagoons. During the autumn, White-fronted Geese *Anser albifrons* are present in the eastern valleys. In winter, an estimated total of 500,000 are reported in Central Anatolia and in the regions of Lakes Tuz, Aksehir, Eber and Karamuk.

Meric Delta and Lake Gala

An area of 3,800 ha (40° 47′ N, 26° 05′ E) (including 600 ha covered by Lake Gala – fresh water).

In summer rice growing is extensive but in winter all the delta is shallow water providing good feeding for ducks, geese and swans and species include Mute Swan *Cygnus olor*, Whooper Swan *C. c. cygnus*, White-fronted Goose *Anser albifrons*, Grey Lag Goose *A. anser*, Pintail *Anas acuta*, Teal *A. crecca*, Mallard *A. platyrhynchos*, Gadwall *A. strepera*, Wigeon *A. penelope*, Garganey *A. querquedula*, Shoveler *A. clypeata*, Red-crested Pochard *Netta rufina*, Pochard *Aythya ferina*, Tufted Duck *A. fuligula*, Smew *Mergus abellus* and Goosander *M. merganser*.

Other important wildfowl areas are:

Lake Kus (Manyas)

An area of 16,200 ha (40° 10′ N, 28° 00′ E).

The shores, with their rich vegetation cover, offer excellent nesting sites.

Lake Ulubat (Apolyont)

An area of 13,500 ha (40° 12′ N, 28° 40′ E).

The western and southern parts of the lake are excellent habitat for wildfowl.

USSR

Caspian Sea

In the region of 10–12 million ducks, geese and swans cross the Caspian Sea each year on migration, many spending 1 to 3 months there. The sea coasts and neighbouring lowlands are regions of mass wildfowl breeding, with production totals each year in excess of 2 million. In summer the territory is used by over 450,000 moulting ducks.

Nearly the entire species populations of Red-breasted Goose *Branta ruficolis* and Greater Flamingo *Phoenicopterus roseus* either visit these places during their seasonal migrations or winter on the Caspian coast.

Matsalu Bay

A protected area of 13,500 ha in Estonia (58° 40′–50′ N, 23° 30′–58′ E).

Grey Lag Goose *Anser anser* and Eider Duck *Somateria mollissima* breed there in substantial numbers. Other breeders include: Velvet Scoter *Melanitta fusca*, Mallard *Anas platyrhynchos*, Pintail *A. acuta*, Shoveler *A. clypeata*, Pochard *Aythya ferina* and Tufted Duck *A. fuligula*.

Kandalakshskaya Bay

This Murmansk reserve extends to 31,000 ha (65° 50′–67° 10′ N, 32° 30′–34° 00′ E).

Many of the small islands are important breeding places for Eider Duck *Somateria mollissima*.

The Bay of Kirov

An area of 160,000 ha (39° 00′–15′ N, 48° 50′–49° 10′ E), with the Kyzyl–Agach Reserve being of greatest interest, and 93,000 ha in area.

An expanse of marshland, large reedbeds and shallow river arms. The Kyzyl–Agach Reserve is a wintering quarter for several millions of waterfowl.

Counted in 1958–9 as 2,894,000 surface feeding ducks, 850,000 diving ducks and 1,700 *Cygnus* species.

[23]

Counted in 1959–60 as 2,944,000 surface feeding ducks, 423,000 diving ducks, 7,000 *Anser* species, 11,000 Red-breasted Geese *Branta ruficolis* and 10,150 *Cygnus* species.

Yugoslavia

Kopački rit Reservation

In the vicinity of Osijek, at the influx of the Drava River into the Danube.

Hutovo blato

Near the town of Čaplijina, is a habitat of importance for both nesting species and migration.

Pod gredom and Prud

Areas covering 750 ha, situated north-east of Metković and are ornithological reservations important for migration and the nesting of waterfowl.

Rakita

Situated on the River Sava in the south-eastern part of Lonjsko. A protected locality important for breeding and migration.

Skadarsko jezero

Montenegro Albania (42° 07'–25' N, 19° 00'–30' E).

A lake of 40,000 ha with extensive reedbeds and seasonally flooded areas.

An important wintering and passage area for Anatidae, with up to 10,000 White-fronted Geese *Anser albifrons* and many thousands of duck, particularly Mallard *Anas platyrhynchos*, Teal *A. crecca*, Shoveler *A. clypeata*, Tufted Duck *Aythya fuligula*, Pochard *A. ferina* and Ferruginous Duck *A. nyroca*.

Zambia

The nine larger wetlands cover 23,500 sq. km, which is a little over 3 per cent of Zambia's total area. The national parks comprise 8 per cent of Zambia and include 30 per cent of its wetlands.

The most common wildfowl include Fulvous Tree Duck *Dendrocygna bicolor*, White-faced Tree Duck *D. viduata*, Red-billed Teal *Anas erythrorhyncha* and Spur-winged Goose *Plectropterus gambensis*.

Kafue Flats

A total area of 6,000 sq. km, comprising the Kafue River and its flood plains, is one of Africa's most important wetlands.

The White-faced Tree Duck *Dendrocygna viduata*, the Red-billed Teal *Anas erythrorhyncha* and the Spur-winged Goose *Plectropterus gambensis* are very common.

Bangweulu Swamps

About 6,000 sq. km, are drained by the Luapulu and Chambeshi Rivers and adjoin Lake Bangweulu to its south and east.

The White-faced Tree Duck *Dendrocygna viduata* is one of the most common species here, and the Yellow-billed Duck *Anas undulata* a fairly scarce species in Zambia is quite common in the Bangweulu Swamps.

Wildfowl of the World

Black-necked Screamer
(Northern Screamer)

Chauna chavaria

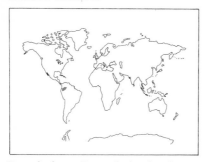

Description Top of the head and crest are grey, the cheeks are white with a patch of bare reddish skin around the eyes. There is a deep, sharply defined black collar around the neck. Upper parts and breast are dark grey with pale edgings to the feathers, under parts are of a paler grey. Tail black. The bill is short and pheasant-like in appearance, the upper mandible sharply down-curved. The pinkish legs and feet are long and stout, and have only very slight webbing between the toes. Sexes are similar. Length 70 cm.

Characteristics and Behaviour The Screamers are distant relatives of the ducks, geese and swans, with some similarities but also a number of distinct differences. There are only three species in two genera, all of them being restricted to tropical and sub-tropical South America. In spite of their unwebbed feet they swim easily along the river edges of the well-forested areas which they inhabit, the long toes enabling them to walk over the top of thick aquatic vegetation. On land they proceed with slow, deliberate strides. When disturbed they usually seek shelter in trees, perching very easily on the branches. The wings are long and broad with two sharp spurs growing from the carpal bones on the leading edge of each wing.

Habitat Marshes, thickly vegetated jungle lakes, and forest lagoons.

Distribution The ranges occupied by the two species of Screamer in the genus *Chauna* are limited in size and well over a thousand miles apart. The Black-necked Screamer is only found north of the Equator, in the northern parts of Venezuela and Colombia, from the Lago de Maracaibo west to the lower Rio Atrato. Sedentary within this range.

Food Consists mainly of vegetable matter such as aquatic plants, grasses, seeds and sometimes cultivated crops.

Voice The name 'screamer' originated from the harsh call, a high-pitched double note uttered constantly during the breeding season. The sound carries for distances well over a mile.

Display During pair formation there is much fighting, sometimes involving use of the sharp spurs on the wings. There is also a great deal of calling, with birds indulging in wheeling, soaring flight. Pairs are usually formed for life.

Breeding The nest is built either in or close to shallow water. It is constructed from sticks, aquatic vegetation and grasses; measuring up to 30 cm high. Normal clutch size is four to six, the eggs are large and smooth, yellowish white in colour. Both sexes share the incubation which takes at least 6 weeks, but the young are well developed at hatching and leave the nest after a very short time. They resemble goslings in their coats of yellow down.

Crested Screamer
(Southern Screamer)

Chauna torquata

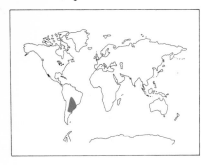

Description The crown and neck are dark grey, with cheeks and throat paler but not white as in the Black-necked Screamer. A patch of bare reddish skin extends from the base of the bill around the eye. The black collar round the neck is much less extensive than in the smaller species. The rest of the plumage is grey, paler below with broad white edging to the feathers. Tail black; bill greyish; legs and feet pink. The claws on the wings are present in both sexes which are generally similar in appearance. Length 90 cm.

Characteristics and Behaviour
The Crested Screamer is the largest of the group. In relation to their bulk the Screamers are very light in weight due to the hollow bone structure which is present to a much greater extent than in most birds, even the bones of the toes are hollow. A complicated system of air sacs beneath the skin also contributes to a low density. So despite their bulk which makes take-off laborious, the Screamers are very efficient in the air, soaring to great heights and capable of remaining on the wing for hours at a time. An unusual characteristic concerns the plumage, which does not grow in definite feather tracts but is distributed over the whole body, a feature shared

only with the ostrich, penguins and colies.

Habitat Marshy regions with small lakes and swamps, open lowlands and wet grasslands, often occurring in large flocks numbering hundreds or even thousands of individuals outside the breeding season.

Distribution South America between latitudes 15° S and 38° S. From Bolivia, Paraguay, south Brazil and Uruguay south as far as the province of La Pampa in Argentina.

Food Aquatic plants and roots, grasses, seeds, grain, etc.

Voice Similar to the Black-necked Screamer. The 'cha-ha' call note is not really a scream but more like the cry of a goose.

Display Not recorded.

Breeding The breeding season usually commences in the southern spring but appears to be quite flexible. The nest is similar to that of the Black-necked Screamer, containing five to six whitish eggs. Incubation and care of the nidifugous young are shared by both adults. Young birds are often caught and kept in captivity, where they prove to be easily domesticated and can be reared alongside the more usual domestic fowl. Screamers can be seen in many zoos and have bred successfully in captivity.

Crested Screamer with 'spurs' revealed by
partly opened wings as a threat display

Magpie Goose

Anseranas semipalmata

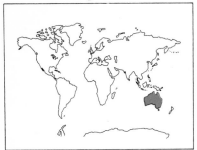

Description Head and neck are black with an extensive patch of bare skin on the forehead, sides of head pinkish with irregular black spots. Mantle, rump and underparts white; flight feathers and tail are black. Bill yellow with a black mark on each side of upper mandible. Legs and feet are orange-yellow. The sexes are similar but the unusual knob on the crown is much more prominent in the male. Length 85 cm. Immatures are browner, with less white on the mantle and rump.

Characteristics and Behaviour A fairly large bird with superficial resemblance to the true geese, but this is the only species in the genus *Anseranas*, and it has no close relatives. It has certain peculiarities of anatomy which are also found in the Screamers, but the Magpie Goose is unique amongst waterfowl in not moulting all its flight feathers at the same time, and thus never loses its powers of flight entirely. It perches readily in trees, often on the highest, most slender twigs, where its long hind toes enable it to balance skilfully. The other toes are only partially webbed, so in general it walks more easily but swims less effectively than other species of waterfowl. With broad wings and tail it flies easily. Gregarious in its habits, it is sometimes encountered in flocks of a thousand or more. Before the settlement of Australia they were much more numerous and widespread than today, but they are easily shot and in some areas their requirements conflict with those of agriculture.

Habitat Marshes, swamps, areas of temporary flood, and open plains.

Distribution Found only in the Australasian region, it is now restricted chiefly to the northern parts of Australia and southern New Guinea. Accidental in Tasmania.

Food Mainly vegetable matter, aquatic plants and grasses. Feeds by wading in shallow water or occasionally up-ending in deeper water. It also grazes on open plains at times, even associating with water buffaloes. It is often attracted to rice paddies and other irrigated areas where it can become a serious pest, feeding on the tender young shoots; but control of water levels is usually successful in preventing the birds breeding amongst the rice.

Voice The call is a high-pitched bugling. The male has an extremely long trachea which gives his voice a deeper tone than that of the female.

Breeding The breeding season is irregular, depending on the onset of the rains and could be any time between July and March. In years of drought breeding may not take place at all. The nest is usually found in wet, well-vegetated areas, built in shallow pools, on tussocks or small islands, from mud, rushes and other plant stems. The normal clutch varies from four to ten glossy white eggs with a pitted surface. Average size 78 × 53 mm. Much larger clutches have been recorded but are probably due to more than one female. Incubation period is about 35 days. The downy young are various shades of brown and buff, darker above, pale below, with buff stripes on the back, and brown eyestripes.

Magpie Goose perching on a tree top

Spotted Whistling Duck
(Spotted Tree Duck)

Dendrocygna guttata

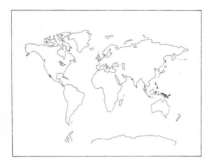

Description The dark brown of the crown extends down the back of the neck. The face, throat and sides of the upper neck are pale grey, sharply defined from the dark brown of the lower neck. There is a dark stripe through the eye. Upper parts are dark brown, upper tail coverts black and white. The breast, sides and flanks are reddish brown, heavily spotted with white, the spots surrounded with dark brown. Belly pale grey. The bill is dark with a reddish tinge. Legs and feet dark. As in all species of *Dendrocygna*, the sexes are similar in plumage. Length about 45 cm. Immatures are duller with fainter spots.

Characteristics and Behaviour Flight is very noisy due to deep notching of the first primaries which beat through the air with a loud swishing note. They are probably more arboreal than any of the other whistling ducks, perching regularly and roosting in trees overhanging or close to water. Flocks numbering hundreds have been recorded, but more frequently they are found in pairs or small groups. Non-migratory, but local movements influenced by monsoons. This is the least known of the whistling ducks, very little has been recorded of its habits and behaviour in the wild.

Habitat Swampy lagoons, rivers and marshes, etc.

Distribution The Equatorial west Pacific, from south Philippines, Celebes, west through Buru and Ceram to New Guinea and the Bismarck Archipelago.

Food Omnivorous, but mainly vegetable matter.

Voice Mainly silent, but has a harsh, low call.

Display Not recorded.

Breeding The breeding season is prolonged and usually determined by the rainy season, March, April and September recorded in New Guinea. Details of nesting behaviour are not well documented, but some nests have been found in hollow trees. The downy young resemble those of the Plumed Whistling Duck (*D. eytonii*), with lines on the back instead of the spots found on the young of the other six species.

Plumed Whistling Duck

(Grass Whistle-duck or Plumed Tree Duck)

Dendrocygna eytonii

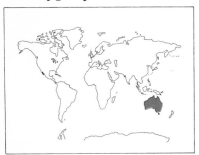

Description Both sexes similar in plumage. Olive-brown above with buff edges to feathers. Face and neck fawny buff, throat creamy white. Pale chestnut breast distinctly barred with black. Long, broad and pointed plumes of creamy feathers with black margins are arranged fanwise from either flank, making this the most handsome of tree ducks. Bill deep pink spotted and mottled with black. Legs and feet are flesh coloured. Length 50 cm. Immatures are of a uniform pale brown with less-distinct breast markings.

Characteristics and Behaviour May be recognized in the field by the characteristics already set out when describing the East Indian Wandering Tree Duck. A shy and very wary nocturnal species. The daytime being spent on the edges of lagoons, swamps or rivers usually in tightly packed groups. In the early evening they set out in a succession of parties to feed in their favoured areas. The flight and wing beat are slow and produce that familiar whistling sound. On land they are graceful and capable of walking long distances; on water they are less adept, swimming both awkwardly and slowly. Although able to dive, they seldom do so unless injured.

Habitat Tropical grasslands, but during the dry season large numbers congregate on the bare edges of swamps, rivers and lagoons. Breeding occurs during the wet season. Then the grass is very tall and so they are widely distributed throughout these grasslands.

Distribution Confined as a breeding species to Australia, but vagrants are occasionally recorded in Tasmania, New Zealand and New Guinea. The principal breeding range extends in an arc north westwards from northern New South Wales across Queensland's grass plains, the Northern Territory, and into Western Australia. Perhaps the highest breeding density being the grasslands of western Queensland.

Food Feeding occurs at night-time when the birds fly out in small groups to feed along swamp edges or on the grassy plains. Whilst feeding in compact groups the birds are constantly on the move and at all times 'whistling'. The diet is entirely vegetable with grasses being the principal food, including barnyard millets and couch, but wild rice, rushes and sedges are also taken.

Voice A shrill whistle by both male and female.

Display Males seem to fight at all times and as the wet season commences so display and posturing by the males increases in frequency. It is quite possible that many birds have a life-long partnership with their respective mates.

Breeding Peak breeding occurs during the months of February and March, but if the season is exceptionally wet this could extend into May and even commence as early as January. A simple scrape in the ground lined with grasses suffices as a nest, and this concealed under long grasses or other vegetation. The clutch usually consists of ten to twelve pure white eggs each measuring 48 × 36 mm. Both sexes share the incubation for a period of 28 days.

East Indian Wandering Whistling Duck

(Water Whistle-duck or Wandering Tree Duck)

Dendrocygna arcuata arcuata

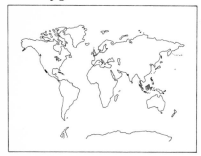

Description The plumage of both sexes is similar. In general this short-tailed species has brownish-black upperparts with feathers edged chestnut. Crown and back of neck are black, as are the primaries and outer wing coverts, the face being light brown. Breast and underparts are bright rufous with occasional black spots on the breast. The elongated flank feathers are buff, edged with chestnut. Bill is black. Legs and feet are black. Length 57 cm. Young similar to the adults but duller.

Characteristics and Behaviour Smaller and somewhat darker than the Fulvous Tree Duck. On land is distinguished from the Plumed Tree Duck in holding the head and neck far less erect; on water it floats lower and the neck is usually not extended. In flight the Wandering Tree Ducks are readily distinguished from other ducks, apart from their shrill and seemingly never ending whistle, the slow beat of short rounded wings, long trailing legs and outstretched neck with depressed head are all very characteristic. They usually occur in dense flocks on the water or out on the banks roosting. When disturbed on water they swim together forming a compact group before flying off to quieter parts. Activity often falls off noticeably during the hotter parts of the day.

Distribution Nominate race ranges through Indonesia to the Philippines.

Food They feed entirely in water either diving, even to the depths of 10 feet or so, in search of food; dabbling in shallow water; or taking seeds and flowerheads direct from aquatic plants. Feeding in flocks is quite usual. Water-lilies, grasses and sedges, pondweeds and duckweeds form a major part of the diet and feeding takes place during both daytime and at night.

Voice A shrill, incessant whistle.

Display Possibly like the courtship display of the swans and it is quite probable that they mate for life; as is usual with other tree ducks. Fighting often takes place between the males, usually at the beginning of the wet season.

Breeding This occurs between December and May. The nest, which is but a scrape in the ground, is usually not far from water and sheltered by long grass, but again often found in areas with little nest cover. The eggs are six to fourteen in number and laid on a lining of grasses, no down is added. They are cream coloured and measure 51 × 37 mm. The job of incubation is shared by both male and female for a period of 28 to 30 days.

Australian Wandering Whistling Duck

Dendrocygna arcuata australis

Slightly larger than *D. a. arcuata* (58 cm), and confined to north and north-west coastal regions of Australia.

Lesser Wandering Whistling Duck

Dendrocygna arcuata pygmaea

The smallest of the three and probably confined to New Britain.

Fulvous Whistling Duck

(Fulvous Tree Duck)

Dendrocygna bicolor

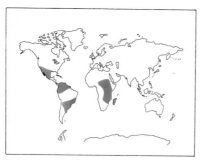

Description Sexes similar. The plumage of the crown is dark brown, continuing in a dark line down the back of the neck, the front and sides of the neck are a paler buff. The mantle and wings are dark brown, or black edged with chestnut. Breast and underparts are a rich fulvous, and the ornamental flank feathers which overlap the wing, are creamy buff and similar to the Wandering Whistling Ducks. Upper and under tail coverts are creamy white, the tail blackish. The bill is dark grey. The legs and large feet are bluish-grey. Length 45 to 50 cm. Immatures are generally paler, less distinctly coloured with the chestnut parts more brown.

Characteristics and Behaviour This species is mainly active during the night, feeding on vegetable matter, some of which is obtained by diving. In flight they progress steadily with a slow wing beat and feet extending behind the tail. The neck is extended downwards when alighting. Not particularly wary but difficult to approach closely when feeding. Most populations are non-migratory or travel only to a limited extent.

Habitat Shallow lakes and swamps in open areas, seldom near the coast in Africa. In America, ricefields, fresh water, and brackish marshes and ponds.

Distribution The remarkably disintegrated distribution, which spans the continents of north and south America, Africa and Asia, is the most noteworthy feature about this species. The separate populations are isolated by thousands of miles, yet there are no sub-species, each population remaining true to type. In north America, mainly south-western United States and Mexico, also Florida and the West Indies; in south America, from Panama south through Brazil to central Argentina. In Africa it occurs south of the Sahara from the Chad region, Sudan and Ethiopia, south to Natal, also Madagascar. In Asia, India and Burma south to Pegu, but scarce in Ceylon.

Food Mainly the seed of weeds and cultivated grain. Also aquatic insects, especially Coleoptera. In some areas of the USA planting of rice treated with insecticides has affected numbers dramatically.

Voice Similar to the Indian Whistling Duck, but shriller. The usual call is a double-noted whistle 'tsii-ee, tsoo-ee', higher pitched in the female.

Breeding Nests are usually placed in reeds or other aquatic vegetation, built up at times as much as 1 m above the water level. Constructed of plant material and usually concealed from above. In Indian sometimes built of sticks in hollow trees or large forks. Clutch size is very variable, up to six eggs are recorded in Trinidad; twelve to seventeen in North America with at times even larger numbers. They are ivory-white in colour, average size 56 × 42 mm. Incubation is by both adults and takes 24 to 26 days. The ducklings are tended by both adults. Fledging period about 9 weeks.

Black-billed Whistling Duck
(Black-billed Tree Duck)

Dendrocygna arborea

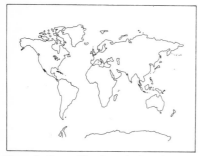

Description Head dark brown, darker, almost black on the crown and nape. The feathers at the back of the head are long and form a noticeable crest. The brown of the head shades into pale buff on the chin and throat, the lower neck being speckled with dark brown. The upperparts are dark brown with pale narrow edging to the feathers. The breast is rusty brown, the flanks pale buff with heavy black spots, and the undertail coverts also pale with smaller black spots, upper tail coverts are black. Bill black, legs and feet dark greenish to black. Sexes are similar. Length 50–56 cm. Immatures are paler and lack the black spots.

Characteristics and Behaviour This species is the largest of all the whistling ducks, with long legs and generally goose-like appearance. It is sometimes known as the West Indian or Cuban Whistling Duck. It walks well and regularly perches high-up in trees, sometimes feeding on the fruits; but swimming is very infrequent. Much of the daytime is spent concealed in the swamps, with the bird becoming active at dusk and feeding mainly at night.

Habitat Fresh- and salt-water swamps in well-wooded regions, mangroves, etc.

Distribution The very limited range is restricted to the West Indies, where the species is entirely absent from some of the islands, and has a patchy distribution on others, although it is fairly numerous in favoured areas. It occurs in the Bahamas, Cuba, Jamaica, Hispaniola, Puerto Rico, Virgin Islands and some of the more northerly Lesser Antilles.

Food Mainly vegetable matter.

Voice A harsh, high-pitched whistling.

Breeding The breeding season is usually late summer. Nests are normally on the ground, close to water amongst aquatic vegetation, occasionally in holes in trees or amongst epiphytic growth. Up to fourteen eggs have been recorded, usually ten to twelve, creamy-white in colour, average size 55 × 40 mm. The incubation period is about 30 days. The downy young are dark above, yellowish below, with a pale band between the crown and the bill, and white spots on the upperparts.

Indian Whistling Duck
(Indian Tree Duck)

Dendrocygna javanica

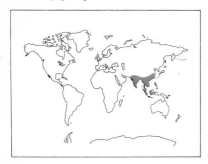

Description This is a small, short-tailed bird with plumage which bears resemblance to the Fulvous Tree Duck. The upper parts are reddish-brown, the feathers of the mantle edged with rufous. The face and neck are greyish-buff, crown darker. Lower breast and under-parts are chestnut. The upper tail coverts, which are chestnut in this species, prevent confusion with the Fulvous in which they are creamy, also the flank feathers are much less orna-mental. The bill is slaty grey to black. Legs and feet are lead grey. Sexes alike. Immatures are duller brown on the upper parts and paler below. Length 40–45 cm.

Characteristics and Behaviour Often found in large numbers in parts of its widespread range, which covers most of southern Asia, but in the breeding season the large flocks disperse and breeding pairs are more widely scat-tered. The broad, rounded wings pro-duce a noisy flight due to peculiarities of the outer flight feathers, but the birds spend much of their time on the water, swimming well and diving to depths of almost 3 m. On land its gait is more of a waddle than some of the other species – but it is quite effective, especially on marshy land. Perches freely in trees and branches overhanging water. They are not subject to any hunting pressures as they are very poor to eat.

Habitat Mainly low-lying areas with fresh-water swamps, shallow lakes with reedbeds and floating vegetation, lagoons, flooded paddy-fields. Not very frequent on the coast.

Distribution India and Ceylon, Burma and Thailand across to southern China and south Vietnam. Southwards it extends down the Malay peninsula to Sumatra, Java and parts of Borneo. It is resident in much of its range, a partial migrant in some areas, with movements determined by local rains and droughts.

Food Mainly vegetable matter, leaves, stems and roots of aquatic plants. Grain, especially rice – in some areas large flocks will descend on the paddy-fields at night and become quite a pest in some farming areas.

Voice A shrill, double noted whistle, used almost constantly when the birds are in flight.

Breeding In India the breeding season extends from June to October depending on the timing of the mon-soon. In Ceylon, eggs are laid in December–January and again in July–August. The nest is often made amongst long grasses, reeds or other vegetation. Sometimes hollows in old tree trunks are used, also forks in large branches 6 or 7 m above the ground and some distance from the water. Occasionally old nests of crows, herons and kites may be taken over. The nest is made of twigs, rushes, leaves and grasses, usually unlined apart from a few feathers. Clutch size varies from seven to twelve but up to seventeen have been recorded. They are white and smooth but become stained brown during incubation. Average size 47 × 37 mm. Both sexes are believed to share the incubation but estimates of the period vary from 22 to 30 days.

White-faced Whistling Duck
(White-faced Tree Duck)

Dendrocygna viduata

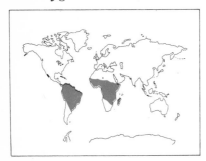

Description The front part of the head and face is white, the rear part of the head and the nape are black, a very striking contrast which makes the bird instantly recognizable even at long range. There is a white spot on the throat, separated from the white of the neck by a variable black collar; lower neck, breast and back are a rich chestnut. The mantle and scapulars are olive-brown edged with buff, the flanks are barred black and white. The rump, tail, underparts and under surface of the wing are all black. The bill is dark grey, bluish round the nostrils and with a pale band near the tip. Legs and feet are bluish-grey. The sexes are similar, but the female has the white of the head and neck tinged with rusty brown. Length 40–45 cm. Immatures have head and neck mainly buff with the crown and nape darker.

Characteristics and Behaviour Very numerous, even abundant in suitable areas throughout its widespread range, often occurring in dense flocks numbering thousands. Crepuscular and nocturnal in its feeding behaviour, usually resting during the day on sandbanks or islands, seldom perching in trees. When disturbed, flocks circle round, calling repeatedly and are so tame they do not disperse even when shotguns are fired. The flight is slow and heavy on rounded wings, but it swims buoyantly and dives well. On land it walks with an upright carriage, neck extended when alarmed. During seasons of drought lengthy movements are undertaken in search of suitable feeding areas, but there are no regular migrations.

Habitat Inland lakes, pools, swamps, river banks and estuaries, temporary floodwaters, salt-water lagoons and coastal islands.

Distribution Found in both the Old and New Worlds. In Africa south of the Sahara to Angola and Natal, but rare in the extreme south. Also Madagascar. In South America, north-east Colombia, north Venezuela, Guyana, Surinam, Brazil, Paraguay, Uruguay and north Argentina. Also Costa Rica, Trinidad and Curacao.

Food Feeds by wading in shallow waters, also by diving. Aquatic vegetation, grasses, weeds, seeds and small aquatic animals.

Voice Very noisy, the call is a clear high-pitched whistle of three syllables.

Breeding The season is very variable and dependant on rains. Recorded in most months of the year in Africa. January to April in Zambia, March to July in Malawi, October to November in Rhodesia, August to October in Trinidad. The nest is often in hollow trees in South America; but in Africa mostly on the ground, well concealed amongst thick vegetation. It is sparsely lined with grasses and no down is added. Eggs are usually eight to twelve in number, creamy-white with a pinkish tinge, average size 47 × 36 mm. The incubation period of 28 days is shared by male and female. The downy young are dark brown above, creamy yellow below, with creamy spots on the back and sides of rump.

White-faced Whistling Ducks – mutual preening

Red-billed Whistling Duck
(Red-billed Tree Duck)

Dendrocygna autumnalis

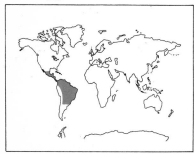

Description Head and upper neck are grey, with crown and back of neck dark brown, the feathers of the nape forming a small occipital tuft. There is a white ring around the eye. Lower neck, breast and mantle are rusty chestnut. Wings dull white and black. Underparts black, undertail coverts white with black markings, tail black. Bill pinkish-red with a blue nail. Legs and feet are pink to pale flesh colour. Sexes similar. Length 50–55 cm. Immatures lack the black of the underparts and have greyish-brown and breast. The southern race *D. a. discolor* from South America has a greyish-brown mantle and breast and is slightly smaller.

Characteristics and Behaviour A fairly large species which breeds colonially and sometimes occurs in huge flocks outside the breeding season. It will associate with Fulvous Whistling Ducks in areas where both species are found. In flight the large white patch on the forewing is very conspicuous. Feeding takes place mainly at dusk or during the night. Migratory in habits in the extreme north and south of its range, but for the most part makes only local movements dependent on the food supply. The habit of perching varies according to locality, dead trees are often used, sometimes low bushes.

Habitat Generally prefers areas of shallow water, well-vegetated lagoons, lakes, muddy areas, and fresh-water marshes.

Distribution The Northern Red-billed Whistling Duck (*D. a. autumnalis*) occurs from south Texas and Mexico through Central America to Panama. The southern race (*D. a. discolor*) is found from Panama south to northern Argentina, Paraguay and southern Brazil. The wintering range extends from south Mexico southwards, although small numbers have been known to winter in south Texas. The extent to which southern populations migrate northwards is not precisely known.

Food Mainly vegetable, especially seeds and in some areas grain when available. Roots and tubers of aquatic plants; sometimes feeding by up-ending. The small amounts of animal matter consists mainly of insects and molluscs.

Voice A noisy species, possessing a variety of notes, but the usual call is a four noted whistle, on a descending scale, high-pitched and musical.

Breeding The breeding season extends from April to October in Texas. The nest is usually in a tree cavity, occasionally on the ground where it is made of grasses and well concealed. The normal clutch size varies from twelve to sixteen, but larger numbers up to fifty or sixty are sometimes found 'dumped' in a communal nest. The eggs are whitish and smooth, average size 52 × 39 mm. Incubation, which is by both adults, varies from 25 to 30 days. The ducklings leave tree nests within 2 days of hatching, being tended by both parents. They are bright yellow with dark brown markings on upperparts and sides, a dark crown and a stripe through the eye. Fledging period is 8 to 9 weeks.

[46]

Coscoroba Swan

Coscoroba coscoroba

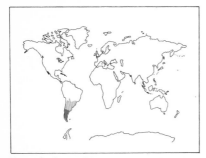

Description Plumage entirely white apart from black tips to the primaries, most conspicuous when the bird is in flight. Its bill is a bright rosy pink tipped with a white nail. The legs and feet are a somewhat lighter shade of pink. It is not yet certain whether the Coscoroba is more closely related to the swans or the whistling ducks (tree ducks). Not being a member of the genus *Cygnus* it is not a 'true' swan. Nevertheless it is quite similar in general appearance. In other respects it resembles the *Dendrocygnae* (Whistling ducks), especially in the construction of its bill, which suggests that it does not graze extensively like the swans. The downy young have dark markings on the head and back, another feature not shared by the swans but very similar to the downy young of whistling ducks.

Characteristics and Behaviour Walks more easily and much more frequently than the other South America species, the Black-necked Swan. It also swims well and is able to take-off from the water without any preliminary run. It is the smallest of the swans, usually weighing no more than 4–4½ kg.

Habitat Well-vegetated lakes and ponds, also in marshy regions.

Distribution In the wild, the Coscoroba is restricted to the southern parts of South America where it breeds in Tierra del Fuego, Argentina, Chile, Uruguay and as far north as Paraguay and the southern tip of Brazil. Distribution within the range is very scattered, with the bird absent from large areas, but sometimes found in large flocks in a few suitable localities. In the austral winter they move farther north but always remaining in the southern half of South America. There is no set pattern to these migratory movements.

Food This species has been little studied in the wild, and there are no recorded observations on feeding behaviour. However, the construction of its bill, which resembles that of the Whistling ducks, suggests that it does not graze as extensively as the true swans, nor does it feed by up-ending in the manner adopted by all other swans.

Voice The call is unusual, consisting of four loud notes on a descending scale. The bird's name, which is an attempt at onomatopoeia, is a passable impression of the four notes.

Display Not recorded in the wild.

Breeding The nest is a heap of mud and aquatic vegetation, usually at the edge of a lake or lagoon and more profusely lined with feathers and down than other swans. Incubation of the eggs is by the female, with the male standing guard. Details of incubation are lacking except from birds in captivity.

Black Swan

Cygnus atratus

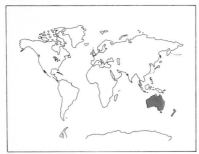

Description On the water, appears almost entirely black; in flight, the white primaries become very conspicuous, creating a most striking and unexpected appearance. The bill is crimson, with a broad white band on the upper mandible. The legs and feet are dark grey. Immature birds are a dull brown, paler below, with a dark brown bill and grey legs and feet. Length 150 cm.

Characteristics and Behaviour Although very graceful on water, rather awkward on dry land. They rise in the air only with some effort, and once airborne their wing beats produce a sound very similar to the Mute Swan. Very active at dusk, when they will often move to other feeding grounds, keeping contact with their loud trumpeting calls. They also move about freely on moonlit nights.

Habitat Favours large lakes with shallow margins, swampy areas, brackish or salt-water lagoons, estuaries and sheltered bays. In the breeding season, mainly on large waters but will take advantage of small temporary floodwaters to attempt breeding almost any time.

Distribution Endemic to Australia and Tasmania only, but has been introduced to New Zealand. Occurs throughout Australia wherever suitable habitat is to be found, except in the extreme north of Queensland and Northern Territory; the largest concentrations are in the south-west. Its introduction to New Zealand in 1864 was so successful, with practically no predators or competitors, that in some areas rather drastic measures had to be taken to control numbers and keep them within reasonable bounds. Although not truly migratory, it has a tendency to wander in response to temporary flooding after irregular heavy rains, or in search of more permanent waters during periods of prolonged drought. It is the state bird of Western Australia, where it was first seen in the estuary of the Swan River by Vlaming in 1697. Flocks of up to 50,000 strong are on record.

Food Appears to be completely vegetarian. Mainly leaves and stems of aquatic plants and much submerged plant life including *Potamogeton* spp. and algae. Some seeds are eaten by young birds but no specific animal food has been recorded.

Voice The call is a high pitched, bugling usually emitted with neck outstretched. There is also a wide-range of more conversational notes.

Display Much like the Mute Swan. When aggressive the wings are arched over the back like the Mute but the neck is held straight and curved sharply near the head so that the bill points downwards at a steep angle.

Breeding The breeding season varies according to the rains, starting in June or July in the south but sometimes as late as December. Not normally territorial, nests are often in large colonies and spaced only a few metres apart. The site chosen is frequently a sedgy island in a lake or lagoon, the nest itself being a bulky but neat arrangement of twigs, rushes and waterweeds, lined with white down and placed in reeds or sedges, occasionally built-up in shallow water. Eggs are pale green with a chalky covering which becomes stained during

incubation. Five or six is the usual number but some clutches have contained as many as fourteen eggs. Both male and female share the incubation, the only swan to do so. The female usually sits at night, the male during the day, with the non-incubating bird standing guard. The incubation period is variable but usually between 34–37 days. The downy chicks are greyish-brown with a black bill tipped grey and dark grey legs and feet. They are occasionally carried on the backs of the adults but not as often as the cygnets of the Mute Swan.

Black Swan in flight

Black-necked Swan

Cygnus melanocoryphus

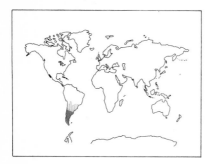

Description Entire plumage of the body and lower neck is white, with the remainder of the neck and head black. The bill is bluish-grey with a conspicuous bright red caruncle at the base, present in both male and female. There is a white line from the forehead round the eye extended towards the back of the head. The legs and feet are a pale flesh colour. Length 100 cm. Immature birds have a lot of grey in the body plumage with dark edges to the primaries. They lack the bright red caruncle at the base of the bill which does not appear until they are fully mature at 3 to 4 years of age. The black and white adult plumage however is attained in the second year.

Characteristics and Behaviour The most aquatic of all the swans, seldom leaving the water except in the breeding season. They move very awkwardly on land, and feeding takes place almost entirely in the water. Flight is rapid and noisy, and the take-off much more laboured than that of the Coscoroba. Occurs in flocks outside the breeding season. Generally of shy disposition and difficult to approach closely.

Habitat Favours lakes and marshes, preferably of large size. In the Falkland Islands it is found in brackish estuaries as well as fresh-water lakes. Outside the breeding season large flocks have been recorded in the fjords of Tierra del Fuego and islands off southern Chile.

Distribution The southern half of South America, barely reaching the tropic of Capricorn at the limit of its non-breeding range. Breeds in Brazil from São Paulo, south to Uruguay, Paraguay and Argentina, in Chile south from Coquimbo, Tierra del Fuego and the Falkland Islands. It is thus found over much the same area as the Coscoroba but is not as frequent in coastal regions. They are most numerous in the southern parts of the range, and these populations probably make the longest migrations north in the southern winter. The Falkland Islands population is non-migratory. In Argentina, flocks numbering hundreds can be encountered, but the species is less numerous than in former years and in need of some form of protection.

Food Mainly aquatic vegetation, with some small amounts of fish spawn and aquatic insects, but few observations in the wild. Different feeding methods from the Coscoroba may minimize competition between the two species. In the Falkland Islands, sometimes feeds in marine Kelp beds.

Voice More of a whistling sound compared to the other swans, soft and musical.

Display The birds circle each other, calling repeatedly while moving the head and neck up and down. Aggressive intention by the male in defence of its territory is signalled by lowering the neck and thrusting the head forward, but the wings are not arched as with the Mute Swan.

Breeding The breeding season extends from July to November. Nests are built in brackish lakes and swamps, in shallow water or amongst waterside vegetation, where a loosely constructed mound of plant material is accumulated. Clutch size varies from three to

seven long cream coloured eggs, average size 101 × 66 mm. The incubation period in the wild has not been determined, but ranges from 33 to 36 days in captivity. The male mounts an almost continuous guard on the nest, and the female will incubate for lengthy periods, sometimes days, without leaving to feed. Breeding is usually territorial, but on large lakes nests have been found within 15 m of each other. The downy chicks are white, with bill, legs and feet black. They are carried on to the water almost immediately on the backs of the adults, where they remain for the first 2 or 3 weeks, the adults feeding more cautiously to avoid dislodging them. In the early stages the tiny cygnets are well protected and often completely hidden beneath the wing feathers of the adults, at these times it can be very difficult or even impossible to detect their presence.

Mute Swan

Cygnus olor

Description All three European swans are large birds with long necks and immaculate white plumage. Features which distinguish the Mute Swan from Whooper and Bewick's are the pinkish-red bill with black base and conspicuous knob which is more prominent in the male. The carriage of the neck in a graceful curve is also distinctive. Legs and feet are black. The male (cob) is larger than the female (pen) with a length of 150 cm. Juveniles are grey-brown in plumage with grey bill and legs. The 'Polish' Swan is a variety in which downy cygnets and juveniles are white from the start, with pale coloured legs which never become black.

Characteristics and Behaviour Many of the Mute Swans to be found in the British Isles are of semi-domesticated origin, but some wild migrants may occur as winter visitors. The characteristic attitude of 'sailing' on the water with wings arched above the back and tail elevated is not shared by other northern swans. In flight, the powerful wing beats create an unmistakable singing swish on the downstroke which is audible up to half a mile away. From the eleventh century most Mute Swans in Britain were domesticated, they were classed as royal birds and permission to keep them was only granted by the Crown – if the birds were pinioned to prevent flight and marked in such a way that the owner could be identified. These marks were usually cut or scratched on the upper mandible, or sometimes on the legs or webs of the feet. This marking of swans still persists on the River Thames, but in general most Mute Swans have now reverted to a free existence.

Habitat Lakes, ponds, reservoirs, slow-flowing rivers, estuaries and sea lochs are all suitable habitats for a pair during the breeding season, provided there are shallow areas with sufficient food to raise a brood of cygnets. Even the smallest ponds can be suitable if there is just sufficient length for the birds extended take-off run. Most pairs are strongly territorial in the breeding habitat except where abundant food supplies occur in a relatively small area, e.g. coastal *Zostera* beds; in these circumstances large numbers may nest in fairly close proximity. Many Mute Swans are more or less sedentary, but in parts of the range, especially in Europe, large flocks build up in sheltered coastal areas during the winter.

Distribution The breeding range is highly fragmented across Europe and Asia, mainly in the temperate zone between 40° and 60° N. It includes the British Isles, Netherlands, Denmark, southern Sweden, Germany, Roumania, Russia, Asia Minor and east to Mongolia and Manchuria. Some populations winter within the breeding range, others go south to the Mediterranean and south-west Asia. The species has been introduced to many countries including Australia, in 1866 to New Zealand, and the USA.

Food, A little more animal matter is taken than by the Whooper and Bewick's Swan, but the diet is still almost entirely vegetable. Mainly submerged vegetation together with stems and roots of aquatic plants. Tadpoles, small frogs, worms, insects and their

larvae, small fish and fresh-water molluscs are taken in small quantities when available. In coastal areas *Zostera* is the favourite food plant.

Voice   Not strictly voiceless. It possesses various grunting, snoring and hissing notes, while the cygnets have a thin piping call.

Display   Little courtship display prior to pair formation, but the aggressive display is frequently seen, with neck drawn back and wings arched over the back.

Breeding   The breeding season usually commences in late April or early May, occasionally a little earlier. The nest is a huge pile of reed stems, leaves, roots, rushes and sticks, etc. placed in shallow water or on a bank or island. Both birds help in gathering the material which is finally arranged by the female. The greyish-white eggs are usually four to seven in number, 115 × 75 mm and take about 5 weeks to hatch. Unlike other European swans, the Mute often carries the cygnets on its back, sheltering them between half-open wings. There is a lengthy fledging period and young birds sometimes remain with their parents through the autumn and winter.

[55]

Bewick's Swan

Cygnus bewickii

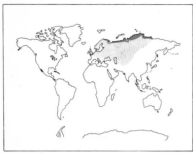

Description Adult plumage entirely white. The bill black with a yellow patch at the base but the yellow area is smaller than in the Whooper Swan and ends abruptly well behind the nostrils.

The pattern of yellow is infinitely variable, and whilst not sufficient to cause confusion with Whooper Swans, it was enough to lead Sir Peter Scott to the remarkable discovery that individual swans could be recognized by this characteristic alone. Legs and feet are black.

Juvenile birds are similar in colouring to young Whoopers, with the bill pattern pinkish or browny-yellow for the first 12 months.

Characteristics and Behaviour Bewick's Swan is the smallest of the three European species of swans having a total length of 120 cm. However, size alone is not a reliable factor for identification unless a direct comparison can be made. This is evidenced by the fact that only one 'wild' swan was recognized in Britain until 1830 when William Yarrell described the smaller species and named it after Thomas Bewick. Nowadays some systematists consider Bewick's Swan to be merely a sub-species of *Cygnus columbianus* – the Whistling Swan of North America. Besides being smaller, it has a relatively shorter neck than the Whooper and a stockier, less-elongated body. It often migrates and winters in family parties, sometimes of three or four generations, but congregates in large numbers at favourite winter haunts and migration stations. Said not to fly in regular formations. Walks easily and grazes on land more than other swans.

Habitat In the breeding season – large river estuaries and shallow tundra pools with rich marginal vegetation. In winter – shallow coastal areas, estuaries and flooded meadows, particularly where food supplies are artificially supplemented.

Distribution Breeding distribution restricted almost entirely to the tundra region of Northern Russia and Siberia, from the Kola peninsula and Petsamo east to the delta of the Lena River; thus complementary to range of the Whooper. Eastwards from the Lena it is replaced by the sub-species known as Jankowski's Swan, supposedly with a slightly larger bill but very difficult to distinguish. Birds from this eastern end of the range winter in China and Japan with the western population wintering in the British Isles, France, Netherlands, West Germany and Denmark. Since the 1950s increasing numbers have been wintering in England, especially at Slimbridge and on the Ouse Washes which frequently hold over a thousand birds. There has been a corresponding decrease in Scotland and Ireland.

Food In summer, chiefly leaves, stems and roots of aquatic plants, with possibly some animal matter in the form of insects and their larvae consumed especially by the young. In winter the diet includes seeds and grasses as well as aquatic plants, also waste left from the harvesting of grain and root crops.

Voice Resembles that of Whooper Swan but softer and more musical. Alarm note is a harsh 'howk' repeated several times. Like the Whooper it also

has quieter buglings used on the water and when feeding.

Display Unlike the Mute Swan, aggressive behaviour is not accompanied by arching of wings above the back. Courtship display is similar to that of the Whooper's, with preliminary pairing activities involving sinuous neck movements observed in mid-winter.

Breeding Nests often made on small islands in river estuaries and lakes, or at the edge of tundra pools. Constructed from mosses, lichens and sedges, they have a deep depression lined with down and feathers. Being used year after year the accumulation of material sometimes stands 75 cm high. The normal clutch is three to five creamy-white eggs of 102 × 68 mm. Incubation is by the female alone and for a period of about 5 weeks. Both adults tend the young which require a further 6 weeks to fledge.

Head of Bewick's Swan

Whooper Swan

Cygnus cygnus

Description Adult plumage is entirely white. The bill is black with yellow markings at the base more extensive than those of Bewick's Swan and usually terminating in a fairly sharp point on the lower edge of the upper mandible. There is no knob as with the Mute Swan. Legs and feet are black. Juvenile birds are mainly ash-brown but greyer than juvenile Mute Swans and with flesh coloured bill, legs and feet. Length 150 cm.

Characteristics and Behaviour Much wilder bird than the Mute Swan, usually difficult to approach closely and avoiding close proximity to areas of human activity other than agriculture, although there are a few notable exceptions. The long neck is usually held fairly straight, especially when the adult is on the alert, but is frequently curved when feeding or if angry. It walks easily on longish legs with a high stepping action. In flight the wings do not produce the loud vibrant soughing of the Mute Swan, merely a swishing comparable with other large birds. Outside the breeding season flocks are formed, and occasionally family parties, but sometimes numbering hundreds of individuals. On migrating flights they will adopt V or echelon formations, usually at no great altitude.

Habitat In the breeding season includes fresh-water lakes, small pools, slow-moving rivers, swampy areas and stony plateaux; seldom in the tundra region. At this time pairs are strongly territorial and defend an area sufficiently large for the feeding requirements of the family. In winter a preference is shown not only for coastal areas, but also for inland lakes, reservoirs, rivers and sometimes quite small pools.

Distribution The breeding range in northern Europe and Asia is very extensive and almost entirely in the boreal forest zone, seldom found beyond the tree-line and there only slightly overlapping the breeding range of Bewick's Swan. The majority of pairs nest within the coniferous forest area with smaller numbers in the birch zone. The range extends from Iceland in the west, parts of northern Scandinavia and Finland, through Russia and Siberia east to Kamchatka peninsula, the Commander Islands and Anadyrland. Small numbers of Whooper Swans occur in Scotland, where breeding was once regular in Orkney Islands but there are no confirmed breeding records for the past 30 years since a pair nested successfully in the Outer Hebrides. In winter, migrates to western Europe, from Britain south to the Iberian peninsula, the Mediterranean, Black Sea and Caspian Sea, northern India, China and Japan. Migrants to Scotland, Ireland, northern England and north Wales are mainly of Icelandic origin.

Food Mainly vegetable, but animal matter recorded includes worms, aquatic insects and fresh-water molluscs. Leaves, stems and roots of aquatic plants are consumed in quantity, also grasses, seeds and winter wheat, etc. In some inland areas feeds in cultivated areas, stubble fields and water meadows. *Zostera* is a staple food of birds wintering in coastal areas.

Voice A loud, double noted bugling with the second note of higher pitch than

the first; it is this whooping call from which the bird's name is derived. The alarm is a harsh, single noted version of the call, and a variety of lower 'conversational' notes have been described.

Display Courtship display is elaborate, commencing with the male moving his head up and down and calling noisily with open wings. As the pair approach each other they rise in the water beating their wings with head and neck extended upwards.

Breeding The nest is a bulky structure of mosses, grasses, aquatic plants and some mud. It is often placed on an islet in a large lake, but also close to pools in boggy areas and along calm reaches of rivers. The same nest may be built up and used again in subsequent years. The usual clutch is five to six creamy-white eggs, averaging some 113 × 73 mm in size. Laying commences from late May in Iceland to mid-June in more northerly regions. Incubation is by the female alone and takes 35–40 days. The male stands guard nearby. Both adults care for the young which can fly after 8 or 9 weeks.

Head of Whooper Swan

[59]

Trumpeter Swan

Cygnus buccinator

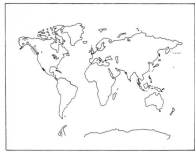

Description Adult birds have entirely white plumage, the sexes being similar, but the male slightly larger. A rusty staining of the plumage is frequent when feeding in iron-rich waters. The bill and lores are normally black, with no yellow marking except a small orange-yellow mark on the lores. Legs and feet are usually grey to black, but sometimes shaded with olive, yellow or orange. Juveniles are browny-grey, with yellowish legs and flesh coloured bill.

Characteristics and Behaviour The largest of all the swans, but accounts of its actual dimensions vary widely; there can be considerable differences between individuals. At 150 cm in length it differs little from the Whooper, but it is heavier, with large specimens weighing over 13 kg. The head has a distinct wedge-shaped appearance with the forehead and culmen being almost in a straight line. The range of the Trumpeter in the USA was formerly much more widespread than at present, the large low-flying birds being an easy and profitable target for the guns of early European settlers. By the early 1930s this southern population had been reduced to a remnant and was finally saved only by establishment of Red Rock Lakes Natural Wildlife Refuge in 1935.

Habitat In the breeding season, shallow fresh-water lakes and small ponds as little as 1 acre in extent, bordered with aquatic vegetation and with adequate submerged plant life for feeding purposes. In winter, suitably vegetated fresh waters not subject to freezing. Also occasionally in coastal areas, particularly in south-west Alaska, and some marshy areas inland.

Distribution Breeding range formerly extended across the USA from Idaho to the Great Lakes, south as far as Missouri. Northwards the range included central and north Canada and Alaska. Today breeding areas in the USA are restricted mainly to Red Rock Lakes National Wildlife Refuge, Yellowstone National Park and half a dozen other Wildlife and Forest Refuges in Montana, Idaho and Wyoming. Numbers in Canada are also much depleted, being restricted mainly to the Grande Prairie region of Alberta, with small numbers in the Cypress Hills. The Alaskan population has been least affected, and this is now the stronghold of the species supporting 3,000–4,000 birds. In winter, Trumpeters have a tendency to remain within the breeding areas so long as waters remain unfrozen or if grain is provided to supplement the diet. The Alaskan population is the most migratory, many moving south to the bays and island-dotted coast of British Columbia.

Food Almost entirely vegetable. Leaves, stems roots and tubers of submerged aquatic plants are consumed in large quantities. Pondweed, duckweed, water milfoil and sedges are some of the preferred items. Feeding methods include submerging the head and neck, up-ending in deeper water, and trampling to loosen roots and tubers. Young birds take a larger proportion of animal matter, such as insects and crustaceans, during their fledging period.

Voice A loud resounding honking, usually of two syllables 'ko-hoh', a much deeper note than the Whistling Swans.

Display Occurs most frequently during the breeding season when pairs are defending territories. Aggression is shown by partly raising and flapping the wings, with neck extended and accompanied by sharp, rapid calling. Pulling the feathers of the intruders; chasing and aerial pursuit are also part of the aggressive display. Successful defence of the territory is followed by the 'triumph' ceremony when the pair swim towards each other with wings trailing and neck folded close to the body. Pumping the head up and down whilst calling is usually an indication of intention to take flight.

Breeding Trumpeters take at least 3 years to reach maturity, with most pairs not commencing to breed until they are 4 or 5 years old. The nest is constructed from sedges and other aquatic plants gathered from the immediate area so that completed nests are usually surrounded by a 'moat' of open water where the plants have been uprooted. The site is usually at the edge of a shallow lake or on a marshy island, but occasionally nests are found on marshy ground some distance from the nearest open water. Numerous nests are built on the top of muskrat houses.

Some four to seven eggs are laid, size 110 × 70 mm originally white but becoming stained during incubation. The incubation period lasts 33 to 37 days, by the female alone, the male standing guard. A further 13 to 15 weeks are required before the young can fly. There is much variation in the rate of development of the young and many are trapped, still unable to fly, by an early freeze.

Swan Goose
(Chinese Goose)

Anser cygnoides

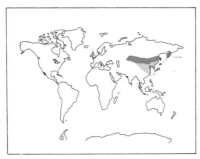

Description Fairly large with a total length of 110–120 cm. Upperparts and flanks are greyish-brown with paler bands formed by creamy edgings to the feathers. Underparts are a more uniform paler brown, whilst the bill is black and unusually long, more closely resembling that of a swan. At the base of the bill is a narrow white band, sometimes inconspicuous. The crown and back of the neck are chestnut, with the rest of the head, front and sides of neck, pale buff. Legs and feet are bright orange, the legs being fairly long. Immature birds are a little paler and lack the white at the base of the bill.

Characteristics and Behaviour Although restricted to Asia in the wild, the Swan Goose has been domesticated for two or three thousand years, and in this form, known as the Chinese Goose or African Goose it has found its way to many other parts of the world. Like all geese the wild species stands with the body horizontal, but domesticated birds hold the body upright. Their general appearance has also changed considerably, the bill is much shorter and has a frontal knob resembling the Mute Swan, they have also become heavier and are unable to fly.

Migratory within the Asian continent but not in the extreme north.

Habitat In the breeding season, the side of large lakes and rivers, marshy areas, even small streams. In winter, mainly on coasts, estuaries and lakes.

Distribution In summer, the breeding range is roughly limited to the area between the latitudes of 48° N and 57° N in a wide belt stretching across Asia from the River Ob in the west to Kamchatka in the east. This area includes most of southern Siberia, northern Mongolia and Sakhalin. In the autumn it migrates south through Mongolia and Manchuria to north-east China and the two largest Japanese islands of Hokkaido and Honshu.

Food Not many facts are recorded about food items in the wild state, but the shape of the bill suggests that it feeds mainly on aquatic plants and grazes less frequently than most other geese.

Voice A loud and high-pitched honking, the note more extended than in the Grey-lag Goose and ending on a higher pitch. The calls of domesticated birds are louder and used more regularly.

Display Typical of the genus.

Breeding The nest is made close to lakes, rivers, in swamps or in grassland on the steppes, during April or May. It is lined with down and usually contains five to eight white eggs, size 82 × 56 mm. Incubation is by the female, with the male on guard nearby, and extends a little over 4 weeks. When the brood leave the nest they are tended by both parents, while later several families may join up together. When danger threatens the goslings, they will freeze in an attempt to conceal themselves, but on the water they will dive to escape danger. Adults will also dive occasionally during the flightless period. Downy chicks have brownish upperparts, paler below, and a black patch over the eyes, their bill, legs and feet are dark grey.

Domestic Chinese Goose

Wild ancestor Swan Goose

[63]

Grey-lag Goose

Anser anser

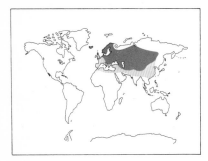

Description General appearance of plumage is greyish-brown, the upperparts lightly barred with pale margins to the feathers. Underparts are similar, shading to ash grey on the lower breast and white on the belly. The head and neck have similar colouring to the body, not darker as in the Pink-footed Goose. The bill is large, orange coloured with a white nail. Legs and feet are flesh coloured. Immature birds have greyish legs and usually lack the spotting or blotching on the breast present on most adults. Length 80 cm.

Characteristics and Behaviour Largest of the 'Grey geese' and the only goose indigenous to the British Isles. Today most of the Grey-lags breeding in Britain are feral, the wild population having been almost eliminated during the past two centuries. Gregarious by nature, they are seen in groups varying from family parties to flocks numbering thousands. Flight is strong and direct, usually in formation when any distance is travelled. On land they move easily and are able to run swiftly to avoid danger during the moult.

Habitat In the breeding season – lowland marshes, open moorland with swamps, extensive reed marshes and even small offshore islands. Formerly in the fens of Cambridgeshire and Lincolnshire. Out of the breeding season – salt- and fresh-water marshes, estuaries, pasture land, stubble fields and potato fields, etc.

Distribution In summer the range extends from Iceland, north Scotland, Scandinavia and Finland east to Russia. Also Germany and Poland. It is replaced by the eastern race, which is slightly larger and has a pinker bill, in south-east Europe, Asia Minor and USSR from the Urals east to Manchuria. In autumn the Iceland birds migrate to the British Isles, arriving usually in October, the rest of the European population wintering in the Netherlands, France, Spain, North Africa and the eastern Mediterranean. The eastern populations winter in north-west India, Burma and south China.

Food Variable. Includes grasses, roots and rhizomes of marsh plants, spilled grain in stubbles, and a wide range of root crops such as potatoes, turnips, swedes and carrots; at times, also small aquatic animals.

Voice The call is the well known, loud, three-noted honking of the familiar farmyard goose, of which the Grey-lag is the ancestor. Calls vary and could possibly help to identify individuals. There are lower conversational notes and hissing is used in threat and anger.

Display Courtship behaviour takes place in winter amongst young unmated birds, older adults being paired for life. The gander drives away all other suitors from his intended mate, and returns cackling in triumph, until he is finally accepted. Pre-mating display takes place in the water and involves the pair swimming towards each other with tail elevated and head dipping in the water.

Breeding The breeding season commences early May in Iceland, late April in Scotland and a little earlier in Mid-Europe. The nest site can be a depression in the ground amongst heather,

built-up amongst reeds or rushes, an elevated site in marshy regions, or on small islets where they are comparatively safe from predators such as foxes. Pairs are usually territorial or in small colonies. The nest is lined with down and feathers, the clutch size varies considerably from three to as many as ten or twelve, but four to six is normal, size 85 × 58 mm. The eggs are creamy-white when fresh but often become stained in the nest. Incubation lasts 27–28 days, by the female alone. Goslings leave the nest almost immediately after drying out, the female leading them to a suitable feeding area with the male guarding the rear of the procession. The downy young are brownish on the crown and upperparts of the body, with pale yellow underparts and a white bar on the wing. Bill, legs and feet are grey. The young birds feed themselves and are fully fledged in about 8 weeks.

White-fronted Goose

Anser albifrons albifrons

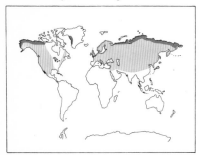

Description Darker and slightly smaller than the Grey-lag. Adults have head and neck dark brown, upperparts also brown but with light edging to the feathers. Front of neck and underparts are greyish, with breast and belly displaying irregular black bars that vary with each individual. Most characteristic is a prominent white patch at the base of the bill. Colour of the bill – various shades of pink, often very pale. Legs and feet are orange, but sometimes a bright flesh colour. Immature birds differ in lacking both the white forehead and black barring of the underparts. Length 70 cm. The Greenland race *A. a. flavirostris* is distinguished by darker head and neck and orange-yellow bill.

Characteristics and Behaviour Similar to Grey-lag in general habits but can be extremely agile, even acrobatic, in its flight. It also has the ability to spring almost vertically from the ground on take-off. On migration they are often seen in association with other species, and though feeding in large flocks, there is a tendency to subdivide into smaller units.

Habitat In the breeding season – arctic tundra, mainly low-lying coastal areas with swamps and shallow lakes. Usually above the tree-line but occasionally in shrub tundra. In North America mainly sub-arctic regions, including open areas in the forest zone.

In Greenland, low arctic tundra and small marine islands in the north of the range with a holarctic distribution between them.

Distribution Four sub-species are generally recognized. The type species breeds along the arctic coast from the Kanin peninsula in north-east Russia, Kolguev Island and Novaya Zemlya east to Siberia as far as the Kolyma River where it probably intergrades with the Pacific White-front *A. a. frontalis*. This race occurs on both sides of the Bering Straits in east Siberia and Alaska and north-west Canada as far east as King William Island. In Greenland *A. a. flavirostris* is restricted to a narrow belt along the west coast. The breeding range of the Thule White-fronted Goose is not yet accurately known.

In winter practically the whole of the Greenland population flies south-east to winter in Ireland and eastern parts of Scotland and England. The Wexford Slobs in Ireland often hold half the population, and another large group winters on Islay in the Inner Hebrides. Some of the Russian breeders migrate to England, Belgium, the Netherlands and Germany. Others winter in south-east Europe, east Mediterranean, Black Sea and Caspian Sea. Pacific White-fronts usually keep to their respective sides of the Bering Straits, with Siberian birds wintering in India, Burma, China and Japan; American birds going south to California, Texas and central Mexico.

Food Mainly grasses, although in some areas birds are adapting to feed more on agricultural land. In North America quantities of berries are consumed in the autumn. Probably small amounts of animal food including insects and molluscs, etc. are also taken.

Voice The call is higher pitched, more musical and delivered more rapidly than other grey geese, usually a double noted 'kow-yow'. The quality of the

sound is such that in some areas the bird is known as the 'laughing goose'.

Display Similar in most respects to that of the Grey-lag.

Breeding Usually nests in large scattered colonies in open tundra, marshes, islets in lakes, rivers or off the coast. Breeding begins in May or early June, the nest being placed on a small mound, ridge or other slightly elevated position with a clear all-round view. It is constructed from plant material close at hand, and rather sparsely lined with down and feathers. Eggs four to seven, creamy-white but becoming stained, average size 79 × 52 mm. Incubation is by the female alone, with the male standing guard, for a period of 27–28 days. When the goslings are dry they leave the nest accompanied by both adults, but not travelling far in the initial stages. Later they move to a suitable moulting area, usually on water, where the young escape danger by diving. Fledging period is about 8 weeks. Downy young are similar to young Grey-lags but are darker brown above.

Western Bean Goose

Anser fabilis fabilis

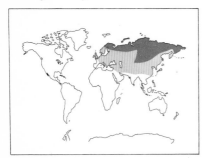

Description A much browner bird than the Grey-lag with a long neck and relatively slender, tapering body. The feathers of the mantle, wings and sides of the body have pale buff or white tips, often prominent, giving a slightly barred appearance. Generally, plumage is more uniform than other grey geese, lacking the paler forewing of the Grey-lag and the dark belly markings of the two White-fronts. The colour and shape of the bill varies considerably with geographical location, and this has led to a complex situation where taxonomists recognize six or more different sub-species, which intergrade in parts of the range. These are sometimes divided into two main groups. The tundra Bean Geese, breeding in arctic tundra regions in the northern part of the range, have a shorter bill with long tapering nail and curved lower mandible. The forest Bean Geese, breeding in coniferous zones south of the tundra, have a long slender bill with short, rounded nail and a straight lower mandible. The bill is orange-yellow and black; tundra geese being mainly black with orange-yellow band near the tip, forest geese (which include the nominate race *A. f. fabilis* or Western Bean Goose) have a mainly orange-yellow bill. Legs are orange or orange-yellow. Immatures are slightly duller but very similar to adults. Length 78 cm.

Characteristics and Behaviour With the exception of the Grey-lag, this is the largest of the grey geese, and in general the most silent. Normal habits very similar to other species in the group, but Bean Geese have a tendency to roost more frequently inland, on lakes and marshes. In the British Isles returning migrants in autumn used to feed on waste left behind from the bean harvest, a crop which was grown much more extensively than at present. This habit gave rise to the bird's common English name.

Habitat In the breeding season inhabits both the tundra and taiga zones across the breadth of northern Europe. Habitat is thus extremely variable, including rocky coastal tundra, marshes, slow-flowing rivers, lakes, and open areas amongst coniferous forest (where our illustration was taken). Winter habitat is also very variable, dry pastures, stubbles, potato fields, muddy seashores and estuaries.

Distribution Omitting the discrete range occupied by the Pink-footed Goose, Bean Geese occur during the breeding season in northern Norway, northern Sweden, northern Finland and Russia across Siberia to the Gulf of Anadyr and south to the Altai and Mongolia. Winter range includes British Isles (small numbers), southern Scandinavia, Germany, the Netherlands and south to the Mediterranean. Central Europe, Black Sea, Caspian Sea, Asia Minor and Turkestan. Eastern races winter in China, Korea and Japan.

Food In summer, grasses, aquatic plants, cotton grass, mosses and lichens. Berries are recorded in autumn by eastern race *A. f. serrirostris*. In winter, in addition to grazing feeds widely in cultivated areas, taking potatoes, spilled grain, growing shoots and clover, etc.

Voice The double-noted nasal call is not unlike Grey-lag and even more simi-

lar to Pink-footed Goose, but deeper and more honking.

Display Courtship behaviour, aggressive display and triumph ceremony, similar to Grey-lag. Immatures pair in winter and usually remain together for life.

Breeding Egg-laying commences mid-May in the southern parts of the range but up to a month later in the north. Forest Bean Geese often make their nest at the foot of a tree or close to a fallen trunk, but in fairly open areas.

Beyond the tree-line, nests may be on islands in lakes, on rocky slopes or amongst tundra vegetation. The nest is constructed by the female from grasses, mosses, lichens but lined with down. Quite often the male escorts the female to the nest area when she returns to incubate, a task undertaken by her alone which takes about 28 days. Clutch size varies from three to seven, usually four or five and measuring 84 × 55 mm. The eggs are white and coarse grained, becoming stained. The young are tended by both adults and are flying after 2 months.

Lesser White-fronted Goose

Anser erythropus

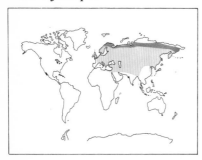

Description General appearance very much like a small White-fronted Goose. Plumage details are almost identical, including the black bars on the belly, but the head and neck are slightly darker and the upperparts a richer brown. Chief points of difference are the more extensive white band on the forehead which reaches the crown of the head above the eyes, the much smaller bill, and the yellow ring which surrounds the eye. For identification in the field, size alone is not a reliable factor. The bill is pink, the legs and feet are orange. Immatures have no white on the forehead, and no barring or dark spots on the belly, but they do have a yellow eye ring, somewhat paler than the adult's. Length 60 cm.

Characteristics and Behaviour Generally more graceful and neater in appearance than the White-fronted Goose, with noticeably smaller head and shorter bill. Whilst not much inferior in external dimensions it is only three-quarters the weight of its relative, but its wing span is proportionally longer, so that the tips of the closed wing extend beyond the tail. When feeding it is more active than the White-front and experts are able to pick out the odd Lesser White-front in a flock of the larger species by the more rapid feeding movements.

Habitat In northern Scandinavia it breeds on rocky hillsides and scrubby tundra with dense thickets of dwarf birch (*Betula nana*) and willow. In Siberia in swamps, along river banks, usually in the boreal zone, but also in tundra, where it overlaps with the White-fronted Goose. It winters on large lakes and rivers, especially with reedbeds suitable for roosting purposes.

Distribution It breeds in small numbers in northern Norway and Lapland, but much more extensively across northern Russia and Siberia, from the Kola peninsula to the Gulf of Anadyr. It winters more or less south of the breeding range from central Europe, Hungary, the eastern Mediterranean, Asia Minor, the Aralo–Caspian region, Turkestan, northern India, China and Japan where it is now much rarer than in the earlier part of this century. In western Europe, including the British Isles, it is only a casual winter visitor. One or two occur in most years on the Severn Estuary with the flocks of White-fronted Geese, and a similarly small number of immature birds occur in the Netherlands with flocks of Bean Geese.

Food Feeding habits are very similar to the White-front. On the breeding grounds almost entirely grass and other plant material, but not known to feed on berries as are the White-fronted and Bean Geese. In winter will augment its diet with grain when available.

Voice The call is high pitched and whistling, of either two or three syllables, 'kwee-yoo, Kwee-yoo-yoo'. Very experienced goose watchers can sometimes differentiate between the call of this species and the White-fronted Goose, but this requires a degree of skill and practice not acquired by the casual observer.

Breeding Egg-laying commences at the end of May in more sheltered areas,

but usually early/mid-June on the higher ground often favoured by this species. The nest is a hollow in the ground about 60 cm in diameter, made from heather stems, twigs, moss and grass, and lined with down and feathers. It is often built on a slight elevation, usually concealed under scrubby vegetation. Clutch size is usually four to five, occasionally three or six. The eggs are a glossy creamy-white, average size 76 × 49 mm. The female alone incubates for a period of just under 4 weeks, sitting closely with the male on guard nearby. The goslings are well guarded by both adults. Their heads and upperparts are a darker brown than young White-fronts. The sides of the face, throat and underparts are yellowish, the bill black, and the legs dark green. Fledging takes about 5 weeks, during which time, while the adults are moulting, families avoid open areas, keeping under cover amongst thickets of dwarf trees and scrub. Lesser White-fronts nest in scattered colonies and after the hatch some families will join up to form flocks of over a hundred strong.

Pink-footed Goose

Anser fabilis brachyrhyncus

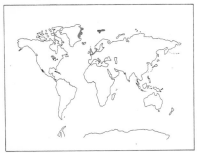

Description Somewhat smaller than the Bean Goose, of which it is here considered a sub-species. Distinguished by its paler grey back and the colouring of its bill and feet. The bill is smaller, black with a pink band, occasionally entirely pink. The legs and feet are pink, easily distinguished from the Bean's orange-yellow. The head and neck are very dark, contrasting strongly in flight with the pale grey forewing. Sexes alike. Immatures lack the pale edging to wing feathers and appear slightly darker. Legs and feet are duller, occasionally yellowish. Most easily confused with immature White-fronted Goose. Length 60–70 cm.

Characteristics and Behaviour Highly gregarious both in the winter quarters and on the breeding grounds. Winter roosts often hold thousands of birds, and are usually situated where there is little chance of disturbance, often on large sand banks, in estuaries, etc. Also on lakes and marshes when not disturbed.

Habitat During the breeding season in a variety of situations including river valleys, swampy plains, rocky coastal areas, cliffs, rock outcrops and steep slopes of ravines. In winter frequently close to estuaries, especially with extensive cultivated areas nearby, feeding in stubble fields, potato fields, pastures, also on moorland fields and saltings.

Distribution Shares with the Barnacle Goose a unique distribution which coincides to a remarkable degree in both summer and winter quarters. The breeding distribution is restricted to the arctic and sub-arctic islands of Spitsbergen, Greenland and Iceland; wintering areas are chiefly Scotland, England, Germany, the Netherlands and Belgium. Ringing recoveries indicate that both Greenland and Iceland breeders winter only in Britain, arriving in September with larger influxes in October, and usually remaining until April or early May. The Spitsbergen population remains isolated in the winter when the majority are found in the Netherlands. On migration, recorded in the Faeroes and Scandinavia with stragglers occasionally reaching central and eastern Europe.

Food In summer, grasses, sedges, roots, stems and leaves of various aquatic plants; horsetail, chickweed and saxifrages, etc. In winter, grasses, spilled grain, potatoes; shoots of young wheat and grasses in spring. Recently, the tops of frost-affected carrots left in the ground.

Voice The normal call consists of two, sometimes three notes, not as high pitched as the White-front, but more variable. The alarm note is a very high-pitched squeal.

Display Similar to the Grey-lag Goose. Pairs are usually formed in the winter quarters, breeding birds arriving on the summer range already paired. Usually commence breeding at 3 years of age, occasionally 2.

Breeding The geese arrive in Iceland early/mid-May, a little later in Greenland and Spitsbergen, and egg-laying usually commences within a few days of arrival. The nest is in a shallow depression, constructed from grass, mosses and lichens, lined with down; but usually in some elevated position with good

all-round views. Some nests are re-used for a number of years. Eggs three to seven, usually four or five, dull white, average size 78 × 52 mm. Incubation period is 28 days and by the female alone with the male on guard close to the nest. Normally the female leaves the eggs no more than once a day to feed. The downy young are yellowish-green in appearance, with a slate coloured bill and dark grey legs and feet. They leave the nest within a day and are tended by both adults, later joining up with other family groups. At this stage the moult of the adults commences and whilst the entire family are flightless they escape danger by taking to the water or running to high ground. Fledging takes about 7 weeks, after which flocks unite for the southward migration.

Lesser Snow Goose

Anser coerulescens coerulescens

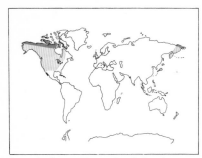

Description Normal adult plumage is pure white with black primaries and grey wing-coverts. The bill is short and stout, pinkish-red in colour tending towards orange at the base. The nail is white and a black line runs along the edge of both mandibles which outlines the conspicuous 'grinning patch' on the side of the bill. Legs and feet are pink. Immatures have greyish-brown upperparts shading to white below. Primaries are blackish; bill, legs and feet are dark grey. There is a distinct colour phase of the sub-species known as the 'Blue Goose' (shown opposite), identical in all respects except for colouring of plumage. Adults have only the head and neck white, the rest of the plumage being a variable ashy blue-grey with pale edging to some of the feathers. Intermediates occur between normal and the blue phase birds with more extensive white on the belly. Immatures of the blue phase are very dark, much like adults but with head and neck as dark as the upperparts. Bill, legs and feet are dark grey. Average length 70 cm.

Characteristics and Behaviour The most numerous of the Snow Geese, the Lesser has an extensive range in the arctic regions of North America and formerly west across the Bering Straits to mainland Asia in north-east Siberia. This Asiatic population is now probably confined to a very large colony on Wrangel Island. The proportion of blue phase birds varies geographically, decreasing from east to west and reaching zero on Wrangel Island, where the entire population is white. Highly gregarious by nature, they occur in huge flocks both on the breeding grounds and in winter quarters.

Habitat Fairly flat areas away from the coast with ponds, streams or shallow lakes nearby. Sometimes on islands in river deltas.

Distribution Mainly on islands off the North American continent from southern Baffin Island west through Southampton Island, Victoria Island to Banks Island, and south to northern Mackenzie and Keewatin, Hudson Bay and James Bay. Also Wrangel Island off the coast of eastern Siberia. At the end of the breeding season the Siberian population migrates across the Bering Straits to spend the winter in California where they mix with some of the Banks Island population. Other wintering areas are Mexico, Texas and Louisiana. Migration takes place along well-defined flight paths, often in huge numbers and at altitudes up to 3,000 m.

Food Almost entirely vegetable matter. The stems, roots and seeds of grasses and aquatic plants are taken in quantity. Berries and insects are eaten on the breeding grounds and during spring and autumn migration. In winter they will feed on waste grain in stubble fields and rice paddies.

Voice The call is a loud, high-pitched 'kowk', uttered in flight or on the ground. A deeper 'kaa-aa' is used as an alarm note on the breeding grounds.

Display Pair formation takes place in winter quarters and involves fighting between males and aerial pursuits, with loud calling. Aggressive behaviour in defence of territory also involves some fighting, with females as well as males taking part. Mixed pairings between

[74]

normal, blue phase and intermediates occur, and mates usually remain together for life.

Breeding Breeding areas are sometimes still under snow when the geese arrive, and the weather is an important factor in breeding success. In poor years very few young are reared. Egg-laying usually commences mid-June. The nest is a shallow scrape on a ridge or hummock, lined with grasses, down and feathers. Eggs, usually three to five, are creamy-white becoming stained; average size 80 × 52 mm. The incubation period is only 22–23 days, by the female alone, rarely leaving the nest after the first week. Goslings leave the nest within a few hours of drying, except in wet weather when they remain there for up to 3 days. Family groups soon join up into flocks of as many as a thousand birds. Goslings are able to fly in approximately 6 weeks.

Greater Snow Goose

Anser coerulescens atlanticus

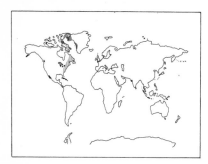

Description Adult plumage is identical to the white phase Lesser Snow Goose, all white with the exception of black primaries and grey wing coverts. The present sub-species is slightly larger with an average length of 78 cm, but there is a slight overlap in size between the two. Unlike the smaller bird, the Greater Snow Goose is not known to be dimorphic, i.e. there is no 'blue' phase. Bill pinkish-red, legs and feet pink. Length 75–80 cm.

Characteristics and Behaviour Much less numerous than the Lesser Snow Goose with a more northerly breeding range in the high arctic. In addition to its larger size, the bill is larger in proportion but the differences are not sufficient to make identification in the field easy – especially with smaller specimens. The feathers of the head are often stained a rusty brown through feeding in iron-rich waters. It is very much a feature common to the smaller sub-species. General behaviour is very similar to that of the Lesser Snow Goose.

Habitat In the breeding season high arctic and variable. Level plains some distance inland; steep slopes and sometimes cliff faces (in Greenland); sheltered sides of ravines (on Bylot Island). During migration, rests on fresh- and salt-water marshes, flooded meadows, grain fields and lakes; generally avoiding forested areas. In winter, mainly coastal bays and shallow estuaries often with marshy areas nearby.

Distribution Breeding range is more northerly and farther east than that of the Lesser Snow Goose, being restricted to various islands surrounding Baffin Bay. The most important colonies are on Baffin Island, Ellesmere Island, Bylot Island and Axel Heiberg Island, with smaller groups breeding on Devon, Somerset and Prince of Wales Islands and north-west Greenland. The southward movement begins in early September and some 4 or 5 weeks later large numbers arrive on the St Lawrence River to the east of Quebec City. A remarkable feature of the migration is that what appears to be the entire population of Greater Snow Geese gather in this one area near St Joachim every year, during both autumn and spring migrations. This makes it possible to estimate the total population with a high degree of accuracy. At the turn of the century there were no more than 2,000 to 3,000 individuals; by 1921 5,000 to 6,000; in 1941 there were 20,000 and in 1951 30,000. The latest estimates are between 150,000 and 200,000, a vast increase during the course of the century.

When the marshes at St Joachim freeze, the geese fly non-stop to Delaware Bay, then gradually move south to winter on the east coast of the US in Maryland, Virginia and North Carolina. The return northwards commences late February, with a return to St Joachim in April/May where the flocks will rest for up to 6 weeks before returning to the breeding grounds.

Food Vegetable matter, roots and stems of aquatic plants, grasses, bulrushes and grain, including wild and cultivated rice.

Voice Similar to Lesser Snow Goose, but lower pitched.

Display In aggressive behaviour the black wing tips are displayed prominently; in the triumph display, pairs point head and neck upwards, calling noisily with half-open wings.

Breeding Birds usually arrive in the breeding area in early June already paired off, but remain in flocks until the thaw. The first nests to be described were those discovered by Peary's expedition in 1892. On mainly level ground the goose usually selects a slightly raised mound on a ridge, and constructs the nest from nearby vegetation. Down and feathers are added when the eggs are laid, which is usually in the latter part of June. Clutch size varies up to six or seven eggs measuring 82 × 55 mm which take 23–25 days to hatch. Incubation is by the female with the male keeping guard. The young leave the nest soon after hatching and make their first flights in about 6 weeks.

Ross's Goose

Anser rossi

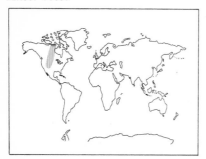

Description Plumage mainly white with black primaries, shading to grey at the base. Seldom any ferrous staining of the head and neck which occurs so frequently with other Snow Geese. The bill is very short and stubby, pinkish with green or bluish-grey patch at the base of the upper mandible. In adults this area is often covered with caruncles, especially in old males. There is no 'grinning patch' at the side of the bill. The feathers of the neck are deeply furrowed. Legs and feet are pink. Length 53–65 cm. Immatures are like immature White Snow Geese, but with paler upperparts; short, smooth, grey bill tinged pinkish; and grey-green legs.

Characteristics and Behaviour Less shy and more approachable than other Snow Geese. A highly gregarious species which has been counted in flocks of over 5,000 strong, it associates freely with other species, especially Lesser Snow Geese, but also White-fronts and small Canada Geese.

Habitat In the breeding season, islands in tundra lakes, river marshes, and flat areas with scrub vegetation and grasses. On migration, saline lakes, flooded stubble fields and river deltas. On wintering grounds, rough pastures, cultivated fields, marshes and wet meadowlands.

Distribution The breeding grounds of this goose were unknown until 1938, when a colony was found in the Perry River region of arctic Canada. At that time the population was believed to be no more than 2,000 birds. Known breeding areas now are to the south of Queen Maud Gulf (Perry River), Southampton Island, and two areas at the west of Hudson Bay, one on the McConnell River near Eskimo Point, the other near Churchill. There are summer records from Banks Island, but no proof of breeding; and there are possibly other colonies as yet undiscovered. The spring migration northwards is gradual, commencing in early March and not reaching the breeding grounds until the first half of June or even later, with a number of stop-overs en route. The return migration is also fairly protracted and also dependent to a large extent on weather conditions. Commencing in September the southward movement continues into December, by which time the majority have reached their final winter quarters. The two main wintering areas are California in the San Joachim and Sacramento valleys, and the Gulf areas of Texas and Louisiana where there has been a considerable increase since the 1960s. Total population is now estimated in the region of 20,000 to 30,000.

Food Chiefly a grazing bird, feeding on grasses, green shoots of crops, etc. Also the roots of grasses and sedges in summer, and spilled grain in the autumn.

Voice The call is a squeaky high-pitched 'keek-keek', a quiet 'luk-luk' recorded on breeding grounds.

Display Territorial display is highly developed, pairs are very active in defending a small area around the nest. When aggressive the neck is stretched out and the bill is open. Any fights are usually of short duration.

Breeding Nests colonially, usually mid-June. The nest is constructed from small twigs, leaves and mosses, and lined with down. Eggs may be two to eight, but usually four, they are pale creamy and average 74 × 49 mm. Incubation is by the female alone for a period of 21 to 23 days. The downy young are dimorphic, with both yellow and grey phases, and others which are intermediate. The down is very long and fluffy. Chicks leave the nest soon after hatching, being led by the adults to marshes or rivers nearby. Breeding success is often dependent on prevailing weather conditions during June/July, in poor years the number of young reared to the flying stage being negligible. Families later amalgamate into groups of a hundred or more which remain together until the moult of the adults is completed. The young are able to fly at about 6 weeks, by which time the adults are able to fly again. Predators of small young include arctic foxes, skuas and gulls.

Emperor Goose

Anser canagicus

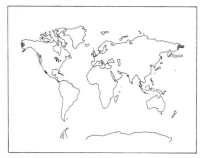

Description Head and rear of the neck are pure white. Chin, throat and front of the neck are black. The upperparts are bluish-grey, the feathers having conspicuous black sub-terminal and white terminal bands, which give the upperparts a distinctly barred appearance but less distinct towards the tail. The underparts are similar but slightly darker and with a more scaly appearance. The flight feathers are dark grey, the tail white becoming grey towards the base. The head plumage is often stained through feeding in iron-rich waters. The bill is short and pinkish with a white nail, the lower mandible being darker, usually nearly all black. Legs and feet are orange-yellow. Sexes are similar. Length 65 to 70 cm. Immatures have a grey head and neck, the crown flecked with white, bill and legs yellowish-brown.

Characteristics and Behaviour Migratory in habits but not to the same extent as most other geese, usually remaining in the area of the Bering Sea throughout the year. The maximum distance travelled between breeding and wintering areas is in the order of 1,500 miles, but most individuals move much shorter distances. The flesh has a strong unpalatable taste at times, due to the habit of eating sea lettuce, but this did not prevent the Eskimos rounding up large flocks of flightless geese for food.

This practice has declined in recent years, but hunting still accounts for large numbers as the Emperors are not very wary, fly low, and are easily shot. In flight the short neck gives a chunky appearance, wing beats are rapid but the flight is not swift and rather laborious. Usually seen in flocks of up to fifty, except during the moult and on migration, when much larger gatherings occur.

Habitat In the breeding season, marshy areas, ponds, lakes and creeks, usually within 10 miles of the coast. For the rest of the year mainly coastal, feeding in the littoral zone.

Distribution Breeds in Alaska from Kotzebue Sound and the Seward peninsula to the Yukon Delta and Kuskokwim Bay. Also on St Lawrence Island and small numbers on Nunivak Island. In Siberia mainly around the shores of the Chuckchi peninsula from Kolyuchin Bay round the Gulf of Anadyr, and south to Cape Navarin. The winter range extends along the entire chain of Aleutian Islands through the Commander Islands to the southeast coast of the Kamchatka peninsula. Smaller numbers remain close to the Alaska peninsula on Kodiak Island and Afognak Island.

Food Mainly vegetable matter, seaweed, eelgrass, algae, grasses and sedges. Also quantities of berries when available. Animal matter includes molluscs and crustaceans.

Voice The call is a double-note reminiscent of the White-front, but shriller and quite distinct. Alarm note deeper and longer.

Display Not recorded.

Breeding Commences late May in early seasons, more usually early/mid-June. The nest is usually close to water, amongst vegetation, a depression lined with a mixture of grasses, mosses, down

and some feathers. Clutch size varies from two to eight, usually four to six, the eggs are creamy-white and smooth, average size 78 × 52 mm. Incubation by female alone for a period of 24 to 27 days. The downy young have smoky grey head and upperparts, with a pale ring around the eye. Underparts paler. Bill and legs blackish. In their early days young goslings are subject to predation by Glaucous Gulls (*Larus hyperboreus*), until families amalgamate and the increased numbers provide greater safety. Fledging period about 48 days.

Bar-headed Goose

Anser indicus

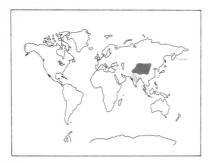

Description Medium sized, pale grey goose with brown and white markings. The head and sides of the neck are white with two striking dark brown bars on the head, one running from eye to eye round the back of the head, the other similar but lower down round the nape. Both front and back of the neck are striped dark brown. The flanks are brownish, tail coverts white, flight feathers tipped with black. The bill is yellow with a black nail, legs and feet are also yellow. Sexes alike. Length 75 cm. Immatures are slightly paler, lacking the bars on the head but with a dull brown line through the eye. Bill, legs and feet a more dingy yellow.

Characteristics and Behaviour Fairly gregarious in its habits, normally encountered in flocks ranging from family groups to numbers in excess of a hundred. It is very difficult to approach on its wintering grounds in India where flocks rest during the day on sandbars in wide rivers where they are fairly safe from hunters. However, in some of the more remote parts of the breeding range where they are not molested they can become remarkably tame.

Habitat In the breeding season is found on islands in high-altitude lakes, where they remain until the lakes freeze over, returning with the thaw in spring. In winter they prefer the larger lakes and rivers which provide safe roosts during the daytime.

Distribution The breeding range is restricted to mountainous regions of central Asia north of the Himalayas. It extends from Ladakh in northern India north to the Altai mountains and Mongolia, and from the Pamir and Tien Shan ranges through Tibet to Lake Ch'ing Hai (Koko Nor) in north-west China. Wintering in northern India, West Pakistan, Kashmir, Punjab, to East Pakistan and Assam. Reaches Mysore in the south regularly but does not occur in Ceylon. Small numbers also winter in north Burma. Crossing the Himalayas on their migratory flight Bar-headed Geese or Grey-lag Geese (possibly both) have been recorded at altitudes of 27,000 feet. Most birds arrive in India about November, leaving in March.

Food Almost entirely vegetable matter. Mainly crepuscular and nocturnal in its feeding habits, flying out from daytime roosts to feed in fields of growing crops, where they cause considerable damage in some districts. Also feeds on grasses and aquatic plants in marshy areas.

Voice Similar call to the Grey-lag Goose but deeper and more nasal.

Breeding Nests are often built in huge colonies, sometimes thousands strong, on islands surrounded by deep swamp or in lakes. The breeding season commences late May or June, the nest being a slight depression amongst grass or other vegetation and lined profusely with down. Also recorded nesting on cliffs. Eggs are usually three to six in number, the ivory-white shells becoming stained during incubation. Average size 84 × 55 mm. The female alone incubates for a period of 28–30 days. The downy young have grey-brown upperparts, pale yellow underparts and a small yellow patch on the wing. They are tended by both adults.

[82]

Hawaiian Goose
(Néné)

Branta sandvicensis

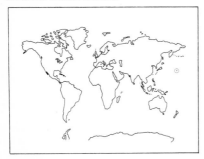

Description Crown, front of the head, throat, and a long band down the back of the neck are all black. The sides of the head and remainder of the neck are buff, the neck feathers are deeply furrowed and the neck appears striped with dark wavy lines. There is a dark ring round the lower part of the neck. Upperparts are grey-brown with pale edging to the feathers giving a barred appearance. The breast is pale brown and flanks are streaked with darker brown. Tail coverts are white; rump black. Bill, legs and feet are black. The sexes are similar. Length 65 cm. Immatures are duller than adults with a greyer neck.

Characteristics and Behaviour
With a weight approaching 2 kg, the Néné is the largest endemic land bird in Hawaii, where it has been adopted as the state bird. Although non-migratory, it is believed to have evolved from the migratory Canada Goose (*Branta canadensis*), but over a long period of isolation it has developed a number of peculiar characteristics. In adapting to dry volcanic regions with very little standing water, it has become highly terrestrial, the feet are only partially webbed; the legs are very strong and set well forward for easy walking without waddling, and the soles of the feet are padded for better protection in rocky

terrain. The rescue of the Néné from the brink of extinction is one of the great successes of wildlife conservation. In 1950 the estimated world population was no more than fifty individuals compared with an estimated 25,000 in the eighteenth century. A number of factors were involved in the decline; the bird's tameness made it an easy target for hunters, and this was aggravated by the fact that the open season for hunting coincided with the breeding season. There was a severe loss of much of the lowland habitat to agriculture, and competition for grazing from sheep and goats. Introduced predators such as dogs, cats, rats and particularly the mongoose had a detrimental effect on breeding success. A breeding programme undertaken by the Board of Agriculture and Forestry in Hawaii, and the Wildfowl Trust in England has enabled numbers to increase beyond 2,000.

Habitat Mainly upland areas to 3,000 m, lava fields and volcanic craters with low vegetation.

Distribution Restricted to the main island of Hawaii and the neighbouring island of Maui where it was reintroduced in 1962 after a total absence since the previous century.

Food Grasses, herbs, seeds and berries.

Voice The name Néné has been derived from the low wailing call, but is normally not very vocal except in the breeding season.

Display Courtship display includes head dipping and ruffling the neck feathers. It is more quarrelsome than many geese and the male can be aggressive in defence of territory.

Breeding The breeding season in the wild extends from October to February and is unusual in commencing at the time when daylight is decreasing. The nest is on the ground, constructed by the

female, and lined with down. Three to six creamy-white eggs are laid, average size 80 × 50 mm. The incubation period is 30 days. The goslings are well developed on hatching but with only short hours of daylight for feeding the fledging requires a period of 10 to 12 weeks.

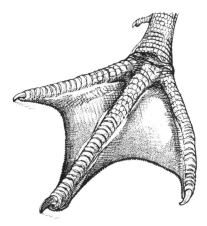

Foot of Néné showing reduced webbing between the long toes

Canada Goose

Branta canadensis

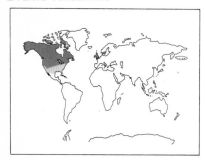

Description Crown, front of head and neck are black with conspicuous white cheek patches which sometimes run in a continuous band under the throat or they may be separated by a black band. There is sometimes a white band round the base of the black neck, but this is absent in some of the sub-species. There is no furrowing of the neck feathers. Body plumage varies from greyish-brown to dark brown with buff edging to the feathers showing as wavy bars. The upper breast and underparts from belly to tail are whitish and there is a white crescent on the rump. Bill, legs and feet are black. The sexes are similar. Length varies from 60 to 110 cm according to race. Immatures are duller with less well-defined markings.

Characteristics and Behaviour An extremely variable species, with many authorities recognizing as many as twelve different sub-species, and weights ranging from 1 kg for the smallest females, to almost 9 kg for the largest males. It is a remarkable fact that both the largest and the smallest of all true geese are found in this one species. Flight is strong with steady wing beats, flocks flying in regular formations on long migration flights, but shorter journeys are undertaken with no set pattern and usually at low altitudes. Birds move easily on land, where most of the food is obtained; they also swim well.

Habitat Varies considerably amongst sub-species and according to season. In summer, marshes, prairies, wooded country, wet and dry tundra, and coastal regions. Winters in open country, feeding in fields or at the edge of ponds, or woods, in estuaries, etc.

Distribution In the breeding season, Aleutian Islands, Alaska, and across Canada from Yukon to Labrador and Newfoundland, south to northern USA. In winter locally in southern Canada, south to Mexico and the Gulf Coast.

Food Mainly vegetable, various grasses, sedges, and aquatic plants. In tundra regions will take berries of *Vaccinium* and *Empetrum*. In wintering areas, shoots of cultivated crops and grain. Also insects, molluscs and crustaceans.

Voice Varies from a loud resonant honking in the large birds, to a high-pitched yelping cackle in the smallest.

Display In pair formation display, the male approaches the female with lowered head and neck swaying from side to side, the final movements being accompanied by a long snoring noise. In aggressive behaviour, a similar attitude is adopted, but with a honking call.

Breeding Usually commences late March or early April in the south of the range, to late May/June in the north. Most nests are on the ground near water, in marshes, tundra, on islands, etc. Clutch size normally four to six but more have been recorded. Eggs are white and smooth, average size 86 × 59 mm for largest sub-species, 74 × 48 mm for smallest. Incubation is by the female and takes about 28 days, a little less for the smaller birds. The goslings leave the nest on the first or second day, eventually being led by the adults to open water. They are able to fly about 8 weeks after hatching, but the family remains together on migration and throughout the winter.

Smallest and darkest race. Cackling Canada *Branta c. minima*, alongside the largest and lighter Giant Canada *Branta c. maxima*

Barnacle Goose

Branta leucopsis

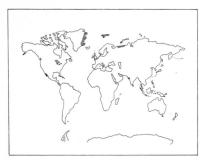

Description Face and forehead creamy-white with a black streak from the bill to the eye. Crown, neck and breast are glossy black. Upperparts dark grey shading to pale grey on the mantle, the feathers have a black sub-terminal band and a white tip, giving a heavy barred effect. Upper and under tail coverts white; tail black. Underparts are pale grey with faint barring on the flanks. The bill is black, short and delicate. Legs and feet are black. Sexes similar. Length 60–70 cm. Immatures have face flecked with dark feathers and have a brownish tinge on the back and underparts. In recent years a number of individuals with all white or nearly white plumage have been recorded wintering in the Solway Firth. They are not true albinos as they have conventionally coloured eyes, bills and legs, and are usually referred to as leucistic specimens.

Characteristics and Behaviour A gregarious species, found in family parties to flocks numbering thousands in favoured localities. They are generally more approachable and less suspicious than other species. More terrestrial than Brent Geese but are occasionally seen on the sea. Feeding birds often appear quarrelsome, and feeding activity continues during the night. Flocks do not normally associate with other species, although odd birds will occasionally be found feeding with grey geese. At the end of the Second World War the Spitsbergen population wintering on the Solway Firth had been reduced to just a few hundred individuals, but total protection and the establishment of a reserve at Caerlaverock have boosted numbers to over 6,000. The total world population of Barnacle Geese is now estimated at almost 80,000.

Habitat In the breeding season, rocky coastal regions, fjords, small islands, steep-sided valleys and marshes. In winter, coastal pastures, salt marshes, tidal flats, occasionally on cultivated land.

Distribution Like the Pink-footed Goose, the Barnacle has a wintering area restricted to north-west Europe, and a breeding range limited to just three isolated localities. The three populations remain segregated throughout the year; birds breeding in Greenland wintering in western Scotland and Ireland. The most important resort for this group is now the island of Islay in the Inner Hebrides where there has been a dramatic increase in numbers over the last 20 years, and the winter population has risen to over 20,000. Birds breeding in Spitsbergen winter only on the Solway Firth in an area centred on Caerlaverock and the Wildfowl Trust Refuge. The third population breeds only on islands to the north of Siberia between the Barents and Kara Seas, wintering in the Netherlands. The latter is the largest group, numbering some 40,000–50,000.

Food In winter the most important source food are the stolons of white clover, horizontal shoots running along the surface of the ground and rich in starch. Also various grasses and seeds. In summer, the leaves and catkins of alpine willow are sometimes taken.

Voice A short shrill bark, usually repeated a number of times in quick succession.

Breeding The nest was unknown until 1891, when the first ones were discovered in east Greenland. Egg-laying commences late May to June, depending largely on the thaw. Breeding is colonial, and nests are placed on the face of steep cliffs, rocky outcrops, and low-lying islands. All these typical sites provide a considerable measure of protection from terrestrial predators such as arctic foxes. The nest site is a small depression with a little moss of lichen, and lined with down. Some sites are re-used for a number of years. There are usually four or five eggs, dull greyish-white but becoming stained, average size 76 × 50 mm. Incubation is by the female for a period of 24 to 25 days, the mate standing guard nearby. The downy young are greyish-brown above, whitish below, with a dark line from the bill to the eye, and a dark band on the upper breast. They leave the nest soon after hatching, accompanied by both adults. For a few days they are very vulnerable to predation by Glaucous Gulls, but experienced adults seldom leave their goslings unguarded. First flights are usually achieved after 6 or 7 weeks.

Red-breasted Goose

Branta ruficollis

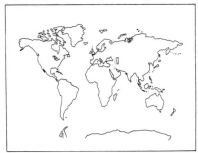

Description   Crown, back of neck, and band through the eye from crown to chin are black. There is a white patch between the bill and the eye, and a chestnut-red patch surrounded by a white border on the side of the head. The front of the neck and upper breast are also chestnut red, separated from the black of the lower breast by a white border. The upperparts are black with a double white wing bar; upper and under tail coverts white; tail black. The small delicate bill, legs and feet, are black. Sexes are similar. Length 50–55 cm. Immatures have chestnut patch on the head more grey-brown; speckled white markings on the back; and markings on flanks less well defined.

Characteristics and Behaviour   The smallest of the European geese, and also the rarest. The total population is probably less than 20,000 and numbers are believed to be still declining. The causes include changes in land use on the wintering grounds, possibly the lower level of the Caspian Sea, and de-salination of lagoons south of the Danube delta may also be significant. Winter flocks are very active, with rapid feeding action and quarrelsome behaviour. Their flight is usually in irregular formation, seldom in lines or chevrons. Flocks normally associate with much larger flocks of White-fronted Geese and the odd stragglers which are recorded in western Europe are nearly always single birds amongst a flock of White-fronts.

Habitat   In the breeding season, chiefly near rivers in tundra regions, with cliffs, or steep banks with rocky outcrops. In winter, formerly steppe grasslands, but now more frequently cultivated lands. Roosting at night is usually in coastal areas, on islands and sandbanks.

Distribution   The breeding range in northern Siberia is restricted to an area centred on the Taomyr peninsula, extending from east Yamal peninsula, to the Khatanga River. The wintering range is equally limited. Formerly numerous in the south Caspian area, the most important area is now in eastern Roumania, at the edge of the Black Sea.

Food   In summer probably feeds mainly by grazing. In winter associates with White-fronts feeding on spilled grain and sprouting wheat shoots. On migration will eat the bulbs of wild garlic.

Voice   The call is a double-noted screech, the second syllable high pitched and strained. Hisses when angry.

Breeding   Usually in small colonies numbering a few pairs. The nests are in open situations near cliffs or rock outcrops and nearly always very close to the nest of some raptor, especially Peregrine (*Falco peregrinus*), or Rough-legged Buzzard (*Buteo lagopus*). This close association is too regular to be accidental, and is believed to benefit the geese by affording protection from predators such as Arctic Foxes, Gulls and Skuas, through the raptor's defence of its own territory. Clutch size is three to eight, eggs are white with a greenish tinge, becoming stained, average size 70 × 48 mm. Incubation is by the female and takes about 25 days. The downy young are sepia coloured on the crown and upperparts, pale greenish-yellow below. Fledging period is about 6 weeks.

Brent Goose
(Brant)

Branta bernicla

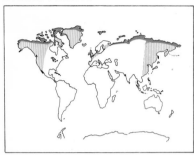

Description Adults have the entire head, neck and upper breast, black with variable markings forming a partial or sometimes almost complete collar round neck. Upperparts dark greyish-brown. Upper and under tail coverts and sides of rump, white; showing as a conspicuous white 'Vee' in flight. Tail and flight feathers are black. The underparts vary from pale brownish-grey to sooty brown, or almost black, depending on the sub-species. The Dark-bellied Brent (*Branta b. bernicla*) (opposite) from western Siberia is intermediate between the Light-bellied or Atlantic Brent (*B. b. hrota*) and the very dark Black or Pacific Brant (*B. b. nigricans*) of North America. Bill, legs and feet are black. Length 55–60 cm. Juveniles have white tips to feathers of upper wing coverts, and usually no white neck markings, although these usually appear in the first winter.

Characteristics and Behaviour Small, dark and highly maritime in its behaviour; the Brent spends most of its life at sea and until very recently has fed inland only during severe weather conditions. Flight is rapid, usually in straggling lines or loose flocks, and fairly low over the water. Feeding times are determined by the tide, so Brents feed by day or night, 'up-ending' more frequently than other geese. At high tide they usually rest on the water.

Habitat In the breeding season, offshore islands, river deltas, marshy uplands and tundra lakes, seldom far from the coast. In winter and on migration, muddy estuaries, bays and tidal flats, usually where there is an abundant growth of *Zostera*.

Distribution In summer the Brent has a circumpolar distribution and a breeding range extending farther north than that of any other goose. It occurs in arctic North America, northern Greenland, Spitzbergen and right across arctic Siberia. Winter range in America is on the Pacific coast, south to California and Mexico, on the Atlantic coast from Massachusetts to North Carolina. In Europe, Denmark, Germany, the Netherlands, the British Isles and the north and west coasts of France.

Food Staple food item is the Eel grass *Zostera* which grows in shallow muddy coastal areas between high- and low-water marks. In the 1930s *Zostera* disappeared from many areas as the result of disease, and the Brent goose populations on both sides of the Atlantic crashed dramatically. The situation is now somewhat improved and numbers are increasing again. On the breeding grounds mosses and lichens are eaten until the thaw enables new vegetation to be grazed.

Voice A guttural honking 'Krronk'.

Breeding Return to the breeding grounds is usually early June, with most clutches complete before the end of the month. The nest varies from a slight depression to a large mound of mosses, profusely lined with down. Eggs are usually three to five, creamy-white, average size 72 × 47 mm. Incubation is by the female alone for about 25 days. The young are led to tidal flats or pools where they consume quantities of insect food as well as grasses. Feeding almost continuously they develop rapidly and make their first flights at the age of $6\frac{1}{2}$ to 7 weeks.

Cape Barren Goose
(Cereopsis)

Cereopsis novaehollandiae

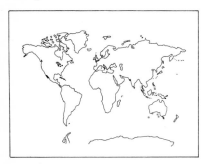

Description Sexes alike. Large, with an overall colour of ashy grey, the head slightly paler and the crown white. Both primaries and secondaries are tipped with black, whilst the tail and rump are entirely black. Wing coverts and scapulars have quite large blackish spots. The bill is covered by a fleshy wax-like skin of yellow tinged with green, bill tip is black. Legs are pink to purplish-pink, the feet are black. Length of male 75–90 cm, the female is slightly smaller. Immature birds are paler but the wing spots are more numerous and the legs at first are grey.

Characteristics and Behaviour Unmistakable in the field, a large grey long-legged goose-like bird, invariably holding head erect when approached too closely. Being grazing birds they naturally spend most of their time on land and only infrequently enter water, except to escape an enemy or if wounded, at such times they take to the sea and are seen to be strong swimmers.

Habitat In the breeding season the Cape Barren Goose inhabits islands of varying size, but essentially small, low-lying and covered with grass and scrub-like growth. At other times they occur on open grasslands in coastal areas of the southern mainland (Australia).

Distribution Confined as a breeding species to the islands off the southern coast of Australia, where it is widely distributed. The range extends from as far west as Albany to Melbourne in the east. It is generally accepted that the Fureaux Group of islands off the north-east coast of Tasmania is the bird's stronghold, but the two large islands, in that group, of Flinders and Cape Barren do not have breeding populations. During the summer months the largest mainland concentrations are recorded in south Australia around Lake Albert and Lake Alexandria, where flocks of up to 500 have been sighted. Formerly persecuted, when large numbers were shot because of the volume of grass they consumed and the odour left by fouling the grass was distasteful to the grazing sheep; and of course they made very good birds for the table, being much enjoyed. Nowadays, thanks to protection, they are slowly recovering their former numbers. A current estimate of birds in the wild would be around 6,000.

Food A grazing bird obtaining its food by the edge of lakes and along the sea shore. Only vegetable matter is taken, and of that the common tussock grass, found on the islands, forms the bulk of its diet. Other grasses eaten include wallaby grass, barley-grass and spear grass, etc. and in smaller quantities, clovers, medics and sedges.

Voice The male a loud trumpeting, the female a low grunting sound.

Display They are found in pairs at all times of the year but courtship and fighting is more prevalent from about February, which sees their return to the breeding grounds. Aggressive by nature, they will not tolerate the presence of others and defend their breeding territories quite strongly. They most probably mate for life.

Breeding Nest building usually commences late May or early June and both birds share this task. A slightly

elevated position is often chosen on or beside a grassy tussock, even a few feet above ground in a bush, and quite regularly in no way sheltered from the prevailing winds. A mound of material is gathered and a cup is fashioned, 7 cm deep by 20 cm across and substantially lined with grey down which is used to cover the eggs when the female leaves her nest. Peak egg-laying is late June to mid-July, a usual clutch would be four to five glossy white but coarsely textured eggs each measuring 83 × 56 mm. The incubation period is 35 days. The young are guarded quite vigorously by both parents even against human intruders and the family remain within their territory for about 6 weeks. On fledging, the young form nomadic parties and leave their island home, these flocks consisting of up to 200 individuals or even more.

Andean Goose

Chloephaga melanoptera

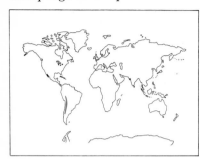

Description The adult plumage is white all over, apart from the black tail and mostly black wings. The scapulars are marked with dark elongated spots, the primaries glossy black with bronze tinge, and the greater wing coverts metallic purple. The iris is brown, bill red with a black nail, legs and feet red. The sexes are similar. Length 70–80 cm. Immatures are like adults but duller and greyer.

Characteristics and Behaviour The largest of the five species of South American Sheldgeese, a group resembling the true geese in their principal feeding habit of grazing, but which is more closely related to the ducks. They are seen on water less frequently than other *Chloephaga*, being poor swimmers, but broods of young are usually led to water for safety. They are quite tame and approachable in their mountainous breeding quarters, but become more wary when forced to lower pastures by bad weather. Flight is strong but heavier than that of true geese; whilst their large size and short neck give the birds a thick-set appearance in the air.

Habitat A montane species of the high Andes, breeding at altitudes between 3,000 and 5,000 m, with nests found as high as the snow-line. In winter flocks move to lower altitudes, grazing in valley meadows and marshland.

[96]

Distribution The most northerly distribution of the Sheldgeese in the high Andes of southern Peru, Bolivia, Chile from Arica to Ñuble province, and north-west Argentina to Catamarca province.

Food Entirely vegetable. Because of their habit of feeding almost exclusively on grasses, all South American Sheldgeese (with the exception of the Kelp Geese (*Chloephaga hybrida*)), are considered pests by the sheep farmers. Any birds straying close to human habitations are usually killed and large numbers of eggs are destroyed, yet populations are believed not to be decreasing.

Voice Notes vary considerably between the sexes. The gander has a high-pitched whistle, the goose a harsh quacking call.

Display More developed than in other *Chloephaga*. The male throws its neck back along the body, then with ruffled plumage and bill depressed utters a series of whistles and low grunts. The female, also with ruffled plumage, replies in a low quacking voice. Males are very aggressive in defence of territory and young.

Breeding The breeding season commences November, in the southern spring, and is rather early for such high altitudes. The nest is a shallow scrape in stony ground scarcely concealed by the thin vegetation, usually on steep slopes above mountain lakes. Clutch size varies from five to ten eggs, greyish-white, average size 77 × 51 mm. Incubation period is 30 days, by the female alone, with the male standing guard near the nest. The downy young are black and white, with black spots on the sides of the head and on the thighs. Bill, legs and feet are black. On hatching, the brood is led to the water, with the gander in front and the goose at the rear of the party. Goslings are eaten, but adults are tough with an unappetizing odour.

Ashy-headed Goose

Chloephaga poliocephala

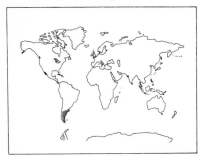

Description Both male and female have the head and neck ashy grey, lighter on the forehead and crown; and a white ring round the eye. Feathers of the nape, lower neck and breast are copper coloured; the breast sometimes lined with narrow black bars. The mantle is coppery brown; back and tail are black. Underparts are white with black barring on the flanks. The wings are white with chestnut scapulars and metallic green speculum. The short narrow bill is black; legs are orange on the outside, black inside; feet black and orange. Length about 55 cm. Immatures are similar but duller, browner and without the metallic green speculum; they do not assume adult plumage until the second year.

Characteristics and Behaviour A fairly small Sheldgoose with very distinctive plumage. Usually found in small flocks, it will at all times associate with Magellan Geese (*Chloephaga picta*) and Ruddy-headed Geese (*C. rubidiceps*). In some areas the species is kept with domestic poultry and is reported to be easily domesticated. Migratory in parts of its range.

Habitat Grasslands, mainly inland, usually avoids coastal regions, but is found on some islands. Grazes in marshy valleys, around the edges of lakes, occasionally on estuaries. In mountains it prefers boggy areas with aquatic vegetation in forest clearings.

Distribution In the breeding season, Argentina from Neuquen and the Rio Negro, south of Tierra del Fuego. In Chile, from Malleco to Llanquihue in the Andes; and from Chiloe island south to islands near Cape Horn. In winter, moves north as far as Buenos Aires in Argentina, and Colchagua in Chile. A scarce breeder in the Falkland Isles.

Food Strictly a grazing species.

Voice The male has a high-pitched whistling call, the female a low harsh cackle.

Display Similar to most other *Chloephaga*, but not quite so elaborate as the Andean Goose. The male stands with breast thrust forward, neck stretched back, and wings extended, calling with a soft whistle. The female adopts a similar, though less exaggerated posture and calls in reply.

Breeding Eggs are laid in October/November in most parts of the range. Nests are usually on the ground, sometimes well hidden in long grasses and concealed from above. Large numbers nest around swampy forest clearings. Recently nests have also been found in the hollows of burnt-out tree trunks (Johnson in *Birds of Chile*) in the Aisen province of southern Chile. Here it was also recorded that they perch regularly in trees, often at considerable heights. All nests have a thick lining of down. The clutch size is usually four to six brownish-white eggs, average size 72 × 41 mm. Incubation is by female alone for about 30 days. The young are usually taken to the nearest water where they remain in family groups and which eventually may join up to form larger assemblies.

Ruddy-headed Goose

Chloephaga rubidiceps

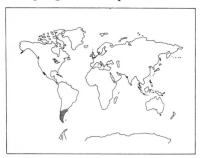

Description Adults have bright chestnut head and neck, with a white ring around the dark brown eye. Breast, flanks and mantle are finely barred grey and black; lower breast, abdomen and under tail coverts are reddish-cinnamon. The wings are similar to those of the Ashy-headed Goose, with speculum metallic green. Rump and tail are black. The black bill is short and narrow; legs and feet are orange-yellow, sometimes with black markings. Individuals with varying amounts of white on the abdomen occur occasionally. Females are smaller and less brightly coloured on the head and neck. Length 45–55 cm. Immatures are greyer than adults and lack the metallic green speculum.

Characteristics and Behaviour The smallest species of Sheldgeese, with a southerly breeding distribution, where it occupies the same sort of habitat and often the same areas as the larger Magellan Goose (*Chloephaga picta*). It is gregarious by nature and flocks numbering many thousands can be found in favoured localities, but it is generally much less numerous than the Magellan Goose. Throughout most of its range it occupies inland areas, but is more of a coastal species in the Falkland Islands. Some populations are migratory.

Habitat Semi-arid open plains, often far from the nearest water, but in the breeding season it prefers some open water nearby, if only a small pond, for protection of the goslings.

Distribution In the breeding season, Tierra del Fuego, the Falkland Islands, Santa Cruz province in southern Argentina, but very scarce in the Magellanes province of southern Chile. Migrants start returning to Tierra del Fuego in early September, leaving again in March and April. The Falkland Islands' population is mainly resident. In winter migrates north to the province of Buenos Aires in Argentina, but is absent from Chile.

Food Essentially a grazing bird, preferring shorter grasses.

Voice The male has a short whistling 'seep' similar to the male Kelp Goose; the female is the more vocal and has a high-pitched cackling note.

Display Generally similar to the other Sheldgeese. In the breeding season the males become very noisy and aggressive and there is a great deal of fighting over territorial boundaries.

Breeding The breeding season extends from September to November. The nests are well concealed in tussocks of grass, rushes, etc. in similar situations to nests of the Magellan Geese, but easily distinguished by the cinnamon coloured down. In the Falkland Islands some nests have been found in old burrows of the Magellanic Penguin (*Spheniscus magellanicus*). Clutch size varies from four to eleven, the eggs are creamy coloured, average size 65 × 48 mm. Incubation is by the female, the male often well away from the nest; period 30 days. The downy young are pale grey and dark grey, with black bill and legs.

Lesser Magellan Goose

(Upland Goose)

Chloephaga picta picta

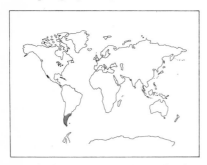

Description The adult male has head, neck and underparts white with black bars on the flanks. The mantle is also barred with black, the wings are dark grey and white with metallic green speculum, the tail black and white. Bill, legs and feet are black. Mature plumage is attained in the third year, immature males have a greyish head and neck, with black barring on the underparts. The female is a dull chestnut with black barring on the mantle and underparts. The bill is black, but the legs yellowish-orange. Males of the typical form, or Lesser Magellan Goose, are dimorphic; some individuals having the underparts barred black and white. Both phases occur in the same regions, but the barred variety is more numerous in Tierra del Fuego. White birds with pure white underparts are in the majority in parts of Patagonia. The Greater Magellan Goose (*Chloephaga picta leucoptera*) occurs only in the Falkland Islands and South Georgia (introduced). It is larger and the males never have barred underparts. Length 60–70 cm.

Characteristics and Behaviour The second largest and the most abundant of the Sheldgeese. Resident in parts of the range but birds in the extreme south migrate in the winter. Greater Magellan

Geese do not migrate. Tame and approachable by nature, but more wary in areas where they are persecuted by sheep farmers – bounties are paid for adults, eggs and young, in some regions.

Habitat Mainly inland, widespread during the breeding season and nesting on high or low ground but preferably near water. In the Falkland Islands, usually near the coast.

Distribution In the breeding, season southern Chile and Argentina south to Tierra del Fuego and Cape Horn; Falkland Islands and South Georgia. In winter north to Colchagua province in Chile, and Buenos Aires province in Argentina.

Food Vegetable matter, chiefly grasses; wild berries in the Falklands.

Voice Much as other Sheldgeese, the male whistles and the female has a low cackling call.

Display Generally similar to other Sheldgeese.

Breeding Occurs from September to October in the Falkland Islands, but August to November in Chile and Argentina. Dry ground is preferred for the nest site, a slight depression lined with grass and a plentiful supply of down. Usually the nest is concealed under long grasses, ferns, bushes or other vegetation. Five to eight cream coloured eggs are laid, occasionally more, average size 75 × 49 mm. Incubation is by the female alone and takes about 30 days. The male is very aggressive during this time, guarding the nest and later helping to rear the brood. Downy young are grey with dark brown markings, but darker and more uniform in the Greater Magellan. Despite the protective colouration and the fierce defence by both adults, the young suffer heavy predation by Skuas and Kelp Gulls. Broods are led to water for safety; usually ponds, rivers or lagoons, but also sea coasts.

Lesser Kelp Goose

Chloephaga hybrida hybrida

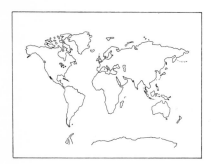

Description   The adult male has all white plumage, the short black bill has a small yellow or pinkish patch on the culmen, and the short legs and feet are bright yellow. Immature males are similar to females in the first year, but with whitish head, neck and breast. In the second year they assume mainly white plumage but they retain black wing tips. Females have the crown light brown, the rest of the head and neck dark brown with a white ring around the eye. Mantle and wings are dark brown, the wings with metallic green speculum and the same white areas as in other *Chloephaga*. The breast and flanks are barred black and white; rump, tail and belly are white. Bill of female is pinkish, legs and feet bright yellow. The Lesser Kelp Goose of Southern Chile has a length of 57–63 cm. The Greater Kelp Goose (*Chloephaga hybrida malvinarum*) of the Falkland Islands has similar plumages but is larger. Length 65–72 cm.

Characteristics and Behaviour   The Kelp Goose is the most distinctive of the Sheldgeese, having a specialized diet and leading a more solitary existence than other species. It inhabits rocky coastlines but seldom takes to the water outside the breeding season, and rarely goes inland except to drink and bathe. The short legs and large feet are probably adapted for walking over slippery seaweed and enable it to hop from one rock to another. Pairs remain together throughout the year. Flocks of any size are unusual except for family parties and displaying groups in spring. Because of its seaweed diet, it is not considered a pest and thus escapes the persecution to which other species are subjected, and so remains relatively tame and approachable. Flight is heavy and usually very low over the water.

Habitat   Rocky coasts, shingle, but not sandy beaches.

Distribution   The coasts and islands of southern Chile from Chiloe Island to Tierra del Fuego, occasionally as far north as Cautin province. Rare on the Atlantic coast of Argentina in Santa Cruz and Chubut provinces. Falkland Islands.

Food   Seaweeds, mainly *Ulva* species (Sea-lettuce). Berries and occasionally grass recorded in Falkland Islands.

Voice   The male has a thin whistling call, the female a low grunting honk.

Breeding   The breeding season is late October to November in Falkland Islands, November to December elsewhere. The nest is built of grasses, profusely lined with distinctive barred down; and placed in a tussock of grass or other vegetation close to the shore. Territories are spaced out all along suitable coastlines, the males on guard being very conspicuous against the dark background, but the sombre females are easily overlooked. A clutch of four to six creamy-white eggs are laid, average size 76 × 52 mm. Incubation is by the female alone and takes about 30 days. The downy young are pale grey with brown markings and a dark line through the eye; bill legs and feet are black.

Abyssinian Blue-winged Goose

Cyanochen cyanopterus

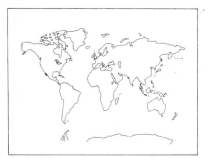

Description Adult birds have the head and neck greyish-brown, with a paler patch below and in front of the eyes. The upperparts are mottled grey and brown on the mantle, bluish-grey on the back, with brownish buff upper tail coverts. The wings have pale blue coverts, black primaries, and metallic green secondaries shading to blue-black on the inner ones. There is a small white mark on the leading edge of the wing close to the bend. Breast and abdomen are greyish-brown with pale tips to the feathers, under tail coverts white, tail black. The short bill is black, iris brown, legs and feet black. Sexes are similar in plumage but female is noticeably smaller. Immatures much as adults but duller. Length 55–65 cm.

Characteristics and Behaviour A monotypic genus restricted to mountainous regions of Ethiopia. It bears a close resemblance to the South American Sheldgeese, but is more aquatic in its behaviour. It is very local in its distribution and does not normally occur below an altitude of 2,400 m, but it can be quite plentiful in suitable habitats. Normally encountered in pairs, but at times large groups assemble. Flight is not very swift, usually low down and following some watercourse. During flight the white patch on the underwing is very conspicuous. It has a rather tame disposition and shows little fear of man, but can be very pugnacious towards others of its kind. During the daytime it can often be seen standing or walking with its head resting on its back and the feathers of its mantle raised; at night it is sometimes more active.

Habitat Lakes, rivers and streams, the edges of swamps, and meadows of short grassland; generally avoiding areas of dense vegetation.

Distribution Restricted to the high plateaux of Ethiopia at altitudes above 2,400 m.

Food Little studied in the wild but probably mainly animal matter. Insects and larvae, molluscs and worms have been recorded.

Voice The male has a very melodious soft whistle, the female a wheezy, cackling call.

Display Not very elaborate, basically similar to the South American Sheldgeese.

Breeding The breeding season is very extensive in the wild, ranging from July to December, in addition, downy young have been recorded in May and July. The nest is on the ground amongst vegetation and from four to seven cream coloured eggs are laid, size not recorded. Incubation by the female takes about 30 days, the male keeping guard nearby. The downy young are black above with silvery white markings on the wings and body, a black patch behind the eye, and yellowish head and neck. Fledging period about 6 weeks.

Abyssinian Blue-winged Goose, showing
characteristic holding of the head back on the
shoulders, seen at rest or even while walking
undisturbed

Orinoco Goose

Neochen jubatus

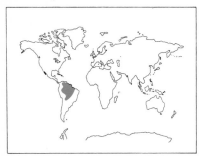

Description The adult male has head, neck and breast pale ashy buff, with fine greyish-brown markings. The upper mantle and scapulars are tawny brown, the wings black with a deep greenish gloss and white speculum. The lower back and tail are also black glossed with green. Flanks and abdomen are chestnut, under tail coverts white bordered with black. The bill is short, high at the base and slightly upturned, mainly black on the upper mandible, but red on the lower mandible. The iris is brown, legs and feet pinkish-red. The female is similar but slightly smaller. Length 55–60 cm. Immatures resemble adults but paler, duller colouring.

Characteristics and Behaviour A tropical South American species with characteristics somewhere between the South American Sheldgeese and the Shelducks of temperate regions of Eurasia and Australasia. In appearance it is superficially similar to the Egyptian Goose (*Alopochen aegyptiacus*) but less adaptable in its habits. Its legs are longer than Shelducks' and set farther forward; its body shorter, and held more upright. Mainly terrestrial in its habits, feeding to a greater extent on vegetable matter. It has a tendency to perch in trees, but flight is rather slow and it is not considered to be a very good sporting bird. Normally encountered in pairs holding territories along river banks, but occasionally in large flocks during the flightless period. Not migratory.

Habitat Banks of slow-flowing rivers and streams, marshes; in savanna and tropical forest regions.

Distribution The llanos (open grassland with scattered trees) of Venezuela and eastern Colombia, Guyana, Surinam, French Guiana; also Brazil south to southern Amazonas and northern Mato Grosso, the provinces of Beni, Santa Cruz and Tarija in Bolivia; Paraguay and northern Argentina in the province of Salta.

Food Adapted mainly to grazing, also takes seeds, insects and worms, etc.

Voice The male has a high-pitched whistling call, the female a loud, harsh cackle.

Display The male struts around with extended wings and breast inflated, head tilted backwards, whistling and grunting continuously. The female also incites the male by stretching her neck forwards, swinging the head low from side to side and cackling loudly.

Breeding Nests are usually made in holes in trees or in the ground, and lined with down. Nesting behaviour is strongly territorial, nests are well spaced out and territories defended vigorously. Clutch size varies from six to ten, eggs are smooth shelled, pale buff colour, and average size is 60 × 43 mm. Incubation is by the female alone and takes 28–30 days, but both adults help in rearing the brood. Downy young are black above, white below, with a black line through the eye, and a large black patch on the ear coverts; wings are black with a broad white band; bill, legs and feet black. Adult plumage is assumed after 3 or 4 months but birds do not breed until 2 or 3 years old.

Egyptian Goose

Alopochen aegyptiacus

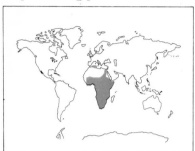

Description Sexes similar, with much variation of colour intensity existing between individuals. The head and neck are of pale grey with the sides and crown mottled brown. A dark yellowish red band occurs behind the neck; a chestnut ring around the lower neck with a similarly coloured patch around the eye, and a line from corner of eye to base of bill. Both mantle and upperparts are reddish-orange with fine black vermiculations, the mantle slightly darker. In the centre of the lower breast there is usually a prominent patch of deep chestnut. The dusky brown scapulars have fine whitish speckles. Back, rump and tail are black; under tail coverts pale cinnamon. Wing coverts are white with a black line; primaries black; secondaries of metallic green. Bill pink with base edges and tip black. Legs pink. Length 70 cm. Immatures are duller than the adults and lack the areas of chestnut on face, neck and breast.

Characteristics and Behaviour A largish Sheldgoose which may be confused with the African Shelduck, but which can be distinguished, even at distance, by the brown patch on its chest, which in shape resembles an inverted horseshoe. In flight the dark markings of the chest are very apparent and prevent confusion between the species. It may be encountered in varying habitats, anywhere that food and water are available.

Usually seen in pairs, but large flocks do occur in the wheat-growing regions. It is the only goose in South Africa that occurs in sufficient numbers to be regarded as a pest by grain farmers; it causes as much damage by trampling the growing shoots as it does by eating them. It is frequently attracted to even the smallest areas of water. A daytime feeder, roosting at night in trees or on sandbanks. A noisy and rather violent bird, with pairs often engaged in fierce combat.

Habitat A tropical to sub-tropical species frequenting marshes, ponds, lakes and the banks of rivers.

Distribution Africa except the Sahara and the north, but does occur in Egypt, northern Algeria and Tunisia; also Palestine and Syria. The deep forest districts of West Africa are usually avoided, but the bird may be met with along the larger rivers.

Food Young grasses and wheat, also leaves and other soft vegetable substances.

Voice The male utters a hoarse breathing sound; the female a harsh trumpeting 'Honk-haah-haah-haah'.

Display In display, with wings half-spread, movements of the extended neck and head are accompanied by the fast repetition of their call notes.

Breeding Old nests of other species are usually chosen, but may utilize a hollow tree, or thick vegetation near water. The down lining is sufficient to cover the clutch. Eggs are laid from July to March with a peak during September and October in the south. A normal clutch would be seven to nine creamy-white eggs measuring 69 × 51 mm, which is a comparatively small egg for so large a bird. Both sexes share the incubation for a period of 28–30 days. It is said that chicks from high-placed nests are taken to the ground in the parent's bill.

Australian Shelduck
(Mountain Duck)

Tadorna tadornoides

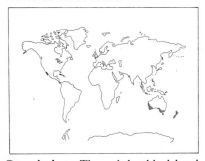

Description The male has black head and neck which are quite often suffused with brown, and a broad white ring separates the black neck from the chestnut breast and mantle. Back, scapulars, flank and abdomen are black but finely lined with buff. Rump, under tail coverts and tail are black; upper wing coverts are white. Primaries black, secondaries green but black towards base. The rich chestnut of the tertiaries is a very prominent feature. Bill, legs and feet are black. The female is somewhat duller than her mate and has a white patch round the eye and a white ring round the base of the bill. Immatures are similar to the adults but duller, and most have an area of white flecks between the bill and the eyes. Length of male 67 cm, female 61 cm.

Characteristics and Behaviour Outside the breeding season, it congregates in large flocks and is regularly seen in numbers that exceed 1,000 individuals. During the daytime, may be encountered resting by the edges of lakes and estuaries before flying out to their feeding grounds in late afternoon. The large wing patches are very prominent when the bird is flying away, and when overhead the white under wings contrast very noticeably with the otherwise dark body. In flight they form long V-like skeins. On land its stance is erect,

on water it floats very high; a strong walker and good swimmer. A bird whose wariness makes it difficult to approach.

Habitat Very much a bird of the muddy shortlines, often encountered on the edges of brackish lakes and estuaries, also found quite regularly in large flocks on fresh-water lakes and lagoons.

Distribution Confined to south-western and south-eastern Australia, being only seldom reported from the central south coast. Also found in Tasmania. In Western Australia, the largest concentrations being found on coastal lakes, estuaries and off-shore islands. Also found in western Victoria and the south-east of New South Wales.

Food A variety of vegetable and animal matter, such as clover leaves and seeds, couch-grass, duckweed, medicks, sedges and pondweeds. Midges and their larvae, water fleas, water-boatmen and a variety of aquatic beetles are also taken. Much time is spent feeding on aquatic plants in shallow water, but grazing also takes place in fields close to the water, stubble fields are sometimes also visited.

Voice A low-pitched honk by the male and a higher-pitched call by the female. These calls are frequently uttered especially so in flight.

Display Soon after they return to their breeding grounds in March the birds become very aggressive towards one another and strongly defend their breeding territory.

Breeding The Australian Shelduck, in all probability, pairs for life. March sees their return to the breeding areas but inland this may well be affected by weather conditions. Both birds prospect for suitable sites, and the nests are almost invariably in tree-holes, but in treeless areas rabbit holes are utilized and occasionally ground nesting occurs

in well-wooded areas. Egg-laying takes place from the middle of June to late September. The clutch consists of from ten to fourteen creamy-white eggs which are said to be laid at intervals of 3 days, size 68 × 49 mm. The female alone incubates for 30 to 35 days whilst the male returns to his territory. When the chicks are hatched they are lead by the female to reunite as a family on the male's territory.

Paradise Shelduck
(New Zealand Shelduck)

Tadorna variegata

The male is similar to the Australian Shelduck but lacks the chestnut breast and mantle and does not have the white collar, these parts being black. The back and mantle are black finely lined with pale grey. The female has head and neck of pure white and the body is of rich chestnut; in other respects as the male. Restricted to New Zealand, but rare in the north. The cream coloured eggs are five to eleven in number and measure 65 × 47 mm. Incubation period 30 days.

South African Shelduck
(Cape Shelduck)

Tadorna cana

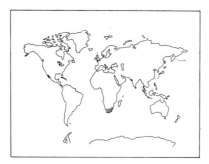

Description   Head and neck of male ashy grey, the thin collar of dark brownish-red is often indistinct. Breast and upper mantle are tawny yellow; upper parts and rest of mantle yellowish-red but lightly lined with grey. The tail and rump are black with fulvous under tail coverts; abdomen dark chestnut. Back, flanks and thighs are fulvous with fine dark brown vermiculations. The wings are as all Shelducks, with white coverts, chestnut coloured tertiaries, secondaries of bright metallic green and black primaries. Bill and legs are black. The female differs mainly about the head and neck; the neck being tinged with brown is therefore darker; the head is variably patterned with white; the body of a more uniform reddish chestnut. Length 63 cm. Immatures are duller than the male and have white lines round the eyes and bill.

Characteristics and Behaviour   The female is often wrongly identified as a White-faced Whistling Duck (*Dendrocygna viduata*). South African Shelducks closely resemble the Ruddy Shelduck, not only in posture and behaviour, but they are of similar shape and general colour. They are bad-tempered birds and can be found inland on river banks, or marshes; usually in pairs or a family group during the breeding season. Many are to be found living around farms, having become semi-domesticated. Under such conditions they are tame birds; otherwise shy and very wary where persecuted. Out of the breeding season often occur in large flocks of up to several hundred and at such times are considered as a pest. Usually the females outnumber the males, on occasions by two to one.

Habitat   They congregate on islands and mudbanks where a great part of the day is spent preening or sleeping. Very partial to dams and shallow ponds with wet muddy surrounds, more so than deeper waters with well-vegetated shores.

Distribution   Widespread in South Africa, Cape Province, Orange Free State and southern Transvaal.

Food   Principally vegetable matter, with *Zostera* (Eel Grass) and *Spirogyra* (algae species) having been recorded.

Voice   The male 'hooogh', the female 'harrk'.

Display   They start to display in February, but pairs do not claim territory until June.

Breeding   Nests in holes and burrows, quite often the disused burrow of an antbear and are composed of down. Breeding commences in late July or early August through to November, six to fifteen eggs may be laid but an average clutch would comprise ten matt white eggs, 71 × 57 mm. The incubation period is 30 days. Both parents show great concern for their young, keeping them together and calling should they become over venturesome and wander too far away.

[114]

Ruddy Shelduck

Tadorna ferruginea

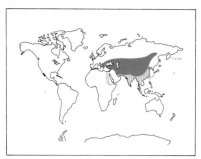

Description The adult male has creamy buff head and neck, paler on the face but more tawny buff on front of the neck. There is a narrow black collar round the neck which is partly or completely lost after the post-breeding moult. The rest of the body is a variable orange-brown with black rump and tail, and chestnut under tail coverts. The wings have black primaries and white coverts which are conspicuous in flight, both above and below; the wing speculum is metallic green. Bill, legs and feet are black. Females have a paler, almost white patch on the face and are without the black collar. Length 65 cm.

Characteristics and Behaviour Very similar to the South African Shelduck (*Tadorna cana*), which is sometimes considered only a sub-species of *T. ferruginea*. It generally favours inland fresh-water areas in preference to the coasts. The flight is strong, with slow and rather heavy wing beats. Feeding activity is mainly out of the water where its upright stance and long legs give it an easy gait. Usually met with in pairs or small parties, except at times of migration. Very noisy and quarrelsome by nature.

Habitat Extremely variable, in the breeding season it can be found at any altitude up to 5,000 m; in winter lower down in river valleys with exposed mud and sandbanks, lakes, marshes and cultivated areas.

Distribution Breeds in Atlas region of Morocco and Algeria; Greece, Roumania, Turkey, Iraq and Iran. Most of central Asia east to Mongolia and China, south to Tibet on almost any type of inland water, including lakes, marshes, saline lagoons, rivers and streams, even in mountainous regions. Some populations are sedentary within the breeding range, others winter south to the Nile valley, India, Burma, Thailand, Vietnam and Korea. Some of the North African populations make an unusual northward migration to winter in southern Spain. Stragglers have been recorded in Japan, Ceylon, western Europe and north America; in the eruption year of 1892 small numbers reached Iceland and Greenland.

Food Very varied but chiefly vegetable in content. Grasses, aquatic plants, corn, rice, also animal food in the form of molluscs, crustaceans, small fish, worms, amphibians, insects and their larvae. Often nocturnal in its feeding behaviour.

Voice The male has a loud honking call, variable in character; the female's call is a louder, more nasal 'kah-hah-hah'.

Display The initial steps in pair-formation are usually taken by the female which selects a mate and then incites him to drive away all intruders. Pairs are very aggressive during the breeding season, but usually ignore other species.

Breeding The season commences from late March in North Africa to late May in the Himalayas. The nest is usually concealed in a hole of some kind, in cliffs in mountainous regions, burrows, sand-dunes, holes in trees or river banks, etc. It is made by the female and consists largely of down and feathers.

[116]

Large clutches of up to sixteen eggs are laid at low altitudes, but eight to twelve is more usual. The eggs are white and smooth shelled, of an average size of 67 × 47 mm. Incubation is by the female for about 28 days. The downy young are dark brown above, white below with a white forehead and face; bill and feet are grey. They are tended by both parents and fledge in about 8 weeks.

Moluccan Radjah Shelduck

(Black-backed Shelduck or Burdekin Duck)

Tadorna radjah radjah

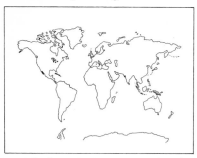

Description Both sexes are of similar plumage. White birds with black mantle, narrow breast band, back, rump and tail. There are grey filamentous lines on lower flanks and under tail coverts. The black line near tips of the greater wing coverts is very distinct. Bill flesh pink. Legs and feet pink. Length 53 cm.

The photograph opposite shows a black and white bird, variations do occur from black and white to dark brown and white.

Immatures are similar in all respects to the adults but the white parts may be flecked or tinged with brown.

Characteristics and Behaviour When resting, not likely to be mistaken for any other species. Very much a black and white bird, the white of the neck and head contrasting sharply with the black back and tail. They are smaller and daintier, with a slightly broader and more upturned bill, than the Common Shelducks. Their flight is swift and they choose to fly in amongst the trees rather than above them. In the daytime they rest on the muddy banks of rivers or lakes and are seen to perch in trees quite readily.

Habitat A bird of shallow brackish water found at the lower altitudes near the coast; only moving inland up the rivers during the dry season. Common in mangrove and sago swamps of New Guinea, also the mudbanks of rivers but not favouring the swampy rain forests.

Distribution The Moluccas, Aru Islands and New Guinea.

Food Small pools or the shallow edges of lagoons are sought out by individuals or pairs and these territories are returned to morning and evenings. On land, wet and boggy areas are regularly visited as feeding grounds. There is a tendency to restrict feeding activities to within their own territory. The diet is predominantly animal matter and such things as molluscs and large insects are taken; also small quantities of algae, but this is only a small percentage of the food intake.

Voice The harsh rattling notes of the female and the hoarse whistles of the male may be heard at all times, whether in flight, swimming or on dry land.

Display Mated males will attack any intruding Radjah Shelduck of either sex should it approach him or his mate too closely. They are extremely pugnacious at the approach of and during the breeding season.

Breeding The selection of breeding territories, by mated pairs, takes place during January and February. This may be a small pool or a stretch of river bank. At such times intruding males are rushed at with outstretched neck by the defending male, with the female often participating in the challenge. Nests are in the hollow limbs of trees, often where a large branch has broken away from the trunk. No nest material is used apart from the addition of a little down. Trees in or near to water are selected. The smooth creamy coloured eggs are usually laid between February and July and the clutch varies from six to twelve. Average egg size is 58 × 41 mm. Incubation continues for 30 days.

[118]

Australian Radjah Shelduck
(Burdekin Duck)

Tadorna radjah rufitergum

Description   Sexes alike. Differs from
the Moluccan Radjah in having rich
chestnut breastband, mantle and
shoulders, and a glossy green wing mirror bordered with black. Also a little
larger at 54 cm.

Distribution   Confined to Australia
where it ranges along the north and
north-east coasts from Derby in the west
round to Rockhampton in the east. The
main breeding areas are located from
Wyndham eastwards to the tip of the
west coast of Cape York Peninsula, and
to a lesser degree along the east coast of
the peninsula and south to Rockhampton.

Breeding   As for the Moluccan Radjah, with most clutches being completed
during May and June.

Common Shelduck

Tadorna tadorna

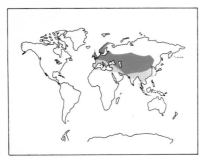

Description The adult male in breeding plumage has the head and upper neck glossy dark green, sharply defined from the white lower neck and upper breast. A broad chestnut band encircles the mantle and breast. The scapulars are black with greenish gloss, the wing coverts white, primaries black, and speculum metallic green. Underparts are white with a wide black band down the centre of the abdomen, black tip to the tail, and pale chestnut under tail coverts. The bright red bill is upturned and has a conspicuous knob at the base of the upper mandible. Legs and feet are pale pink. The female is slightly duller, noticeably smaller and lacks the knob on the bill. After the post-breeding moult in summer both adults have a duller plumage, the chestnut band is less distinct and greyer, the frontal knob disappears and the bill is paler. Length 60–65 cm. Juveniles have a dark grey head with white ring round the eye and lack the chestnut colouring; in first winter plumage they resemble adults but are duller and browner.

Characteristics and Behaviour A large, handsome species with some goose-like characteristics and with predominantly coastal habitat preference. Gregarious by nature but strongly territorial in the breeding season. In flight has slower wing beat and progresses less rapidly than most ducks, but walks easily and runs occasionally in pursuit of elusive food items. Swims buoyantly and will sometimes up-end, but seldom dives; generally spends more time out of water than other ducks.

Habitat Saline or brackish areas, especially sheltered estuaries with extensive banks of sand or mud, shallow bays; flat shores of inland lakes in central Asia.

Distribution In the breeding season, the British Isles, northern France, the Netherlands, Germany, Denmark, Scandinavia, the Balkans, the Caucasus, and across central Asia to northern China. The west European populations are mainly sedentary but large numbers undertake a moult migration in late summer to the Heligoland Bight, where numbers in the order of 100,000 have been estimated. Other populations are migratory and wintering areas extend south to Spain, the Mediterranean, north Africa, Iran, northern India, southern China and Japan.

Food Mainly animal matter, molluscs, small crustacean, also algae, grasses, roots and seeds, etc.

Voice The male has a low whistling call, the female a harsh barking quack.

Display During pair formation the males circle the females whilst performing sinuous neck movements accompanied by low whistling. The greeting ceremony is similar. Drakes defend a feeding territory and small area round the nest.

Breeding From early May onwards. The nest is usually in a rabbit burrow in sand-dunes or banks. In central Asia the burrows of steppe marmots are used. Occasionally holes in trees. Clutch size varies from seven to twelve, larger numbers being the product of more than one female; eggs are creamy-white with an average size of 66 × 48 mm. Incubation by female for a period of 28–30 days.

The downy young are brown above, white below, with blue-grey bill and legs. Soon after hatching they are escorted from the nest by both adults and taken to the nearest suitable water. Families are usually deserted by the parents, sometimes after only a few days, when the moult migration starts. At this stage several broods may join together forming a large crêche of ducklings which are then looked after by a small number of adults, probably non-breeding. The young are fully fledged 6 to 8 weeks after hatching.

Patagonian Crested Duck

(South American Crested Duck)

Lophonetta specularioides specularioides

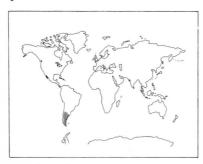

Description Adults have the crown and nape greyish-brown; paler on the forehead, sides of head and neck. Throat almost white. Mantle and flanks are greyish-brown, the breast marked with dark reddish-brown. The wings are olive-brown with a bright bronzy-green speculum; the tail and under-tail coverts black. The bill is grey, with orange edging to the lower mandible. Legs and feet are dark grey. Females are similar to males in plumage, but slightly smaller. Length 50 cm. Immatures are like the adults but paler and duller.

Characteristics and Behaviour This is the only species in the genus *Lophonetta* and there are two sub-species. The Patagonian Crested Duck (*L. s. specularioides*), and the Andean Crested Duck (*L. s. alticola*) which is larger – 60 cm and has plain buff underparts. It is an unusual kind of duck considered to be a link between Shelducks and dabbling ducks. The elongated shape of the body, together with the long pointed tail and long narrow bill give it a distinctive outline, making identification possible at a considerable distance. There is a long straggling crest which is not usually very conspicuous. The feet are set well forward, so the bird walks easily and quite gracefully. During the breeding season Crested Ducks are very aggressive and bad-tempered, frequently attacking birds of other species as well as its own.

Habitat Outside the breeding season the Patagonian Crested Duck is found largely on the coast, in salt-water creeks and small bays, but many pairs move inland to breed. The Andean Crested Duck is a high-altitude race, found farther north on mountain lakes up to 5,000 m altitude, moving down to the valleys in winter only in the extreme south of its range.

Distribution *L. s. specularioides* is restricted to the colder parts of South America from Tulca in Chile and Mendoze in Argentina, south to Tierra del Fuego and the Falkland Islands. *L. s. alticola* is found in the high Andes of north-west Argentina, northern Chile, Bolivia and Peru to 11° S.

Food Mainly animal matter, small crustaceans, molluscs, insects, worms and even domestic refuse.

Voice The drake has a rather deep, hoarse whistling call; the duck has a very low-pitched barking quack.

Display During display the drake's plumage is compressed very close to his body, thus exaggerating his normally slender shape. His wheezy calls are accompanied by head shaking and extending his neck upwards. Tail wagging and swimming backwards are also part of his performance.

Breeding The breeding season is very prolonged, eggs or young have been recorded in almost every month of the year, but most eggs are laid between September and November, or a little later in the mountains. Possibly double brooded. Breeding pairs are strongly territorial and nests are well spaced, often in long grass and usually fairly close to water. Occasionally nests are made in holes in the ground, and old

nests of Horned Coot (*Fulica cornuta*) have also been used. Eggs are cream coloured, usually five to eight sometimes more, average size 60 × 40 mm. Incubation lasts about 30 days, after which the duckling are immediately led to the nearest water. The downy young are brown above and grey below, with white patches on the wings and back, and a dark line through the eye.

South African Black Duck

(Black River Duck)

Anas sparsa sparsa

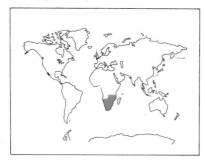

Description Both male and female are of similar plumage, blackish-brown (the duck being somewhat blacker than her mate) with upperparts showing patches of buff or white. A striking wing mirror of iridescent bluish-green occurs between bands of black and white, the very broad upper bands being formed by the secondary coverts whilst the tips of the secondaries make a narrow terminal line. On the outer bend of the wing there is a knob, as in Hartlaub's duck, the underwing is white.

Bill greyish-blue with a broad black central patch and nail. The legs and feet vary from orange to yellowish-brown with darkish webs. The female is much smaller than the male which has a length of 56 cm.

Immature birds are more brownish than the adults, have no patches of white or buff and a far less bright wing mirror. The feather edges are speckled buffish and the underneath parts are silvery-white.

Characteristics and Behaviour The African Black Ducks bear a superficial resemblance to the Mallard but have a slightly larger and wider tail, and a broader but shorter bill. They are the only ducks in Africa with large white spots on wings, scapulars and tail.

Because of their shyness are not easily observed in the wild. They are scarce, very seldom recorded in numbers and are noted for being unsociable. These surface feeding ducks are most active at dusk and dawn when they leave the wooded streams and rivers for dams and other more open water, during the day-time usually resting or sleeping in deep vegetation under overhanging branches or under banks, and are very difficult to flush. They rise with a loud quacking and despite their plump appearance are fast in flight when at such times a whistling sound is produced. If unobstructed by vegetation fly low over the water with wing tips almost touching surface. They are usually seen in pairs unless accompanied by young. When in search of food they are said to dive regularly.

Habitat Essentially a highland bird which is never found at sea level therefore does not occur in estuaries, wide rivers and lowland swamps where the majority of this family are encountered. During spring and summer, streams, stagnant ponds and pools, profuse with aquatic vegetation, and particularly in wooded areas, are much frequented; they also show a liking for the clear running water on high mountain slopes. There seems to be a seasonal movement when, in winter they journey to warmer districts.

Distribution From Cape Province and South Africa as far north as Malawi and Mozambique. Sometimes a numerous species on the reed-covered rivers and rocky streams of Natal and the Transvaal.

Food Mainly small aquatic animals, but vegetable matter is also taken.

Voice Has been described as a rather weak and wheezy whistle made by the male, with the female uttering a harsh sort of quack not unlike that of the Mallard.

Breeding The nest is built in a variety

of situations, but usually a hollow in the ground amongst thick sedges, reeds, under cover of a bank or tree and at times even a hole in a tree. Often nests on small islands. The clutch consists of five to eleven eggs, creamy or pale yellowish and glossy, measuring 60 × 43 mm thus being quite large and somewhat enlongated. The South African Duck breeds at differing times depending on distribution for example: May to August in Rhodesia and July to February in South Africa.

Abyssinian Black Duck

Anas sparsa leucostigma

Very similar to *A. s. sparsa* but the bill is greyish-pink with a central black patch not greyish-blue.

The patches on mantle, tail and flanks are buff, not white.

Habitat Can be found on wooded streams and lakes up to 14,000 feet.

Distribution Ethiopia, central Sudan, Uganda, Kenya and eastern Zaire to Tanzania.

Breeding February to March in Ethiopia and January in Uganda.

Gabon Black Duck

Anas sparsa maclatchyi

Smaller than *A. s. leucostigma* but similar in all other respects. This rare duck is very difficult to locate but can be met with on rivers at low altitude, it also frequents forest pools in the hilly areas of Gabon and Cameroon.

[125]

Bronze-winged Duck
(Spectacled Duck)

Anas specularis

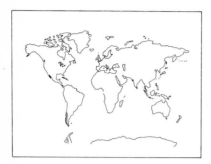

Description   The plumage of both sexes is very similar, but that of the female is somewhat duller. Neck and head are blackish-brown with two striking patches of white, one between the bill and eye and a second, much larger one, extending from the chin and throat to each side of the neck. The brown feathers of the mantle are edged a lighter shade, whilst the wings and tail are of purplish-black. At times, the large bronzy-purple mirror formed by the secondaries, exhibits reflections of pink, and lines of black and white form a border below. Brown underparts contrast with the paler flanks which are boldly marked with large black spots. The bill is a deep slaty grey in both duck and drake. The legs are of dull orange. Length 58 cm. Immature birds have little or no white on face or neck but otherwise are very like the adults.

Characteristics and Behaviour   In shape and size resembles a Mallard, it is a sociable bird often gathering in small parties or flocks.

Habitat   Principally a bird of the rivers and forest streams, but regularly frequents lakes in the more mountainous regions.

Distribution   Restricted to Chile and Argentina where it is to be found on the slopes of the Andes. From Talca on the west and Neuquen on the east, down to Tierra del Fuego. In winter months there is a northward movement to Aconcagua, Chile and Buenos Aires, Argentina.

Food   The diet consists of both animal and vegetable matter; it is on record that small snails are sometimes taken.

Voice   The males make a whistling sound. In the breeding season females produce a bark-like quack said to be very similar to the bark of a small dog.

Breeding   Nesting commences in September but the breeding season is long as is usual amongst the waterfowl of South America. The eggs are yellowish and measure 60 × 40 mm. Details of clutch size and incubation are wanting.

Female Bronzewing inciting male to attack real
or imaginary adversary

Mallard

Anas platyrhynchos platyrhynchos

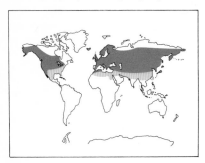

Description The drake has a most impressive breeding plumage with the metallic green of the head and neck separated from the purplish-brown breast by a very distinct white ring. The body is grey, the tail grey and white with the black central feathers forming a tight curl. A mirror of iridescent purple between two bars of black and white is formed by the secondaries, in otherwise brownish-grey wings. The bill is greenish-yellow in the male. Length 58 cm.

The female's dress is of a simple mottled buffy-brown, she has a pale eyebrow and a dark stripe through the eye. Her wing displays a purple mirror, but less bright than in the male. The bill is olive-brown and mottled with orange towards the edges.

In eclipse the male resembles a dark female, but with a ruddier breast, darker crown, brighter speculum (mirror) and a greenish-yellow bill. Immatures are less strongly marked and duller than the adults.

Characteristics and Behaviour This fairly large and very well-known duck, which is the most widespread species and common almost everywhere, has adapted itself to the changes made by man better than any other duck species.

Habitat Can be met with, and will breed, in practically any type of habitat where water is present, if they are not over-persecuted. During winter months, sea coasts and estuaries are often frequented.

Distribution Resident wherever climatic conditions are not too severe. The breeding range is extensive throughout the Northern Hemisphere, but excludes most of northern Siberia, the northern part of Alaska, much of Canada (east of the Mackenzie River and the Great Lakes), Baffin Island, Greenland, below 40° N in America, most of North Africa (but including Morocco, Algeria and Tunisia), India, Burma, Thailand and the southern half of China. Its wintering range extends almost to the Tropic of Cancer and in Africa as far south as the northern Sudan.

Food In North America and western Europe mainly vegetable matter, such as the seeds and stems of aquatic plants, with only a 10 per cent intake of such things as tadpoles and aquatic insects, etc.

Voice The male utters a quiet 'yeeb' but the female quacks loudly.

Display The social play of the male Mallards in the presence of females consists of the 'grunt-whistle' by one of the males with a response from the rest of the drakes involved of the 'head-up-tail-up' movement. This commences with a loud whistle and, with chin indrawn, the head is thrust backwards and upwards, at the same time curving his rump upwards with tail feathers ruffled; the body then sinks to a normal position and, with head held high, the bill is pointed to the female of his choice. Next comes the 'nod-swimming' with the drake stretched flat on the surface of the water he swims in a circle around the duck he is courting.

Breeding The nest is usually concealed beneath undergrowth in the vicinity of water, quite often in old tree

nests, only occasionally in holes. It is
lined with down and the clutch usually
consists of ten to twelve buffish-green
eggs. The average size is 58 × 41 mm
and the incubation lasts about 28 days.

Greenland Mallard

Anas platyrhynchos conboschas

Somewhat larger and lighter coloured
than *A. p. platyrhynchos*. Breeds in southern Greenland. Nesting from May to
July along fjords and on fresh-water
lakes. It winters along the south-western
coast when fresh water is frozen.
Entirely dependent on the sea for food
and lives in flocks close to the coast.

Hawaiian Duck

Anas platyrhynchos wyvilliana

No bigger than a Teal, with the drake's
plumage intermediate between the
common drake Mallard in eclipse and
the female Mallard but with no white ring
round the neck. The duck resembles the
female Mallard. Both sexes have a green
wing mirror. Individual variations of
the drakes considerable.
 Distribution restricted to Hawaiian

Islands. Rare, with an estimated population of 300.

Mexican Duck

Anas platyrhynchos diazi

Strongly resembles female common
Mallard, with the drakes occasionally
having traces of bright colours. The
wing mirror is slightly greenish-blue
and set between lines of black and white.
Similar in size to the common Mallard.

Distribution From Pueblo on the
highlands of Mexico as far north as the
Rio Grande Valley in New Mexico.
Elsewhere only accidental.

Florida Duck

Anas platyrhynchos fulvigula

Closely resembles the Mexican Duck,
but only has a very narrow line below
the greenish-blue wing mirror and no
white line above it.

Distribution From Florida and the
Gulf Coast to the Mexican border. Par-
ticularly common in southern Florida,
Louisiana and Texas.

[129]

Laysan Teal

Anas platyrhyncos laysanensis

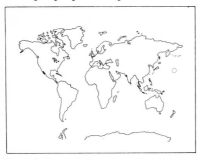

Description The adult drake has a dark head and neck with a wide white ring around the eye and other white markings of irregular configuration. The remainder of the plumage resembles female Mallard, but is a darker and more reddish-brown. Speculum is metallic green and black with a white border behind. The greyish-green bill is narrow at the base, wider at the tip. Legs and feet are orange. The female has a brown rather than green speculum, and has more distinctly mottled upperparts.

Characteristics and Behaviour The Laysan Teal is here treated as an isolated island form of Mallard, although some authors consider it differs sufficiently to warrant the status of a full species. Prolonged isolation has resulted in the loss of sexual dimorphism, reduced powers of flight and relative tameness. Since the species was first named in 1892 it has been on the verge of extinction a number of times. The population has frequently been counted or estimated during the course of the century, not always with the same degree of accuracy, but sufficient to illustrate the wild fluctuations in numbers. There were under 100 in 1903, twenty-four later that year after Japanese feather hunters had visited the island. Only six were found in 1911 after another visit from the feather hunters 2 years previously, and only seven in 1912. An ornithologist found twenty in 1923 and promptly collected six of them. Between 1950 and 1957 numbers rose from thirty-three to between 400 and 600, an increase attributed to the renewal of plant cover after the introduced rabbits had been eliminated. In 1957 the population was considered healthy enough to withstand the removal of eight individuals, with a further thirty-six the following year, to launch a captive breeding programme. This proved an immense success, and within 7 years over 150 birds were thriving in zoos and other collections. But as recently as 1963 another catastrophe befell the Laysan Teal and numbers slumped to about 200 shortly after a hurricane struck the island.

Habitat Areas of low vegetation, seldom nowadays on water.

Distribution Laysan Island only.

Food Mainly insects and their larvae, also crustaceans.

Voice Similar to the Mallard but higher pitched.

Breeding Nests are usually placed under *Chenopodium* or *Scaerola* bushes. The clutch consists of five or six greenish-white eggs, average size 55 × 38 mm. Incubation is by the female for a period of 26 to 28 days. The downy young are dark brown above, pale brown below, and with a dark line through the eye. They are very active and the bill shows signs of the distinctive shape as soon as they hatch.

Head of Laysan Teal

[131]

American Black Duck

Anas rubripes

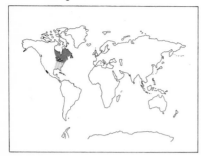

Description Does not have the bright colours of the common Mallard and although much darker it is similar in both shape and size. In breeding plumage the drake has a blackish crown with the feathers having narrow borders of buff. The dull light brown of neck and rest of the head is streaked with black; a dark line passes through the eyes. A laced effect to the general body plumage is produced by the pale brown borders to the blackish-brown feathers. The wing mirror of purplish-blue is set between two black lines and usually with a narrow edge of white below. White under wing. Bill is yellowish shading to olive at base. Legs are coral red. Length 62 cm.

The male in eclipse has head and neck greyer and less streaked, also a dull green bill.

The female bears close resemblance to eclipse male but markings are more irregular, being striped in appearance rather than laced. Bill of olive-green with black mottling. Legs greenish-yellow or dull orange.

Characteristics   and   Behaviour
Very tame on refuges and where they are fed and protected, but extremely wary where hunted. In flight the silvery white of the underwings contrast sharply with the darker body plumage but when on water no well-defined markings are apparent. During late May and early June the drakes gather in large groups, on lakes and estuaries, to moult, leaving their mates to attend to the incubation.

Habitat Although they frequent a variety of habitats, they show more of a preference for wooded areas than any other *Anas* species. May be found on fresh, brackish or salt water depending on place and season.

Distribution Its north-eastern breeding range extends from the west coast of Hudson Bay, Labrador and Newfoundland then south to Iowa, Illinois, Ohio, North Carolina and out westwards. Wintering from Wisconsin eastwards to Nova Scotia, south to the Gulf Coast and northern Florida, and westwards to Houston in Texas.

The Black Duck is quite numerous and easily the most common species in the eastern USA.

Food Mainly vegetable matter such as the seeds of sedges or rushes, the leaves and stems of various pond weeds are also taken. Animal matter accounts for less than 20 per cent of its diet and includes marine worms, grasshoppers, shrimps and even small crabs, etc.

Voice Very similar to that of the common Mallard.

Display The males' display consists of 'nod-swimming' which is frequently performed, but unlike the common Mallard this is independent of the 'head-up-tail-up' activity.

Breeding The Black Ducks breed from late April until June, the nest may be in a tussock of grass in a marsh or other damp site; under cover of grasses or other low vegetation; it sometimes uses old nests of other birds or even holes in trees. The clutch size is usually ten to twelve buffish-green eggs, the average size is 58 × 40 mm. Incubation lasts about 28 days.

Wherever they overlap with the common Mallard, interbreeding takes place.

Indian Spot-billed Duck

Anas poecilorhyncha poecilorhyncha

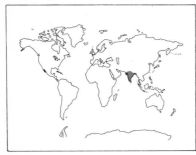

Description Sexes are similarly marked, having a blackish crown and a broad dark line through the eyes, the neck and rest of the head being of pale fawny-grey slightly streaked with blackish-brown on the sides. The lower back, rump, tail and vent are black. On blackish-grey wings the secondaries form a green mirror which is edged with black and white lines. Perhaps the most prominent feature is the pure white on the broad outer web of the two innermost tertiaries. Positioned at the base of the bill are two swollen orange-red spots, these are not present in the duller and slightly smaller female. Bill blackish with a yellow spot at the tip. Legs and feet are yellowish-orange. Length 61 cm. Immature birds are similar to the female.

Characteristics and Behaviour Large and Mallard-like in appearance with rather short legs and wings but a longish neck. Indian Spot-bills are rather heavy ducks and do not fly so well as the common Mallard, but otherwise their behaviour is very similar. A non-migratory bird moving only when the rains and availability of water dictate.

Habitat They are birds favouring lower altitudes, not being met with above 4,000 feet. Their preference is for small ponds and streams to the larger lakes and confine themselves to fresh water only.

Distribution Across India from Sind and Gujerat in the west to Manipur and Assam in the east, then south to Ceylon.

Food Mainly vegetable. Leaves, stems and roots of aquatic plants; seeds of grasses and sedges; grain, including cultivated rice. Often causing extensive damage to crops by trampling more than they eat. Animal food includes aquatic insects and their larvae, molluscs, worms and water snails.

Voice Normally a silent bird, but when used the voice is very difficult to distinguish from the Mallard. The duck has a loud quack and the drake a deep wheezing call.

Breeding The nest in situated on the ground and in the vicinity of water. The season is long, from May to December depending on locality and circumstances. Eggs are white or greyish and eight to fourteen is the usual size of clutch. On average the eggs measure 55 × 41 mm and incubation lasts for 28 days.

The downy young are like those of the Common Mallard but the eye stripe is slightly blacker and a little bolder.

Burmese Spot-billed Duck

Anas poecilorhyncha hartingtoni

Description A little smaller than *A. p. poecilorhyncha* but otherwise very similar in appearance, the underparts less spotty being more uniform in colour. The red dots at base of bill are either absent or quite small.

Distribution Burma, Yunnan and Indo-China where it is scarce.

Habits and eggs as for Indian Spot-bill.

Chinese Spot-billed Duck

Anas poecilorhyncha zonorhyncha

Description Lacks the two red spots on bill and is rather duller and less conspicuously marked than the Indian Spot-bill. From base of bill to the ear coverts runs a broad line heavily speckled with black. The lilac blue wing mirror has only very narrow white borders, the outer webs of the two inner tertiaries are white and less striking than other spot-bills.

Characteristics and Behaviour Similar to the last described species but also frequents the sea coast, not being confined to inland waters. After breeding, undergoes migratory movements to the southern parts of Japan, Korea and China, wherever open water is available. They are wary birds at all times and despite persecution seem to be maintaining their numbers.

Distribution From Kiakhta to Vladivostock and north of the Amur River to Khabarovsk in Siberia, Mongolia, China, Korea and Japan. In Japan it is a common resident, breeding on marshy areas on all the islands, also breeds in the north of Korea from April to July. Nests have been found as far south as Hong Kong.

Australian Black Duck

Anas superciliosa rogersii

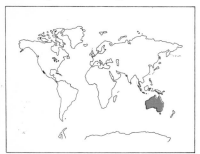

Description Sexes similarly marked. These ducks are closely related to the Spot-bills but do not have a yellow tip to the bill. They are blackish-brown birds with feathers edged in brownish-buff. The head is dark and the face distinctly marked with lines of buff and black; throat white, wing mirror green and black. Bill is lead grey with a black nail. The legs and feet are yellowish-green with dusky webs. Length of male 57 cm, on average the female is a little smaller at 53 cm.

Characteristics and Behaviour In behaviour they are like the common Mallard. Either partial or non-migratory depending on water supplies. These large birds are fast and powerful in flight with a very swift wing beat and a conspicuous long slender neck. Somewhat crepuscular by nature but if persecuted resort to nocturnal habits.

Habitat Although they occur throughout Australia in fresh, brackish, and salt-water habitats, they are nevertheless most frequent in the more deep and permanent waters where thick vegetation abounds. For this reason most swampy areas, both inland and coastal have a resident population.

Distribution Probably the most numerous duck in Australia, greatest numbers occur in the Murray–Darling Basin, the south-west corner of Western Australia and the coastal districts between Cairns and Sydney. Also present in Tasmania, East Indies, Molucca and parts of New Guinea.

Food A typical dabbling duck obtaining food in shallow waters by dredging the mud or by up-ending to reach food from the bottom. Chiefly vegetable matter, with a liking for seeds, but a small percentage of animal matter is also taken.

Voice and Display As the common Mallard.

Breeding In coastal areas the nests are usually on the ground, a preference being shown for the thick vegetation of swamps. Inland, where ground cover is somewhat sparse, nesting in elevated positions is the rule such as in trees or in the old nests of crows, etc. This is possibly a habit taken in those areas where the fox and other predators have been introduced. Occasionally a tree hole is used, in which case a red gum tree is commonly chosen. They are able to breed in every month of the year but the normal season is July to September. During periods of prolonged drought they must, by necessity, wait for the first rains. The eggs are pale greenish-white, size 58 × 42 mm, an average clutch would be eight to ten with an incubation period of 26–28 days.

New Zealand Grey Duck

Anas superciliosa superciliosa

Description Much more strikingly marked than *A. s. rogersii*, especially on the face. The dark feathers are edged with greyish or buffy white. Wing mirror green and black. Legs and feet yellowish with dusky webs. The most handsome of all the Grey Ducks. Immatures are duller than the adults.

Characteristics and Behaviour As the common Mallard.

Voice and Display As the common Mallard.

Habitat, Nest and Eggs As *A. s. rogersii*.

Distribution New Zealand and neighbouring islands. Whilst common on North Island it is not so on South Island.

Food Chiefly vegetable matter with smaller quantities of animal.

Breeding The main breeding season extends from September to January. Since the common Mallard was introduced to New Zealand the two species cross readily.

Lesser Grey Duck

Anas superciliosa pelewensis

Similar to, but smaller than, *A. s. rogersii*.

Characteristics and Behaviour As other Grey Ducks.

Distribution The northern lowlands and Orange Mountains of New Guinea. Numerous Pacific islands to the north of New Zealand and east of Australia, such as New Caledonia, Samoa, Fiji, New Hebrides and Tonga, etc.

Philippine Duck

Anas luzonica

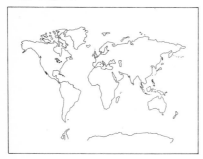

Description Plumage similar in both sexes. Crown, nape, and broad line through the eye to base of bill of very dark brown; the neck and rest of head are ferruginous yellow – this is a Mallard of outstanding beauty. The body is pale fawny-grey, darker above, there is a tinge of tawny-yellow in the breast. It has a dusky rump and tail, and a green wing mirror set between broad lines of black and white. Bill grey-blue. Legs dusky brown.

Immatures are slightly duller.

Characteristics and Behaviour An elegant arch to neck and back, high rounded forehead, slender in shape and with a long tail. In northern Luzon flocks of over a hundred birds have been recorded.

Habitat A very local and far from common species that frequents tidal creeks, small ponds and small mountain lakes.

Distribution Seems confined to the Philippine Islands.

Food Mainly vegetable matter with a small intake of aquatic insects.

Voice Similar to that described for common Mallard.

Display Again similar to the Mallard with the characteristic head-up, tail-up, and grunt-whistle and often an independent performance of 'nod-swimming'.

Breeding An average clutch would be ten pale green eggs. Incubation period is 25–26 days.

Representatives of the Mallard Group can be found all over the world with the exception of South America. They include the Black Ducks, Grey Ducks, Spot-billed Ducks and Yellow-billed Ducks; all with fairly extensive ranges. Two island species have a more restricted range: the Philippine Duck and Meller's Duck. The latter occurs only on the island of Madagascar.

Meller's Duck

Anas melleri

In both sexes the plumage of this large duck is of dark reddish-brown and not unlike the female common Mallard. Wing mirror green with narrow borders of both black and white. Bill large and greyish-green, tip of nail is black.

Found in the eastern half of Madagascar from sea level to 6,000 feet. Common on open ponds and bays, etc. often in the vicinity of forest land. Also met with on sluggish streams and in rice fields. May occur in pairs or small groups. Breeding extends from July to September.

Philippine Duck — showing bold eye stripe,
found in both sexes, and seen in many of those
species derived from Mallard type ancestors

South African Yellow-billed Duck
(Yellowbill)

Anas undulata undulata

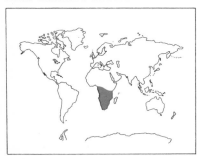

Description Sexes alike. Head and neck are deep dusky brown and densely streaked. The brownish-grey feathers of the upperparts have pale grey or buffish borders; underparts are similarly marked, but have an overall mottled effect. Wing mirrors are greeny-blue between black and white lines. Bill yellow with a long central patch which does not extend to tip; nail black. Legs are yellow and black. Length 50–57 cm. Immatures are both browner and duller, also less distinctly marked.

Characteristics and Behaviour Probably the best known of all the South African ducks, whose yellow bill with black central patch is sufficient to distinguish it from the African Black Duck with which it might be confused. The green wing mirror with its white edges is obvious when in flight. Of all the Mallards this is the most slender and graceful in build, perhaps resembling the Pintail in many respects, the neck being particularly thin. A gregarious species out of breeding season when it occurs in large flocks; somewhat shy and wary, seldom seen at close quarters.

Habitat May be found up to altitudes of 3,000 m; frequenting open waters, rivers and estuaries.

[140]

Distribution From southern Uganda and Kenya down to the Cape.

Food Feeds by up-ending or simply submersing the head. Its diet is vegetarian and includes grasses and seeds.

Voice The male a loud 'queerk-queerk', the female a coarse 'quark'.

Display As other Mallards.

Breeding The nest may be in a damp situation, or many yards away from water; it is built in vegetation and constructed of fine grasses. Down is usually added when the clutch has been completed. Breeds throughout the year, but mainly from August to October. The six to ten eggs are laid on consecutive days, they are yellowish-ivory and measure 54 × 41 mm. Incubation 26 to 28 days.

Abyssinian Yellow-billed Duck

Anas undulata ruppelli

Much darker and browner than *A. u. undulata*, with narrower buffish borders to the feathers. The bill is also of a deeper shade.

Distribution Ethiopia, northern Uganda and Kenya.

Breeding August to May.

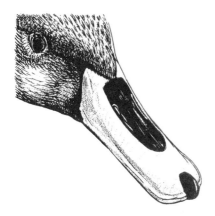

Characteristic long central patch on bill

Australian Grey Teal

Anas gibberifrons gracilis

Description Sexes are only distinguishable by plumage differences with great difficulty and after much experience, even then there is no certainty. A dull brown bird whose back feathers have a brownish edging. Tips of the secondaries and inner wing coverts are white, outer coverts white. The glossy greenish-black wing mirror is banded with white above and below. Both crown and nape are blackish-brown and much speckled with a lighter shade; sides of head are browny white; throat and chin off-white; underparts are greyish-buff the central part of each feather blotched with dark brown. Legs, bill and nail are black. Length of male 44 cm, female 42 cm. Immatures are paler than the adults and especially so about the head.

Characteristics and Behaviour Seemingly a naturally tame bird and one which is easy to approach. Can be met with practically throughout Australia, varying in numbers from a single bird to several thousands that make up the large nomadic flocks on the flood waters of the inland plains. Its flight is rapid and the white on each wing is sufficient to separate it from the Black Duck. On the water it floats high and at long range is sometimes confused with the Pink-eared Duck, single birds are often mistaken for a female Chestnut Teal, but in a mixed flock where direct

comparison is possible they are readily differentiated; the head and neck of the Grey Teal are of a much paler plumage.

Habitat Although it may be encountered in almost any water, fresh, brackish or salt, it much prefers the inland lagoons and flooded plains. Only in times of drought do the bays and estuaries along the coast support other than a sparse population. A bird much affected by rains and always the first to occupy newly created water areas as and when they occur.

Distribution Found throughout Australia, Tasmania and New Guinea. Also (but not common) in New Zealand, and is occasionally reported from some of the neighbouring islands.

Food Feeding takes place within a few feet of the water's edge and consists of dredging mud, filtering insects and seeds from the water surface, and also up-ending in the shallows. Seeds are also stripped from nearby plants. *Polygonum* and *Carex* species provide much of the vegetable food, the larvae of mosquitoes, midges and caddis flies are regularly taken.

Voice The male's call is something of a stifled 'peep', whilst the female utters a loud, rapidly repeated, almost laughing quack which is sometimes repeated upward of fifteen times.

Display In many respects resembles that of the Mallard.

Breeding Inland it has successfully adapted its breeding period to coincide with the availability of wetland areas, hence there is no set month in any one year. However, we find a more regular pattern in the southern coastal regions and in northern Australia, where breeding occurs in late winter to spring, and late summer to autumn respectively. Holes in trees are much favoured sites, but nests can also be found on the ground in almost any situation. The

[142]

duck plucks grey down from her breast and, over a period, will add this as a lining. A usual clutch size would be seven to nine creamy coloured eggs measuring 50 × 36 mm on average. Incubation period is 24 to 26 days.

East Indian Grey Teal

A. g. gibberifrons

Description Slightly smaller and a little darker than the Australian Grey Teal. Similar in other respects.

Distribution Confined to Indonesia where it is common in Celebes but less so in Java, also occurs in the Lesser Sunda Islands to Timor.

Two other races are recognized:

Rennell Island Grey Teal

A. g. remissa

This restricted to Rennell Island and the Solomons. In colour this race is intermediate between *A. g. gracilis* and *A. g. gibberifrons* and smaller than other races.

Andaman Teal

A. g. albogularis

Restricted to the Andaman Islands. Similar in size to *A. g. gracilis* but may be distinguished by a white ring around the eye which is more pronounced in the male. A white-headed form also exists.

Chestnut Teal
(Australian Brown Teal)

Anas castanea castanea

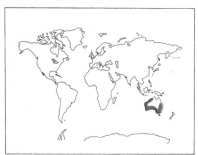

Description The adult male has a glossy green head and neck, the dark brown back feathers are each fringed with chestnut. Breast and undersides are for the most part chestnut, each feather being prominently blotched with dark brown. Back, rump and tail are black to glossy black. The dark brown wings have a glossy dark green mirror with a broad white band in front and a narrower white band behind. A white patch is very prominent on the rear flank. Bill blue-grey. Legs and feet greenish-grey.

The female's general colour is brown. Dark above, each feather with a pale brown margin; and pale below but each feather dark at the centre. Crown dark brown, and the fawn face is streaked with dark brown. The wing mirror as the male's. Immature birds are very similar to the female.

Characteristics and Behaviour When on water, seen to be a small and very dark bird floating high and occurring in pairs or small groups. In the company of Grey Teal, the female Chestnut Teal is readily differentiated, being a much darker bird and not having a white throat. The white patch to the rear of the male's flank readily distinguishes him from a Grey Teal. They seldom leave the water, only rarely feeding on land, but during the breeding

season are often seen running quite adeptly as they negotiate the larger stones of some small rocky island.

Habitat A bird of coastal regions where it frequents brackish lagoons, river estuaries, small bays and inlets, and is a common species in this kind of habitat within its range. In Tasmania whilst it is most numerous in coastal areas, it is also to be found on inland swamps and lakes throughout.

Distribution Principally Tasmania; the islands off southern Australia; and coastal regions from Perth in the west, to Sydney in the east, except the arid areas of the Great Australian Bight between Eyre and Ceduna.

Food Probably similar to that of the Grey Teal as both species may be seen dabbling together on the same water, which would suggest that quantities of water weeds and grasses are consumed along with a small percentage of insects.

Voice The loud quack of the female is that most usually heard and consists of seven to nine syllables. The whistle of the male is not distinguishable from that of the male Grey Teal.

Display Pair-forming display commences in the flocks during March and extends throughout the winter months. Several males compete to gain the attention of a female. Mated pairs leave the flock by August and together inspect the lake edges, small islands or maybe holes in trees as sites suitable for nesting purposes.

Breeding The main breeding stronghold is undoubtedly Tasmania, but major breeding areas do occur in the coastal regions of Western Australia between Augusta and Esperance, also in Victoria and New South Wales from Adelaide to Sydney. October would seem to be the month when most egg-laying commences. The nest is a simple

scrape on the ground in rushes or long grasses, etc. also in Tasmania hollow trees are regularly used. Down is used as a lining. The eggs number seven to fifteen they are cream with a smooth surface and measure 52 × 37 mm. An incubation period of 28 days is usual. Many clutches are lost to the predation of foxes and snakes. The male quite often stays with the female and her ducklings until they are fledged.

There are two further related species which are found in the same geographical region.

New Zealand Brown Teal

A. aucklandica chlorotis

Slightly larger than the nominate subspecies and less brightly coloured.

Auckland Islands Teal

A. a. aucklandica

A short winged bird which has a very weak flight. Confined to Auckland Island.

Baikal Teal
(Spectacled Teal)

Anas formosa

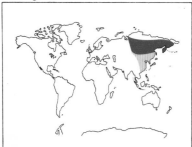

Description   The adult male has an unmistakable appearance about the head. The crown is black, bordered below with a narrow white band; the face is creamy buff divided by a black line curving down from the eye to the throat; and at the back of the head is a crescent-shaped patch of metallic green, bordered behind and below with another white band separating it from the black nape. The buff face patches are finely bordered with white. The mantle is blue grey, finely vermiculated with black; the scapulars are elongated, rufous and white with black centres. Speculum metallic green and black, bordered rufous in front, and white behind. The breast is brown with a vinous tinge and speckled with black; flanks vermiculated bluish-grey with a white bar below the bend of the wing, and another below the base of the tail. Under tail coverts black with reddish-brown edges. Bill slaty grey, legs and feet dull yellowish and grey. The female is similar to that of the Common Teal (*A. crecca*), but larger and with a white spot on each side of the base of the bill. Length 40 cm. Immatures as female, but without the white spots.

Characteristics and Behaviour   Not a great deal is known about the habits of this eastern Asiatic species. At one time it was very abundant, occurring in enormous flocks at favourite wintering areas: one flock in Japan being estimated to number 100,000. The present declining numbers are believed to be the result of excessive hunting and the draining of marshland for agriculture. Migration is along regular, well-defined routes. The flight not so swift or aerobatic as the smaller teal.

Habitat   In the breeding season, in dry parts of forested zone, near pools and streams, etc. and farther north, along the main river valleys of northern Siberia. In winter, shallow fresh-water areas, marshes, and also sheltered coastal areas.

Distribution   Breeds in central and eastern Siberia, from the deltas of the Lena, Yana and Indigirka rivers on the arctic coast, south to Lake Baikal, and from the River Yenisei east to the Andyr and Kamchatka peninsula. Migrants follow routes through Sakhalin and Korea to the main wintering area in southern Japan, others winter in south-east China. A vagrant to India and Burma.

Food   Mainly seeds and small aquatic invertebrates. In winter feeds in rice paddies, also on soya beans. On the spring migration, feeding on acorns has been recorded in south-east USSR.

Voice   The drake has an unusual voice; his call is a loud disyllabic clucking note. The duck has a weak, low-pitched quack.

Breeding   Most birds leave the wintering area in March and the breeding season extends from late April to early July. Nests are usually close to water but in a dry situation amongst grasses or low scrub. A clutch of eight to ten eggs are laid, pale olive colour, average size 49 × 35 mm. Incubation period is about 24 days. The downy young are similar to those of the Common Teal, brown above, yellowish below, with a bright yellow face and dark stripe through the eye.

Female Baikal Teal

Falcated Duck

Anas falcata

Description The drake in breeding plumage has the crown, front of the head and cheeks a bright metallic bronzy-purple; the remainder of the head from the eye back to the long, sleek nuchal crest is a deep glossy green. The iris is dark brown and there is a white spot on the forehead at the base of the bill. The chin and throat are white, bordered below by a black collar with white fringe. The mantle is grey with black markings; the elongated tertiaries are falcated or sickle-shaped, black with a dark blue sheen and narrow white edges. Underparts are pale grey, heavily marked with black on the breast, and more lightly vermiculated on the flanks. The rump and tail are grey with black upper tail coverts and buff under tail coverts with black border. Bill black, legs and feet grey. The female is similar to female Gadwall but has black and green speculum and a short crest. Length 45 cm. Immatures are like females but without crest and with duller speculum.

Characteristics and Behaviour The general outline of the drake suggests a squat, thick-set bird, the size of the head being exaggerated by the crest; while the drooping tertiaries, obscuring the tail, give a false impression of the body proportions. With a distribution broadly similar to that of the Baikal Teal, equally little is known of its habits in the wild. It differs considerably from the Teal, showing closer affinities to the Gadwall. It is migratory in habit, travelling in large flocks but dispersing into small groups on the winter range. The autumn migration extends from September to November with the return journey commencing in February.

Habitat In the breeding season, ponds, rivers, small lakes and marshes in the forest zone. In winter, lakes, marshes, rice paddies and regularly on the sea in Japan.

Distribution Breeds in central and eastern Siberia from 58° N to Lake Baikal and northern Manchuria, and from the Yenisei River east to Sakhalin and Kamchatka. In Japan only on Hokkaido. Winters in southern Japan, east China, Taiwan, Hainan, Laos and Burma. A vagrant to India and Iran.

Food Mainly vegetable matter, seeds, rice and some aquatic plants, also small invertebrates. At times it will dive for food.

Voice The low trilling whistle of the drake resembles that of the Teal, the female has a quack not unlike the Mallard.

Display The drake has a head-up-tail-up display which shows off his crest and buff under tail coverts to good advantage. Females also display with head movements similar to the drake.

Breeding The breeding season extends from May to early July, the nest is concealed in thick vegetation close to water but in dry surroundings. Clutch size varies from six to ten creamy-white eggs, average size 56 × 40 mm. Incubation lasts for about 25 days. The downy young are dark brown above, buff below and with a yellowish face.

[148]

Falcated Drake showing 'falcon beak' like
tertiary feathers hanging over the tail

[149]

Gadwall

Anas strepera

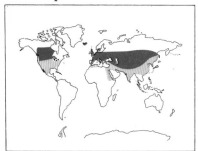

Description From early autumn to early summer, the drake has head and neck pale buff, spotted and streaked with brown, with the crown darker. Both mantle and flanks are finely vermiculated creamy buff and dark grey. The wing is mostly grey with white speculum sometimes concealed by long pointed scapulars, greater coverts black, and median coverts chestnut. The breast has dark crescentic markings but some individuals appear more blotched or spotted. Abdomen and vent are white, upper and under tail coverts black, tail greyish-brown with paler outer feathers. The bill is slaty grey and narrow, legs and feet orange-yellow. The female is browner, with coarser markings; under tail coverts speckled grey and brown, very little or no chestnut in the wing. Bill slaty grey with a dull orange border. Immature females are very similar to adults; male in eclipse and immature males are similar to female. Length about 50 cm.

Characteristics and Behaviour The general appearance of both sexes on water is of dull grey-brown birds with no outstanding field marks. Noticeably smaller than Mallard, with which it freely associates; females may be distinguished by the white speculum, while the black tail coverts readily identify the male especially in flight when they make a strong contrast with the white belly.

The wings are fairly long, more pointed than the Mallard's, and with a quicker wing beat. On water appears more buoyant and swims with tail well elevated.

Habitat Fresh-water lakes and pools with plenty of cover, marshes and streams. Not very numerous in salt-water habitats and generally more numerous inland than in coastal regions. Also prairies of North America.

Distribution A holarctic species, well distributed in temperate regions, the range does not extend beyond 60° N in summer and not much below 20° N in winter. In the breeding season not very numerous in western Europe, from Iceland, British Isles, southern Sweden and Denmark, south to Spain. Central Europe, the Balkans, the Caucasus and across to the Pacific coast of Asia. Also western North America. In winter, south to the Mediterranean and North Africa, the Nile valley, India, Burma, China and Japan. In America, south to Mexico.

Food Mainly vegetable, leaves and stems of aquatic plants, grain; also small molluscs, amphibians and aquatic insects.

Voice The male has a harsh croaking call; the female a quack similar to the Mallard.

Display Similar to the Mallard but less complex.

Breeding From May to June. The nest is usually well concealed in thick vegetation and fairly close to water. It is constructed from grasses, sedges etc. and lined with dark grey down. The clutch size varies from eight to twelve but occasionally more, eggs are pale buff, average size 54 × 39 mm. Incubation, by the female, takes about 26 days. Downy young are dark brown above, creamy below, with a dark stripe through the eye.

Chilean Teal

(South American Green-winged Teal)

Anas flavirostris flavirostris

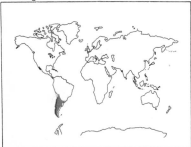

Description Adults have greyish-brown head and neck, dark brown upperparts with pale margins to the feathers, and greyish underparts marked with heavy black spots on the breast. The speculum is black and bright metallic green with a narrow white border. The narrow bill is yellow with a black band along the culmen and a black tip. Legs and feet are dark grey. Sexes are similar but the female is duller and slightly smaller. Length 40 cm. Immatures have only lightly spotted underparts.

Characteristics and Behaviour Four sub-species are recognized, all restricted to South America. The Chilean Teal (*A. f. flavirostris*) is as described; the Sharp-winged Teal (*A. f. oxyptera*) is larger and paler, with long pointed scapulars; the Andean Teal (*A. f. andium*) is also larger than *flavirostris* but is darker, has a bluish-grey bill and purplish sheen on the speculum; the Merida Teal (*A. f. altipetens*) is much like *andium* but paler and lacking the purplish sheen on the speculum. The Chilean Teal has the most southerly distribution and is probably the most numerous small duck in many parts of its range, and the southernmost populations are the only members of the group which are migratory. They are swift in flight, and tame by nature often nesting close to human habitation. Gen-erally sociable, they are usually found in small flocks of up to twenty, occasionally associating with Cinnamon Teal (*Anas cyanoptera*) and Silver Teal (*Anas versicolor*). They perch readily in high trees where they are able to evade predators by manoeuvering at high speed through the branches. Habits of the two grey-billed high-altitude forms have not been extensively studied.

Habitat Small pools and lakes, rivers, coastal lagoons and lakes of the high Andean plateaux.

Distribution The Chilean Teal occurs in Chile from Coquimbo province south to Tierra del Fuego, southern Brazil, Uruguay, Paraguay, Argentina and the Falkland Islands. The Sharp-winged Teal is found in northern Chile, north-west Argentina, Bolivia and southern Peru, mainly at high altitude but also river valleys and coastal areas in desert regions of northern Chile. The ranges of the Andean and Merida Teal are isolated from the others by some 800 miles, the former occurring in the central Andes of Colombia and Ecuador, the latter in the eastern Andes of Colombia and Venezuela.

Food Chiefly vegetable matter; feeds mainly on the water surface but has been recorded diving for food.

Voice Resembles the Northern Green-winged Teal in voice and display.

Breeding The season is very variable and dependent on local factors, two broods are frequently reared. Generally, September to November is the peak period, with second broods from January to February. Nests are usually on the ground, close to water and well hidden in long grasses or other vegetation, in forested areas nests built in large forks of Eucalyptus trees are not unusual; whilst Sharp-winged Teal regularly nests in holes in banks and cliffs. Clutch size varies from five to eight eggs, buff

coloured, average size 52 × 38 mm for
Chilean Teal. The incubation period is
about 26 days, and unlike the Northern
Green-winged Teal, the drake helps in
rearing the brood. The downy young
resemble Mallard ducklings, being dark
brown above, creamy below and
yellowish-brown on the sides of the
head, with a dark stripe through the eye
and another one below.

European Teal
(Common Teal)

Anas crecca crecca

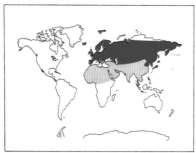

Description The Northern Green-winged Teal are widely distributed throughout the Northern Hemisphere, the nominate *A. c. crecca* in Europe and Asia, and *A. c. carolinensis* in North America. They were at one time considered to be distinct species but are here treated separately simply for convenience. A third sub-species *A. c. nimia*, the Aleutian Green-winged Teal, is indistinguishable from the European Teal except for its slightly larger size, being restricted to the Aleutian Islands and is non-migratory.

The drake European Teal has a rich chestnut head and neck with a metallic green patch running from in front of the eye back to the neck and enclosed with a pale buff border. The mantle and flanks are vermiculated pale grey and black, with a pale line along the body above the wings produced by white patches on the long scapulars. The speculum is metallic green and black, with white borders in front and behind. The upper breast is pale creamy with large dusky spots, rest of the underparts white, with slight barring on the abdomen and vent. The central under tail coverts are black and there is a creamy-yellow patch on each side of the rump. Bill dark grey, legs and feet greenish-grey with dark webs. The female is mottled and streaked dark brown and buff, with dark crown and white underparts. The drake in eclipse resembles the female but with darker upperparts. Length 35 cm. Juveniles also like females but with underparts spotted brown.

Characteristics and Behaviour The Teal is the smallest duck resident in Europe. It is swift and dashing in flight, flocks performing co-ordinated manoeuvres with the agility of small waders. It also has the ability to spring almost vertically from land or water when flushed. Feeding takes place mainly at dusk or at night except in areas where it is undisturbed.

Habitat In the breeding season, small pools or lakes with thick cover, grassy or heather moorland, marshes, peat bogs, areas of low scrub. In winter, on ponds, lakes, marshes, flooded meadows, estuaries and mudflats.

Distribution Breeds in Iceland, Scandinavia, British Isles, central and southern Europe, the Balkans, and across Asia to the Gulf of Anadyr, Kamchatka, the Kuriles and Japan. Winters south of the breeding range to tropical Africa, Arabia, India and south-east Asia.

Food Seeds of grasses and aquatic plants, insects and larvae, molluscs, worms, crustaceans and some grain in winter quarters.

Voice The call of the male is a high-pitched whistling 'krit', the female has a short high-pitched 'quack'.

Display Highly developed and containing some elements similar to display of Mallard. A number of drakes will display to one female and pursuit flights often follow.

Breeding Late April to May, but early June in north of range. The nest is usually in a dry situation well hidden amongst grasses, sedges, heather, bracken and low scrub, etc. Constructed by the female and lined with a small quan-

[154]

tity of down and dead vegetation. Eggs eight to ten as a rule, but larger clutches have been recorded; they are creamy-white with a greenish tinge, average size 45 × 33 mm. Incubation by the female takes about 21 days, after which the drake sometimes assists in rearing the brood. Fledging period 4 to 5 weeks.

North American Green-winged Teal

Anas crecca carolinensis

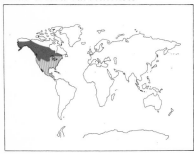

Description The adult drake in breeding plumage is generally similar to drake European Teal, but has a vertical white band on the side of the breast instead of the horizontal white band along the scapulars. It is thus easily distinguished for approximately half of the year. Minor differences include a narrower pale border surrounding the green patch on side of head, usually incomplete and sometimes lacking altogether. The upper breast has a more tawny or cinnamon tinge. Females and immatures cannot be distinguished in the field. Length 35 cm.

Characteristics and Behaviour The smallest duck in North America. Not quite as wild or difficult to approach as the European Teal. The average annual 'bag' in North America of a million birds indicates that they are fairly easily hunted.

Habitat In the breeding season prefers grassy areas with some scattered trees, but avoids forested areas. In winter, areas of brackish water in coastal regions in addition to freshwater pools and lakes. Will also visit rice fields.

Distribution Breeds from Alaska, north-west Canada and British Columbia across southern Canada to Labrador, Newfoundland and Nova Scotia.

In western USA south to California. Also to northern New Mexico, northern Nebraska, Minnesota, Ohio, New York and Maine. Winters in small numbers south Alaska and British Columbia but chiefly in the USA and south to Mexico where it is numerous on both the Atlantic and Pacific coasts. Also to Cuba, Nicaragua, and northern parts of Colombia and Venezuela.

Feeding behaviour, voice, display and breeding Similar to those of the European Teal.

European Green-winged Teal

American Green-winged Teal

European Wigeon

Anas penelope

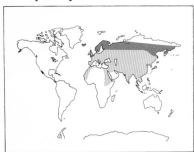

Description The male is easily identified by a variety of fairly conspicuous features. The head is chestnut with a creamy-yellow crown. The breast is pinkish and the body mainly grey with a white line at the edge of the wing. Black under tail coverts form a sharply defined contrast to the underparts which are mainly white. In flight the prominent white patch on the front of the wing is the most useful identification feature.

The female does not possess any outstanding field marks, being mainly brown above and white below. It lacks the creamy-yellow crown, white wing patch and black under tail coverts of the male. At long range or in poor light, identification can sometimes only be assumed by the presence of a male, but the general shape, especially of the high rounded head, can be a very useful aid to identification.

Bill slaty grey with a black tip, duller in female.

Male in eclipse plumage is similar to the female, but with white wing patches.

Legs and feeet vary from brown to grey. Length approximately 46 cm.

Characteristics and Behaviour Intermediate in size between Mallard and Teal, Wigeon are usually seen in small groups or flocks and not normally in close association with other wildfowl species. They rise straight from the water with rapid wing beats, numbers of birds usually maintaining a compact flock formation.

Feeding behaviour is somewhat varied, in addition to paddling in shallow water Wigeon are frequent grazers and will also up-end on occasions. However, diving for food has only been recorded on rare occasions.

Habitat In the breeding season found on small lakes and pools, chiefly in the coniferous zone of northern Europe and USSR. In the British Isles, moorland tarns, islands in lochs and bracken slopes are favoured.

In winter, large flocks, occasionally numbering thousands of birds, can be found in shallow coastal waters, estuaries and saltings; with smaller numbers on inland lakes and reservoirs.

Distribution The breeding range is very widespread throughout most of northern Europe and Asia, from 24° W in Iceland to 180° E in Anadyrland, including the British Isles, Norway, Finland, northern Russia, across Siberia to Commander Isle.

The wintering range extends as far south as North Africa, the Middle East, India, China and Japan. This species is also recorded in North America, outside the breeding season, from both the Atlantic and Pacific coasts, but only in very small numbers.

Food This consists mainly of vegetable matter, chiefly eel grass and seaweed in coastal areas, but the Wigeon is also an efficient grazing bird and can be found cropping the short grasses on saltings and also flooded water meadows well inland, often in very large flocks. For example, on the Welney washes in East Anglia in England flocks in excess of 30,000 have been counted. Animal food recorded includes cockles and dipterous insects.

Voice The call of the drake is a melodious whistling 'whee-oooo' whilst the duck has a low purring note.

Display A number of males usually display to one female, with outstretched neck and raised feathers on the crown, all the time whistling loudly. The pair bond is stronger than in many other wildfowl species.

Breeding The nest is placed on the ground, usually in thick waterside vegetation or under the shelter of a low bush, and lined with grasses and down.

There are normally seven to ten creamy-buff eggs, but larger clutches have been recorded. Egg size approximately 54 × 38 mm.

The breeding season commences in early May but is later farther north. The incubation period is about 3½ weeks, with a fledging period of a further 6 weeks. Sometimes the male will reunite with the family when the female takes the ducklings to the water.

American Wigeon
(Baldpate)

Anas americana

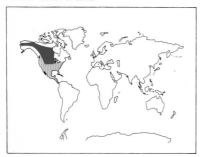

Description In shape and size, very similar to the European Wigeon, but the drake has an obvious colour difference, particularly about the head and upperparts. For instance, the crown and forehead are white and there is a much larger area of metallic green from behind the eye attenuating downwards to nape. The remaining areas of head and neck are spotted black on a creamy-white background. Upperparts are dusky lilac with fine black vermiculations. Breast, sides and flanks are pinkish-lilac shading dusky towards flanks. Bill is slaty grey with a black tip and a touch of black at extreme base. Otherwise as *A. penelope*.

The female falls between the grey phase and reddish phase of the female European Wigeon, but has white background to head with crown and throat distinctly spotted, and bars on upperparts more pronounced.

Characteristics and Behaviour A duck of medium size and seemingly sociable towards other species when afloat. It shows more of a preference for fresh water than *A. penelope*. When both species are in flight together, the drakes are readily differentiated by comparison, with the light head and darker body of the Baldpate being reversed in the European Wigeon. Much time is spent on land grazing. When observed

flying in small groups, an impression of speed is given, but they seldom if ever fly in excess of 30 m.p.h. (48 k.p.h.).

Habitat During the breeding period prefers the marshy areas associated with the larger expanses of open water, whereas the European Wigeon seems happy with any marshland, the expanse of available water being irrelevant. Even in winter many will stay inland on fresh water until such time as it becomes frozen over, only then visiting the coast; whilst a few may seek out large lakes and rivers not affected by frost and remain there to winter.

Distribution The main breeding areas are Alaska east to the Mackenzie River delta then south and east of Great Bear Lake to Churchill on Hudson Bay, along the south-west coast of the Bay and on to the St Lawrence River and as far south as the Great Lakes, then westwards including, Ontario, Manitoba, Saskatchewan, Alberta, Yukon, British Columbia, the eastern half of Oregon, Idaho, Montana, Wyoming, parts of North and South Dakota, Nebraska, Colorado, Utah and Nevada. Wintering occurs along the west coast from British Columbia in the north and including almost the whole of Mexico, then east to Florida and north to Nova Scotia. Also the islands from Cuba to Puerto Rica.

Food In the main, a vegetable diet of grasses, sedges, algae and seeds, with a little animal matter including insects but more usually snails.

Voice The drake's call is somewhat unmusical and comprised of three syllables, these being repeated rapidly. Does not have the long terminal note at the end of its whistle that one associates with *A. penelope*. The female's call has been described as 'qurr qurr' or as 'qua-awk qua-awk'.

Display The majority of birds are already mated by February. The drake swims either behind or alongside his

intended, at times with neck out-stretched, head held low, and bill agape; occasionally uttering his whistling notes.

Breeding The nest is constructed from pieces of grass and stems, etc. in a dry, partly concealed spot on the ground and is lined with down. The clutch size is variable, but on average five to seven creamy-white eggs are laid from the end of May to the first half of June. These measure 55 × 39 mm and the period of incubation is $3\frac{1}{2}$ weeks.

Chiloë Wigeon

Anas sibilatrix

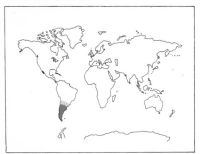

Description Similar in size to the American Wigeon, but with little plumage difference between male and female. The drake has a white forehead with the rest of the head and upper neck black. Two metallic green patches on the sides of the head extend down to the nape, and there is a white spot behind and slightly below the eye. The upperparts are black with white or pale buff edging to the feathers, the breast white heavily marked with short black bars. The flanks are an orange-brown except in the dull phase where they are a drab dark brown. Underparts and tail coverts are white, the tail black. The lesser wing coverts are white, as in other wigeon, showing up as a prominent wing patch in flight. In the female the patch is greyer. The speculum is black tinged with metallic green. The bill is blue-grey with a black nail. Legs and feet are dark grey. The female is slightly smaller and duller, with the white markings on the head not so clearly defined. Immatures are very much like the female with duller head and breast. Length 45–50 cm.

Characteristics and Behaviour The Chiloë Wigeon is quite a numerous species despite a limited breeding range, restricted to the southern third of South America. Flight is strong and birds rise easily from the water. In areas where they are not hunted they are often quite tame.

Habitat Generally prefers fresh-water lakes, rivers and marshes where there is abundant vegetation.

Distribution The breeding range extends from Tierra del Fuego in the south to Atacama province in Chile, to Cordoba province and Buenos Aires in Argentina, also parts of Uruguay and southern Brazil. In winter, migration occurs from the colder southern regions with the limit of the wintering range extending north to Paraguay and Rio Grande do Sul (Brazil).

Food Mainly vegetable, grasses and aquatic vegetation.

Voice The call of the male is a three-note whistle not unlike the American Wigeon, but with final note loud and more prolonged. The female has a rather hoarse quack.

Breeding The breeding season extends from August to January, the actual timing depending on water conditions and location. The nest is a depression in the ground, concealed amongst vegetation. Six to nine creamy-white eggs are laid, average size 58 × 40 mm. Unlike the Wigeon of the Northern Hemisphere the male shares the task of caring for the young. The ducklings are dark brown above, paler below, with a black crown and black line behind the eyes.

[162]

Chiloë Wigeon family, the drake playing a protective role – unusual behaviour amongst ducks

Lesser Bahama Pintail
(White-cheeked Pintail)

Anas bahamensis bahamensis

Description A small slim duck with sexes fairly similar in plumage but different in size. The head and back of the neck are dark brown, the cap extending to just below the eyes. Cheeks and front of neck are white, sharply defined. The upperparts are dark brown with paler feather margins, underparts a rich tawny-brown mottled with darker spots and blotches. The tail is pale fawn coloured, long and pointed, the central feather more elongated in the male than the female. The speculum is green, bordered in front with a narrow cream bar, behind with a narrow black band and a wider band of buff. The bill is greyish-blue at the tip, red towards the base, with black line on the top of the culmen. Legs and feet are greyish-blue. Immatures similar to female but duller. Two sub-species are recognized, *A. b. rubrirostris* from South America south of the Equator, is larger; *A. b. galapagensis* from the Galapagos Islands is the smallest and has the white cheek patches less clearly defined. Length 38–46 cm.

Characteristics and Behaviour Found only in tropical and sub-tropical regions of America, most populations are non-migratory except in the extreme south of the range. Very shy and wary in most parts of the Caribbean where it is a highly prized game bird and suffers nest predation by introduced mammals; but remarkably tame in the Galapagos Islands. Associates frequently with Yellow-billed Pintail in southern South America.

Habitat Well vegetated fresh-water ponds, swamps, and salt-water lagoons, but will also feed well away from water.

Distribution This the nominate race breeds in the Bahamas, Cuba, Hispaniola and Lesser Antilles south to Guadeloupe, Curaçao, Trinidad, Guyana, Surinam, French Guiana and north Brazil. *A. b. rubrirostris* breeds in Brazil, Paraguay, Uruguay, north Argentina, east Bolivia and north Chile. *A. b. galapagensis* is restricted to the Galapagos Islands.

Food Mainly vegetable, grasses, plant leaves and stems, seeds, some aquatic insects and snails.

Voice The drake has a low squeaky call and the female a harsh, high-pitched quack.

Display The drake's display commences with vigorous head-shaking, followed by a posture with head and tail held high and the breast submerged. Females also display, inciting the drakes in a similar way to Pintail (*Anas acuta*).

Breeding The breeding season varies from late spring in the Caribbean; October–November in the south (*A. b. rubrirostris*); and possibly the year round in the Galapagos. The nest is well concealed in thick vegetation or among mangrove roots. Eggs are deep creamy colour, six to eleven, average size 55 × 37 mm. Incubation period is 25–26 days in captivity. Ducklings are dark brown above, pale yellow below, with bright yellow face and neck.

Bahama Pintail courtship – 'down-up' phase of
display with speculum exposed

[165]

Chilean Pintail
(Brown Pintail)

Anas georgica spinicauda

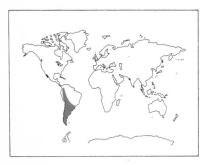

Description A dull brown bird with plumage not unlike the Common Pintail (*Anas acuta*) but with both sexes similar in markings. The crown and back of the neck are dark brown, flecked with black, shading to buff on the sides of the head, and pale buff on the throat. The upperparts are greyish-brown, marked with black; underparts similar, heavily spotted with black on the breast and larger black blotches on the flanks. The speculum is glossy black with a buff border in front and behind. Lower breast and belly are buffish white. The bill is yellow with a dark line on top of the culmen. Legs and feet are grey-green. Length 65 cm. Females are slightly smaller and duller.

The nominate race *A. g. georgica* is restricted to South Georgia only. It is the smallest and darkest sub-species. Length 55 cm. *A. g. spinicauda* (illustrated) is lighter coloured and with two fewer tail feathers. A third sub-species *A. g. nicefori*, Niceforo's Pintail is believed extinct.

Characteristics and Behaviour General behaviour much like Common Pintail, frequenting fresh-water habitats from sea level to the Andes, but non-migratory in the northern parts of its range. Southern populations do migrate, others wander sporadically.

The most numerous of all South American ducks.

Habitat Fresh-water lakes, marshes and rivers. The South Georgian Pintail also occurs regularly on salt water, in bays and fjords around the coast.

Distribution Southern Colombia, Ecuador and Peru (in the Andes only); Chile, Bolivia, southern Brazil and Argentina south to Tierra del Fuego and the Falkland Islands. Migrants are generally within this range. (*A.g. georgica*, South Georgia Island.)

Food Mainly vegetable, grasses, seeds, etc. but in South Georgia animal matter is also taken.

Voice The drake has a wheezy whistling call, the female has a variety of notes including a Mallard-like 'quack'.

Breeding The breeding season of the South Georgian Pintail extends from November to February, that of the Chilean Pintail from October to December except in the Andes where it may be more protracted. The nest is on the ground amongst tall vegetation. Eggs are cream coloured, six to twelve are laid by the Chilean Pintail but clutches in South Georgia are smaller.

Size 52 × 40 mm. Incubation period about 24 days.

Northern Pintail

(Common Pintail or Blue-billed
Pintail)

Anas acuta acuta

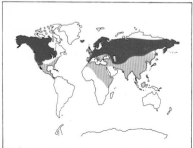

Description   The adult drake has a
distinctive appearance with chocolate
coloured head and neck, the white of the
breast extending in a narrow line at the
side of the neck; and a long pointed tail.
The back and flanks are finely vermiculated dark grey and white; belly
white; under tail coverts black. The
speculum is bronzy-green, with a tawny
border in front and white-edged behind.
Bill bluish to lead grey with black stripe
on top of the culmen. Legs and feet are
grey. Female resembles a Mallard female
but is more graceful with a longer neck,
pointed tail, and obscure speculum.
Juveniles are like the female but with
darker, more uniform upperparts.
Length of drake 65 cm, duck 55 cm.

Characteristics and Behaviour   The
long neck, slender pointed wings and
pointed tail, together with swift flight
and rapid wing beat are characteristic,
making the Pintail unmistakable in the
air. On water they feed from the surface
or by up-ending, their long necks enabling them to exploit slightly deeper water
than other dabbling ducks. They will
also feed on land, walking gracefully and
easily. Generally rather wary in
behaviour, adopting crepuscular and
nocturnal feedings habits. Next to the
Mallard, Pintail is the most numerous
species of duck in the holarctic region.
Associates readily with other species.

Habitat   In the breeding season, shallow fresh-water lakes and marshes,
tundra pools, generally surrounded by
extensive level areas and with dry rather
than swampy surroundings. Grasslands, dry meadows near rivers, not
normally in well-wooded areas. In
winter found more regularly in coastal
regions than inland.

Distribution   Breeds   in   Iceland,
British Isles, northern Scandinavia,
Russia, Siberia, Alaska, Canada, western USA south to California, and west
Greenland. Two isolated sub-species
breed in the Southern Hemisphere, *A. a.
eatoni* on Kerguelen Island, and *A. a.
drygalskii* on the Crozet Islands. Winters
in western Europe, Mediterranean
coasts, tropical west Africa, Black Sea,
Arabia, India, Burma and Pacific
Islands. In America from the Gulf of
Alaska, south to central America; on the
east coast mainly south of New England.

Food   The seeds of grasses, sedges and
pondweeds, some aquatic insects, molluscs and crustaceans, occasionally
grain from stubble fields. In the breeding season also large quantities of larvae
of caddis flies and midges, abundant in
shallow water.

Voice   Not very vocal, the drake has a
low melodious whistle, usually double-
noted, the female a low quack.

Display   Male swims close to female
with elevated tail and bill depressed,
whilst uttering whistling notes. If a
number of males are present the display
often develops into an aerial chase.
When alarmed, tail is depressed and
neck stretched upwards.

Breeding   From early May onwards
depending on location, with replace-
ment clutches up to August. The nest is
loosely constructed from dry vegetation,
lined with down and feathers, and less
concealed than that of most other ducks.
Eggs usually seven to nine but more

[168]

have been recorded; greenish-buff or creamy. Size 55 × 38 mm. Incubation by female alone 23 days. The downy young are dark brown above, whitish below; the crown is dark, sides of the head paler with two dark lines extending from the eye towards the back of the head. Bill and legs are dark grey. The young birds fledge in approximately 6 weeks during which time they are tended by the female but feed themselves. It is not unknown for the drake to be present in the early stages of the fledging period.

Red-billed Teal

Anas erythrorhyncha

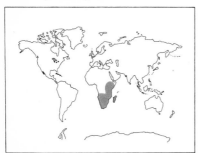

Description Sexes are similar. Crown and nape dusky brown, extending to below the eye and sharply defined from pale buff of throat and sides of head. Upperparts and wings greyish-brown with pale edging to the feathers. Underside of wings grey. Breast and underparts are pale buff with dark brown markings. The bill is bright red with a brown line on top of the culmen. Legs and feet dark slate coloured. Immatures are like adults but with narrower markings on the underparts and a duller bill. Length 43–48 cm.

Characteristics and Behaviour Similar in general appearance to Bahama Pintail, but with a much shorter tail. Flight is swift, the buffish wing bar very prominent. Common throughout much of its range, it is fairly gregarious and also associates freely with other species. It swims quite high in the water and also walks easily, spending much time on dry land and occasionally causing damage to crops, especially rice. Where undisturbed they are reasonably tame, but very active usually swimming away rapidly when approached.

Habitat Found on practically any stretch of fresh water inland, from large lakes to the very smallest pools. They feed regularly in swamps and weed-covered pools, and prefer well-vegetated waters during the breeding season.

Distribution South Africa from Angola, Luanda, Tanzania, Uganda, Kenya and Ethiopia south to Cape Province. Also Madagascar. Common on Rift valley lakes in East Africa.

Food Mainly vegetable, aquatic vegetation, seeds and some cultivated grain.

Voice Generally very silent, but the male has a soft whistling note and the female a low harsh quack.

Display Very poorly developed in this species, limited to some head shaking and calling by the drake, which is otherwise silent for most of the year.

Breeding The breeding season is very variable throughout the range, being determined to some extent by the irregular rainfall. It has been recorded breeding all the year round in South Africa, February and March in Zambia, February to May in Rhodesia, July in Malawi, June to July in East Africa, and January to February in Madagascar. The nest is a deep cup of sedges, lined with down, usually close to water in reeds or rushes. The clutch size is five to twelve eggs greenish-white, and smooth. They are highly variable in size, average 54 × 41 mm. The precise incubation period is not known. The downy young have brown upperparts with a dark line through the eye and a creamy eye stripe above. There are dark patches on the ear coverts and creamy-buff patches on wings and rump.

Red-billed Teal

Marbled Teal

Marmaronetta angustirostris
(Anas angustirostris)

Description Sexes similar. Head and neck creamy colour with brown markings, and a dark brown patch around the eye extending back to the nape. The feathers of the nape are long, forming a short crest which gives the head a distinctive appearance. The rest of the plumage is creamy-white and greyish-brown, spotted and mottled, giving a 'marbled' effect at close range, but at a distance the appearance is more of a uniform pale brown. There is no well-marked speculum but pale secondaries and whitish tail are noticeable in flight. The long straight bill is blackish, the female's with a paler patch at the base. Legs and feet greeny-brown with dark webs. Immatures are duller, being yellowish below and lacking creamy marks on the upperparts. Length 40 cm.

Characteristics and Behaviour Rather skulking and shy in behaviour, hiding in vegetation and remaining silent for much of the time. Numbers in Europe have been much reduced in recent years. Usually found in pairs or small groups, but very large flocks winter in Iran. Non-migratory in most parts of its range, but some populations winter outside the overall breeding range even to the extent of crossing the Sahara Desert. When disturbed the flight is swift, low and usually of short duration.

Habitat Fresh-water lakes and ponds overgrown with lush vegetation, brackish pools and marshes. In winter often found on more open, larger waters, bare banks, and even on temporary pools in the Sahara Desert.

Distribution Mainly sub-tropical. The breeding range includes southern Spain, Morocco, Algeria, Tunisia, Libya, Egypt, Turkey, Syria, Iraq, Iran, Turkestan, Afghanistan and north-west India. Formerly bred in the Canary Islands, Cape Verde Islands and southern France. In winter to west Africa, south of the Sahara.

Food Feeds by dabbling, up-ending and occasionally by diving. Mainly vegetable matter but specific details are lacking.

Voice The drake's call is a wheezing squeak, the female's a feeble quack which is barely audible.

Display Not well developed. Male recorded swimming with head in shoulders and neck withdrawn, then suddenly extending longish neck and raising crest.

Breeding The breeding season does not commence until May in Europe and North Africa, sometimes early June or even later. Nests are placed in rushes, reeds or grasses alongside river banks, occasionally some distance from water. They are small and well hidden, sometimes with a tunnel-like approach, and are constructed from dead reeds and grasses, copiously lined with down. Eggs are yellowish-white, nine to fourteen or more, average size 47 × 34 mm. Incubation period 25 to 27 days. The downy young are brown above and grey below with greenish-grey bill, legs and feet.

Male Marbled Teal with crest raised

Cape Teal

Anas capensis

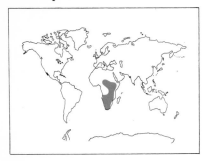

Description Sexes are similar. Crown and sides of the head are white or pale buff, finely speckled with dark brown. Upperparts mottled and spotted dark brown on buff. Wings brownish-grey, speculum bright green and black with broad white borders. Breast and underparts almost white, heavily mottled with grey-brown. Under tail coverts are white barred with brown. The bill is long, upturned and broad near the tip, it is pinkish in colour with black at the base and shading to bluish-grey at the tip of the culmen. Legs and feet are yellowish-brown with dark webs. Immatures also very similar but with markings on upperparts less clear. Length 40 cm.

Characteristics and Behaviour A surface feeding duck with a distinctly pale appearance about the head. In flight the amount of white in the wing is also very conspicuous. Generally silent and retiring by nature, keeping well out on open water in most areas, but will behave more tamely where unmolested. Despite a widespread distribution it is not very numerous, although reported to be increasing in the south of its range. It is often referred to as the Cape Wigeon, but has closer affinity to the Pintails than to any of the Wigeon.

Habitat Found on both large and small expanses of water, fresh or brackish, only occasionally in coastal areas. Wanders regularly, visiting temporary flood regions, marshes, salt pans and soda lakes.

Distribution Africa only, from Cameroun, Lake Chad, Durfur province of the Sudan and central Ethiopia through Tanzania, Malawi, and the whole of southern Africa where it is more numerous and less migratory. In East Africa it is fairly common on the Rift valley lakes including Lakes Rudolf, Nakuru and Elmenteita.

Food A surface-feeding duck; eats mainly vegetable matter.

Voice The drake has a short, high-pitched whistle, uttered mainly in flight; the female has a subdued nasal quack.

Display The courtship display of the male consists of swimming around in circles then scudding rapidly along the water for a short distance.

Breeding The season is very variable, nests have been recorded from July to November in Cape Province, also in March; April in Zambia; and March to October in Transvaal. The nest is a depression in the ground in grass or under bushes, lined thickly with down. The eggs are usually seven to nine, yellowish or creamy-brown, average size 51 × 34 mm. Incubation is by female alone. The downy young are grey-brown above, white below, with white patches on the upperparts and a broad white eyestripe.

[174]

Male Cape Teal uttering 'burp' call

[175]

Hottentot Teal

Anas punctata

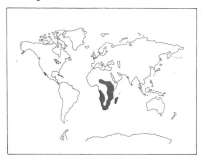

Description The male has blackish crown and nape which gives the head a distinctly capped appearance. Cheeks and throat are buffish with black markings on the side and back of the neck. The mantle is black-brown, scapulars are edged with buff. The wings are dark brown glossed with green, and there is a white bar below the green speculum. The underparts are cinnamon-buff, mottled and spotted blackish, with finer streaks on the belly and under tail coverts. The bill is black with blue edges. Legs and feet are lead grey. The female is similar to the male but with lighter underparts, and spotted rather than streaked on the belly. Length 32–36 cm. Immatures are paler still, with smaller and fewer markings below.

Characteristics and Behaviour The smallest of the dabbling ducks, and the only one with glossy green wings. In flight the dark rump and broad white wing bar are conspicuous. Usually occurs in pairs or small groups, seldom in large flocks. It is said to be sluggish in movement and rather tame in some areas, preferring to take cover in aquatic vegetation rather than fly, but once in the air it has a very swift flight.

Habitat Found on fresh and brackish waters inland, preferably with dense growth of reeds and sedges providing good cover. Sheltered lakes, shallow pools, papyrus swamps and flooded marshland, etc.

Distribution The breeding range includes most of southern Africa from Angola in the west to Malawi and Tanzania in the east, south to Cape Province, but absent from much of the Congo and Zambia. Does not occur on the Cape peninsula. Outside the breeding season some birds wander northwards reaching northern Nigeria and Ethiopia. Widely distributed throughout Madagascar.

Food Specific details are lacking, mainly vegetable matter.

Voice Generally very silent, the drake has a shrill, reedy whistle which is sometimes heard in flight; the duck has a soft quack.

Display Not recorded.

Breeding April to June in Madagascar, June in South Africa and June to August in Malawi. The nest is placed in reeds in shallow water or close to the water's edge amongst thick vegetation. It is made of grasses or reeds and lined with very dark down. The clutch size is usually five to eight creamy-buff eggs, with an average size of 44 × 33 mm. Incubation period is about 20 days.

Puna Silver Teal

Anas versicolor puna

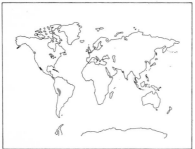

Description   Adults have dark brown crown, nape, and sides of the head to below the eye; contrasting sharply with the pale buff cheeks. The mantle is barred with dark brown and buff, the breast buff heavily spotted with dark brown, flanks barred black and white. The wings are mainly greyish-brown with metallic blue-green speculum, bordered white in front and behind. The rump, tail and abdomen appear silvery grey from a distance but are actually very finely barred with black and white. The long, heavy bill is blue-grey with a black band on the culmen. Legs and feet are dark grey. Sexes similar but the female is smaller and duller. Length 43–48 cm. Immatures are like the female but with markings not so clear.

Characteristics and Behaviour There are three sub-species of this South American genus, the Northern Silver Teal (*A. v. versicolor*) is the smallest. The Southern Silver Teal (*A. v. fretensis*) is larger and darker. The Puna Silver Teal (*A. v. puna*) is the largest of the three, with a much longer bright blue bill that lacks the orange patch at the base present in both *versicolor* and *fretensis*. The plumage is generally duller and less clearly marked. These differences are considered by some authors sufficient to treat it as a separate species. In general, Silver Teal are fresh-water ducks usually found in small parties. They are

fairly tame but rather quiet and do not normally mix with other species. The population breeding in Tierra del Fuego is mainly migratory, but in general most birds are sedentary.

Habitat   Fresh-water pools with well-vegetated margins, reedbeds, marshes and flooded areas near lakes and rivers. The Puna Silver Teal is a high altitude form, frequenting lakes of the high Andes puna zone (dry tussock grass moorland) above 4,000 m.

Distribution   Northern Silver Teal occurs in southern Bolivia, Paraguay, Uruguay, southern Brazil, central Chile and northern Argentina. Southern Silver Teal is found farther south, in Chile from Aisen province to Tierra del Fuego, in Argentina from Chubut south, and in the Falkland Islands. Puna Silver Teal is restricted to the *puna* zone in northern Chile, Bolivia and Peru.

Food   Mainly vegetable matter, seeds of aquatic plants and some insects.

Voice   Usually silent but the drake's call resembles the Garganey's rattling. The female has a low harsh quack.

Display   Drake swims near the female with compressed plumage and extended neck, but display is poorly developed.

Breeding   The breeding season is rather variable in the northern parts of the range, usually October to January elsewhere. The nest is placed in reed-beds or long grasses. The clutch size is eight to ten, possibly less for *puna*. Eggs are cream-coloured with a pinkish tinge, average size 45×35 mm, for *versicolor*, but larger for *fretensis* and *puna*. Incubation period about 25 days. Both adults take part in caring for the brood. The downy young have a dark brown crown, not extending to the eye as in adults. The face and sides of the head are whitish with a dark line through the eye and a dark spot on the ear coverts. The upperparts are dark brown with white marks on the wings and sides.

Garganey

Anas querquedula

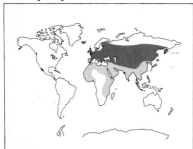

Description Adult male has crown of dark brown, face and neck rusty brown, with a very conspicuous superciliary stripe extending from in front of the eye to the nape. Upperparts are dark brown with pale feather-edgings. Wing coverts are pale bluish-grey. The speculum is metallic green with white borders and is concealed by the long ornamental scapulars. The breast is brown heavily barred with black, flanks are greyish and finely vermiculated, the belly is white. Bill dark grey. Legs and feet are lead-grey. Length 38 cm. The duck is similar to that of the Teal but slightly paler and with throat white. The drake in eclipse is like the female except for the wing. Immatures are very much like females.

Characteristics and Behaviour In the air the very rapid flight and blue-grey forewing are noticeable. Huge flocks occur on passage and in winter quarters; but during the summer, in Europe, usually seen in pairs or small flocks only. Large flocks are usually more densely packed together than other wildfowl, both on the water and in the air. A surface feeder which seldom up-ends but often dibbles along the surface in the manner of Shovelers. When disturbed, springs from the water with the agility of Teal.

Habitat During the breeding season frequents shallow pools, meres and ditches that are well sheltered with thick vegetation, occasionally met with on brackish waters. In winter quarters sometimes occurs on the sea, but more usually on extensive shallow waters and marshes. Avoids mountainous and well-wooded areas. Replaced in similar habitat in North America by the Blue-winged Teal (*A. discors*).

Distribution In the breeding season a rare visitor to England. Regular through most of Europe north of the Pyrenees and the Alps, reaching Denmark, Sweden and Finland. Also in the Caucasus, Iran and across Asia to Kamchatka and Sakhalin, reaching the boreal zone but not crossing the Arctic Circle. The winter distribution is equally widespread, very small numbers occasionally remain in south-west Spain and southern France, but nearly all European birds winter south of the Sahara in tropical Africa. Asian breeders winter in large numbers in India and Burma, southern China, Malaysia, Borneo and the Philippines.

Food A mixture of animal and vegetable matter with a much higher animal content than Teal. Molluscs, crustaceans, aquatic insects and their larvae are taken in quantity during the summer, also seeds and grain.

Voice The drake has a harsh rattling note, the female a low quack. Neither sex is very vocal outside the breeding season.

Display In courtship display the drake swims close to the female, spreading the long scapulars and showing-off the head markings to good advantage. The head is moved backwards and forwards, the rattling note being heard when the neck is fully extended. There are frequent pursuit flights.

Breeding The nest is well concealed amongst thick vegetation, close to marsh or open water, from May

onwards. It is a neat hollow lined with grasses and down. Eggs may be seven to twelve, but usually nine or ten and are of creamy-buff, the average size being 45 × 33 mm. Incubation is by female alone for a period of about 22 days. The downy young are dark brown above with face and underparts paler yellowish-brown. Two dark lines run almost parallel from the bill to the back of the head, one through the eye, one below it. Fledging period is 5 to 6 weeks.

Blue-winged Teal

Anas discors

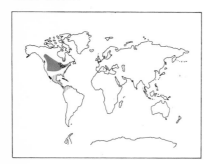

Description The adult male in breeding plumage has the crown, forehead and throat black; the sides of the head and neck are dark slaty grey with a purplish gloss. There is a conspicuous white crescent-shaped patch between the bill and the eye. The mantle is dark brown with buff markings. The metallic green speculum is bordered with white, broad in front, but very narrow behind; and the light cobalt-blue forewing is similar to the Garganey (*Anas querquedula*) but brighter. Underparts are tawny brown with black spots, variable in size and number. Tail dark brown; under tail coverts black; and a white patch on each side of the rump. Bill black, legs and feet yellowish with dusky webs. The female is very much like the female Garganey, but easily distinguished in flight by the blue forewing. Length 35 to 40 cm. Immatures resemble adult females.

Characteristics and Behaviour A small duck bearing closer relationship to the Shoveler (*Anas clypeata*) than to the Common Teal (*Anas crecca*), it occupies an ecological niche in America similar to the Garganey in Europe. Usually migrates in small flocks, but very gregarious in parts of the winter range. Associates freely with other waterfowl, especially Black Duck, Shoveler and Cinnamon Teal; is often very tame and unwary in its behaviour. Frequently rests out of water, perching on tree stumps, logs, boulders, etc.

Habitat In the breeding season, small fresh-water ponds, lakes, marshes, sluggish rivers and small streams, usually in open prairie country. In winter, more extensive areas of shallow water, marshes, and flooded rice fields.

Distribution In the summer, from British Columbia across southern Canada to Quebec and Nova Scotia, and north to parts of Alaska and Yukon. In the USA, south to New Mexico, Texas and Louisiana. Almost the entire population is migratory, leaving the breeding grounds early in the autumn and returning late in spring. Individuals cover great distances and recorded flights include Alberta to Venezuela (3,800 miles), and Manitoba to Peru (4,000 miles). The wintering range extends from the Gulf Coast of the USA through central America and the West Indies to Venezuela, Colombia, Ecuador and northern Peru.

Food Feeds mainly by dabbling amongst vegetation at the surface of shallow water, occasionally submerging head or up-ending, but seldom diving. Takes a lot of animal food, mainly insects, molluscs and crustaceans, in addition to various seeds, grasses, sedges and pondweeds, etc.

Voice Often silent, but male has a high-pitched sibilant whistling call, and female a rather faint quack.

Display Includes vertical bobbing of the head, as in closely related Shoveler, to which the female responds with similar actions. Pursuit flights are frequent in spring and include aerial fighting between drakes.

Breeding Peak laying period is usually late May to early June in most parts of the range. The nest is generally close to water but in a dry situation, well concealed amongst grasses or sedges, a

slight depression lined with dead grasses, down being added during the laying period. Eggs normally nine to twelve, creamy or buffish white, average size 47 × 33 mm. The incubation period is 23 to 24 days, after which the duck-lings are taken to nearby water by the female. In a few weeks family groups may join up, not always accompanied by adults. Fledging period is roughly 6 weeks, and juveniles are able to under-take migratory flights on their own.

Northern Cinnamon Teal

Anas cyanoptera septentrionalium

Description Males in breeding plumage have most of the head and body a deep chestnut red, with very dark crown and black under tail coverts. The breast and sides are sometimes marked with black spots, depending on the subspecies. The wing is similar to Blue-winged Teal (*Anas discors*), with upper wing coverts blue and speculum metallic green bordered with white in front and buff behind. The bill is black, legs and feet are yellow-orange. The female is mottled and spotted in shades of brown and can be impossible to distinguish from the female Blue-winged Teal, but sometimes she is more reddish. Drakes in eclipse are as females but brighter and with a reddish tinge. Length 35 to 47 cm. Immatures resemble females but are duller and paler.

Characteristics   and   Behaviour Widely distributed in North and South America, four of the five races recognized are found only on the southern sub-continent. The Argentine Cinnamon Teal (*A. c. cyanoptera*) has the most southerly range; the Andean (*A. c. orinomus*) is the largest; Borrero's (*A. c. borreroi*) is the scarcest; the Tropical (*A. c. tropica*) is the smallest, the drakes heavily spotted on breast and sides; and the Northern (*A. c. septentrionalium*) is more cinnamon coloured, with the males un-spotted and the females occur-

ring in both pale and dark phases. Their general habits resemble those of Blue-winged Teal, Cinnamon Teal being considered a link between that species and Shovelers. In flight, which is rapid, the blue wing patch is conspicuous in both sexes. Migratory in North America and the southern part of South America, other populations making only local movements. Usually encountered in small parties rather than large flocks.

Habitat Shallow fresh-water areas, ponds, the edges of lakes, reedbeds, small streams and marshes with plenty of cover. Whilst *orinomus* frequents lakes of the Paramo Zone of the Andes at altitudes of 3,700 m and upwards; *borreroi* occurs lower down, between 2,200 and 3,500 m; and *tropica* is usually found in valleys below 1,000 m.

Distribution In the breeding season, south-west Canada, USA west of the Rocky Mountains and south to Mexico; *tropica* and *borreroi* are restricted to Colombia; *orinomus* to Peru, Bolivia and northern Chile; *cyanoptera* is widespread in southern South America from southern Peru and Brazil to Tierra del Fuego and the Falkland Islands.

Food Mainly vegetable matter, seeds of aquatic plants and grasses. Also aquatic insects and larvae, small molluscs and crustaceans. Feeds mostly on the surface but also dives.

Voice Not very vocal, the male has a rattling call, the female a low quack.

Breeding The breeding season is late April to mid-June in North America, September to December in South America. The nest is well concealed, often with a tunnel entrance, in thick vegetation usually close to water. It is constructed of dead grasses, etc. and lined with down. Clutch sizes varies from six to fourteen but usually nine or ten, the eggs are pale buff colour and average size is 47 × 34 mm. Incubation by the female takes up to 25 days, after which the ducklings are led to the water

by the female who also rears the brood. The downy young have dark brown crown, upperparts and wings. Sides of head, neck and underparts are yellowish buff. There is a dark eyestripe, dark spots on ear coverts, and buff markings on wings and sides. Fledging period is about 7 weeks.

Red Shoveler
(Argentine Red Shoveler)

Anas platalea

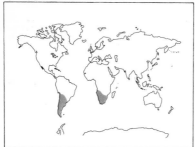

Description   The male has a pale buff head spotted with black, crown darker, chin and throat white. The mantle is reddish brown with large black spots, back and rump are black with a greenish gloss. The wing is like that of other Shovelers with a pale blue shoulder and metallic green speculum. Breast, sides of body and underparts are cinnamon, densely spotted with black. Upper and under tail coverts are black, tail is black and white with a white patch on each side of the rump. The bill is black, iris yellowish, legs and feet pale orange. Females and immatures closely resemble those of the Northern Shoveler. There is no eclipse plumage. Length 45 cm.

Characteristics and Behaviour   The most graceful of the four species of Shoveler, with a slightly smaller bill and long pointed tail. It is swift in flight and swims buoyantly. The species is partly migratory, birds breeding in the south of the range moving north in the austral winter.

Habitat   Shallow lakes and pools with dense reedbeds, marshes and brackish lagoons.

Distribution   The southern half of South America from Cuzco in Peru, Bolivia, southern Brazil, Paraguay, Uruguay, Chile and Argentina (except in the Andes), south to Tierra del Fuego. A rare vagrant in the Falkland Islands.

Food   Omnivorous. Seeds, aquatic vegetation, small crustaceans, molluscs and insects, etc.

Voice   Mainly silent, but the male has a squeaky chattering call, the female a harsh quack.

Display   Essentially similar to that of Northern Shoveler.

Breeding   The season is from September to December. Nests are on the ground in reeds, or amongst coarse grasses. Normal clutch size is six to eight pale creamy eggs, average size 54 × 36 mm. Incubation takes about 25 days. The downy young are brown above, yellowish below, with a dark line through the eye. Bill and feet are dark grey.

Cape Shoveler

Anas smithi

Description   Head of drake is slightly browner than that of Red Shoveler; also mantle and breast are brown and boldly barred black; sides of body and underparts are cinnamon, these too, are boldly barred black rather than densely spotted black. Rump and tail coverts are very dusky green; longest scapulars dark green and blue. There is no white patch on side of rump, and the tail is less pointed. Very similar in other respects. Female is a duller version of male, but with no cinnamon on sides of body and underparts.

Distribution   The southern part of Africa – north to Lobita, Angola, in the west; north to Beira, Mozambique in the east. These are quite probably its boundaries.

Close-up of Red Shoveler bill showing intake of
surface water and the filtration of small animal
and plant food by the lamellae

Australian Shoveler

Anas rhynchotis rhynchotis

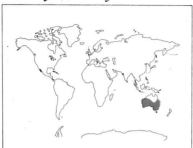

Description The male in breeding plumage has a very dark brown crown and chin, rest of head and neck greyish-blue with a crescent of white between eye and base of bill. The black back and rump have a greenish gloss. Breast, front of neck and tail are dark brown, the brown feathers of breast and front of neck are broadly tipped with a lighter shade of brown and bear a whitish crescent. The deep chestnut feathers of the remaining underparts are broadly edged and banded with black. Each side of the tail has a very prominent white patch. Upper wing coverts are pale blue and the dark green wing mirrors have a white band in front. Bill dark olive brown. Legs and feet pinkish-yellow. In eclipse plumage, the male has neither the white patches on either side of the tail, nor the white facial crescent.

The female is altogether much duller, being mainly buff or dark brown; the under surface of pale chestnut with a dark brown centre to each feather. Length of male 49·5 cm, female 48 cm. Immatures are similar to the females.

Characteristics and Behaviour Australian Shovelers are medium-sized ducks and readily identified by the shape of their head and the heavy bills; they also float much higher in the water than the Teal. The white patches on the male's rump are clearly visible even at long range. Its take-off from the water is almost vertical and is accompanied by a very audible whirring of the wings. The flight is swift and direct, at such times the bright pinkish-yellow legs of the male are very obvious. Only occasionally do they flock in numbers, and even though up to 300 birds have been seen at one time, it is usual to find them swimming in small groups or pairs. They are quiet, unobtrusive and very wary, soon showing signs of awareness when approached. Much of the daytime is spent resting in thick cover and they never perch in trees.

Habitat Even though it can be found in almost any habitat, it shows a distinct preference for permanent and densely vegetated swamps, and any such areas usually maintain a permanent breeding stock. Out of the breeding season is often found in the company of other ducks on shallow lakes and billabongs.

Distribution A rare species confined to Australia and Tasmania. It occurs in the south-western region of Western Australia and practically throughout Queensland, New South Wales and Victoria; with the greatest intensity in the deep swamps of the Murray–Darling Basin and Tasmania. Compared with other ducks, it would seem that the Australian Shoveler has at no time in its history, ever been a numerous species.

Food It feeds by filtering the water for aquatic insects, small shells and seeds, etc.; with insects such as beetles and water boatmen making up the major part of its diet. Having established themselves in a particular swamp they seldom move to other areas. Formation feeding either in echelon or arrowhead, is quite common, the birds disturbing insects with their feet as they paddle along. Feeding by dredging the mud in shallow waters has also been observed.

Voice A silent bird, the female has a very soft quack and the male utters a soft 'took took'.

Display Similar to the European species. The female swimming along followed by one or many chattering suitors who swing their bills upwards uttering a kind of grunting sound, and with feathers of head and neck raised one or other of the males will dash swiftly in front of her. The female in turn, whilst keeping her bill parallel to the water will lower and raise it with ever increasing frequency, finally taking flight and followed in close pursuit by one or more males.

Breeding The selection of a suitable nest site is a joint affair by both male and female, and whilst it is almost invariably a depression in the ground, occasionally the top of a hollow stump may be chosen. A lining of dead grasses with a small quantity of down is usual.

Although nests are to be found 200 yards or so from water, the general rule is to choose a site close to the water's edge. August to December in coastal areas; but for those Shovelers breeding inland the season is likely to be as erratic as with any other inland breeders. Being governed by the occurrence of severe flooding which could be sufficient to induce breeding in any month of the year. A regular clutch would contain nine to eleven creamy-white eggs each faintly tinged with green and measuring 54 × 37 mm. The incubation period is 24 days.

New Zealand Shoveler

Anas rhynchotis variegata

Similar to *A. r. rhynchotis* but confined to New Zealand.

Northern Shoveler

Anas clypeata

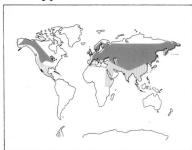

Description The drake in breeding plumage has a metallic green head, with a darker, almost black sheen on the crown, nape, face and neck. The mantle is dark brown with white-edged feathers; the scapulars vary, the shorter ones white, the longer ones blue, white and black. The wings are mainly sepia with pale blue median and lesser coverts, and green speculum bordered with white in front and behind. The lower neck and breast are white, flanks and abdomen dark cinnamon brown to chestnut. Rump and upper tail coverts are black with greenish gloss, sides of rump white, tail brown and white with dark centre. The large spatulate bill is black, legs and feet orange-red. The female is mottled in shades of brown and buff; and is best identified by the bill which is greyish-brown, and the blue shoulder patch. Length about 50 cm. Immatures are similar to females.

Characteristics and Behaviour The most notable feature of the Shoveler is the bill, the tip of which is twice as wide as the base. In flight the white breast of the male is conspicuous, and the pale blue wing patch is evident in both sexes, whilst the rapidly beating wings produce a 'whirring' noise. Usually occurs in small numbers up to twenty, but larger groups can be seen during migration. The bill is usually carried with a downward tilt, even in flight. Feeding birds up-end only occasionally and very seldom dive.

Habitat In the breeding season shallow pools, meres, marshes with good cover and dry areas near by suitable for nesting. In winter fresh-water marshes, swamps, flooded areas, infrequently on salt water except when disturbed.

Distribution Widespread in summer throughout the temperate regions of the northern hemisphere. Less numerous in western Europe than in other parts of the range. Breeds in Europe from the British Isles and France eastwards, also very small numbers in Iceland which was colonized in the 1930s. Asia between latitudes 38° N and 68° N, east to Sakhalin, Kamchatka and north-west China. Western North America from Alaska east to Manitoba, and south to California and New Mexico. Summer and winter ranges overlap slightly but nearly all populations migrate south. Winters to tropical Africa, India, Burma, Ceylon, Vietnam, southern China and Japan. In America to Mexico, Louisiana and Florida.

Food Feeds largely by drawing water through the front of the bill and pumping it out through the sides where the fine lamellae sieve out minute food particles. Also takes insects and larger items directly from the water. Diet consists mainly of small seeds, weeds and molluscs.

Voice Mainly silent; drake has a low-pitched double note 'tok-tok', female a hoarse quack.

Display Consists mainly of raising and lowering the head by both sexes, swimming round in circles, short hovering flights by the drakes, and pursuit flights of female by two or more males.

Breeding Early April in southern parts, and on to June. The nest is usually on dry ground close to water and in a fairly open situation, built of dead grasses and lined with down and

feathers. Clutch size varies from six to fourteen, but is usually nine to twelve, eggs are pale buff with a greenish tinge, average size 52 × 37 mm. Incubation by the female for 23 to 25 days. The downy young resemble those of Mallard, but with a longer bill which begins to assume characteristic shape after only 2 or 3 weeks. Fledging period about 6 weeks.

Ringed Teal

Anas leucophrys

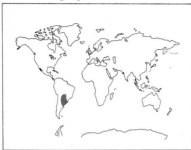

Description The adult drake has top of head and nape black, sides of head greyish-white with fine black streaks. The mantle is greyish-brown; the back, rump and tail glossy black with a greenish tinge. The wings are black with a white patch on the secondary coverts and a bronzy-green speculum; scapulars bright chestnut. Breast pinkish with round black spots, flanks and abdomen grey with fine black lines on the flanks. Undertail coverts black with a white patch on each side of the rump. The bill is bluish-grey, legs and feet pink. Although the male and female are very different in appearance, the drake has no drab eclipse plumage. The female has a dark brown head with a broad white line above and behind the eye, upperparts similar to male but browner and with brown scapulars, underparts greyish with irregular brown bars. Length 35 cm. Immatures resemble female, but young males have no white markings.

Characteristics and Behaviour Very little has been recorded about the habits of Ringed Teal in the wild state where they have a rather limited range and are not very numerous. They are normally very active, swimming buoyantly but seldom diving for food, although they will up-end readily. They are strong fliers, frequently perch in trees, and may in fact have closer affinities with the Perching Ducks than with the Dabbling Ducks. Gregarious by nature, flocks of up to a hundred occur in suitable localities.

Habitat Open pools, swampy and marshy areas, in regions of light tropical woodland, intermediate between dense rain forest and arid pampas.

Distribution South America, in eastern Bolivia from Santa Cruz to Tarija province, southern Brazil in Mato Grosso and Rio Grande do Sul, Paraguay, Uruguay, and north-eastern Argentina from Tucuman to Buenos Aires province.

Food Mainly vegetable matter.

Voice Not very vocal. The male has a long whistling note, the female a Pochard-like quack.

Display The drake swims round the duck, sometimes reversing direction and describing a figure-of-eight pattern. The low whistling call is emitted with the head thrown backwards and bill raised

Breeding Nests are usually made in holes in trees, birds in captivity taking readily to nest boxes. Clutch size varies from five to eight whitish eggs which are incubated for a period of 23 days. Egg size not recorded. The downy young are dark grey above, white below, with white patches on wings and body, and a dark line through the eye.

Ringed Teal wing stretching – revealing white
ring on fore wing

[193]

Australian Pink-eared Duck

Malacorhynchus membranaceus

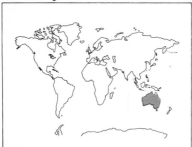

Description In plumage both sexes are alike. The white head is delicately shaded with fine bars of dark brownish-grey on the crown, as are the sides of the face and the neck. A patch of blackish feathers surrounds the eye and extends as a bar to back of neck. Beneath this black bar and immediately behind the eye a small pink patch is evident; with the eye itself being narrowly ringed in white. The neck, breast and flanks are white and strongly barred with dark grey. The back and wings are of a brownish-grey. Tail and rump are blackish-grey, and a broad white band spans the tail coverts. Bill and legs are lead-grey. The very large spatulate bill has membranous flaps at the tip edges. Average length of male is 42 cm and the female 39 cm. Immatures are paler than the adults and the pink ear patches are not distinct.

Characteristics and Behaviour On water the Pink-eared Duck floats high and is seen as a small light-coloured duck. The enormous spoon-like bill is very obvious even at distance and unlike the Shoveler, which is dark in appearance, its forehead is quite distinct – the top of head and top of bill not forming a straight line. It flies with a slower and shorter wing beat than does the Grey Teal, and with head held high and neck less extended than other ducks the flight is characteristic. During the breeding season it appears most confiding and chooses to swim away from the intruder rather than fly. Seldom leaves the water except to roost but may be seen perching on fallen trees a few inches above water level.

Habitat Shallow stagnant water is preferred and it is often in the company of Grey Teal. Has a tendency to flock and on occasions such flocks can be very large. Occurs less commonly in vegetated swampy areas and lakes. Very much a bird of the drier inland regions and where the annual rainfall is below 15 inches.

Distribution As a breeding species restricted to Australia; rare in Tasmania where it does not breed. Western and South Australia support the highest concentrations but small numbers do occur each summer in the coastal regions of Victoria.

Food To acquire food the Pink-eared Duck filters water and /or mud through the dense fringe of fine lamellae, a feature of its large bill. They can often be seen swimming in echelon sifting the muddy water stirred up by the bird in front. Foraging also occurs in pairs or small groups. An analysis of stomach contents has shown that of the microscopic animal and plant intake about 80 per cent were insect, the remainder a mixture of fresh-water algae, small seeds and copepods, etc.

Voice In flight it utters a kind of 'chirrup', that of the female is at a lower pitch. When fighting, a continuous trill is produced.

Display There is a feeding ritual similar to that of the Shoveler. Heads are held face to face or side by side and with bills turned inwards each bird circles anti-clockwise, their bills following one another around and describing a circle of 4 to 6 inches diameter. Some times a small flock participates in the display

[194]

and the pool becomes covered with small rotating groups. A mated male will rush across the water, neck erect and bill swinging at any intruding bird who dares to approach the vicinity of his mate and fighting often takes place.

Breeding Breeds most extensively in those areas of the inland plains where temporary shallow water is available. Only small numbers utilize the permanent swamps. The highest breeding concentration usually occurs in the Murray–Darling region. There is no regular breeding season, the Pink-eared Duck must wait for suitable shallow water conditions to occur, and at such time quickly comes into condition for breeding. However, in those regions with a regular cycle of flooding peak breeding periods do occur. Winter rainfall would produce a peak of August to October and a summer rainfall March to May. The nests are constructed in elevated positions over the water. Such a position may be a few inches high on the top of a log, or 30 feet high in a tree fork or tree hole. A rounded nest, in the form of a mound some 10 inches across, is constructed of dark grey down into which the eggs are buried. An average clutch would be six to eight white or creamy-white eggs, 49 × 36 mm and more pointed at the narrow end than the normal duck egg. The incubation period is 26 days.

Mountain Blue Duck

Hymenolaimus malacorhyncos

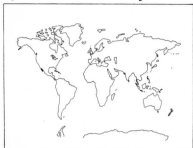

Description Male and female in adult plumage are very similar, with bluish-grey head and neck, shaded with olive on the crown, and dark grey lores. The remainder of the plumage is dove-grey with a deep bluish sheen, heavily spotted with reddish-brown on the breast and abdomen. There is no wing speculum, but the secondaries are bordered with black, and there are narrow white tips to the inner secondaries. A small knob occurs at the bend of the wing, and the underwing is pale grey. The bill is prominent, narrow, and yellowish in colour with a black tip; there is a flexible membrane on each side which is also black. Legs and feet are dark brown, iris yellow. Females are slightly smaller with less extensive reddish-brown spots on the breast. Length 50–55 cm. Immatures are paler than females, with brownish head and without spots on the breast.

Characteristics and Behaviour An aberrant species with a highly specialized bill and rather obscure relationship to other ducks. It is well adapted for life in rapid, turbulent streams, swimming with head low down and elevated tail, diving effortlessly and perching on boulders or clinging to submerged rocks when feeding. It is a strong flier but prefers to avoid danger by swimming and diving. Generally avoids land, where it moves slowly and with some difficulty. Not very gregarious, it is usually seen in pairs or family parties. By nature it is remarkably tame, a characteristic which has hastened its decline at the hands of man. Blue Ducks have become extremely scarce through extensive hunting, disturbance of their habitat, and the introduction of ground predators; but with complete protection numbers are believed to be recovering slightly.

Habitat Swift-flowing streams in hilly and fjord areas, occasionally moving down to lakes or to the sea. Formerly much more frequent at lower altitudes, but the range has been reduced in places where human activity has impaired the clarity of the streams.

Distribution Confined to New Zealand, where it is restricted to the South Island and the mountainous regions of North Island south of the Coromandel peninsula.

Food Almost entirely animal matter; chiefly caddis-fly larvae obtained by diving, and other insects caught on the surface of the water.

Voice The drake has a shrill whistle from which the Maori name of *Whio* has been derived; the female has a rattling call.

Breeding An early breeder, egg-laying commences in August and the season extends to November. The nest is made under cover of thick vegetation or bushes at the edge of water, or in hole in a bank. Some nest sites may be re-used in the following year. Eggs usually four or five, but larger numbers have been recorded, they are cream coloured with an average size of 64 × 42 mm. The downy young are greyish-brown above, creamy-white below, with a dark stripe through the eyes. They are very energetic and active, swimming and diving repeatedly with both the adults maintaining close attendance.

[196]

European Eider
(Common Eider)

Somateria mollissima mollissima

Description The male in breeding plumage has black crown, this extending to just below the eye and forward as a narrow line towards the nostril. The back of the head has a central white line which continues to a point above the eye. Nape is pale green, there is also a patch of pale green on side of head, separated from nape by a narrow white band, this does not extend to below eye. Upperparts, cheeks and throat are white; breast white but with a heavy suffusion of pinkish buff. Remainder of underparts, along with tail, rump, flight feathers and greater coverts, are black. Bill grey, lightly tinged with green. Legs and feet olive-green with blackish webs. Male in eclipse blackish-brown with dusky fawn crown, upper breast and around neck boldly speckled with brown and white. Wing coverts and tertiaries are white. First year males are similar to male in eclipse but have a whitish breast. Females are boldly barred, entirely, with light and dark brown; the barrings being finer below and more subdued on head and breast. Length 58 cm. Immatures of both sexes are a dusky version of female but with smaller and less-pronounced markings.

Characteristics and Behaviour The drake appears as a rather bulky sea duck with a white back and pale breast. Outside the breeding season Common Eiders are only to be found at sea, but usually close in to shore. They favour both rocky coastlines and muddy or sandy coasts, especially where plentiful supplies of mussels are to be found. Their feeding coincides with the falling tide, resting on a rising one. They are strong in flight keeping low to the water and in single line formation at 90° to line of flight. Rocks and sandbars are often frequented for resting purposes, and when on land their walk is slow with a rolling gait but at all times maintaining an erect posture. Usually met with in small groups, although on occasions large flocks may be encountered. On migration flights flocks of between 25 and 100 birds are common but up to 400 have been recorded.

Habitat During the breeding season, sheltered low-lying terrain near the coast, islets in fjords and estuaries, also islets out at sea with sheltered shallow coves and bays. At other times strictly maritime, but keeping close in to shore.

Distribution Breeds in Iceland (about 200,000 pairs), Denmark, Norway, Sweden and Finland (about 300,000 pairs in the Baltic), Russia, south to Scotland and northern England; islets off Ireland; the Netherlands and Brittany. Winters within the breeding area and south to the Mediterranean and central Europe. The total European population is estimated at around 2 million individuals.

Food Acquired either by diving or dipping and consists almost entirely of animal matter. Principal items are molluscs and crustaceans; when vegetable matter is taken this is probably accidental in most cases and occurs when feeding in localities where filamentous algae is present. The Blue Mussel is their chief food and small ones up to 25 mm are usually taken. These are swallowed whole, being readily crushed by the muscular action of the gizzard. Ducklings feed mainly on small snails and shrimps.

[198]

Voice The drake's best-known call is 'a-oooo' a muffled sort of cooing which is heard during certain displays. When alarmed, he utters a harsh 'cor-corr-cor'. Female makes groaning or croaking sounds when in search of a nest site.

Display Cooing by the drake with his breast puffed-out and head thrown back, is followed by jerking the head forward with bill pointing downwards during which the call 'a-oooo' is uttered. Another movement is, holding the head high then pulling it in towards the neck with bill touching water, at such time a bulge appears in the neck and the call 'woo-hooo' is made. Much has been written concerning the display and pair formation of Eider Ducks, far too lengthy to detail within these pages.

Breeding As a rule, the Eider is a colonial nester, and eider farms exist in Iceland; but high density colonies do exist that are strictly wild. For over a thousand years 'down' has been collected from the nests of Eiders, not only in Iceland but also in parts of Norway; farming continues today and the birds have become almost domesticated. The nest is a deep cup in a depression on mossy ground or some other suitable situation. It is copiously lined with down and four to six olive-grey eggs are laid, these measuring 77 × 51 mm. The incubation period is 25 days. Because the female does not feed during this period she must build up her body weight in advance, and prior to breeding the duck feeds at twice the rate of the drake. Nests are often in the same site year after year. When the eggs hatch the ducklings are taken to the water by the female and she is often escorted by other females. Quite often flotillas of ducklings are to be seen on the water and these may be with or without adult birds in attendance.

Sub-species are: **Faroe Eider** *Somateria mollissima faeroeensis*; **Northern Eider** *Somateria mollissima borealis*; **American Eider** *Somateria mollissima dresseri*; **Pacific Eider** *Somateria mollissima v-nigra*.

[199]

Spectacled Eider

(Fischer's Eider)

Somateria fischeri

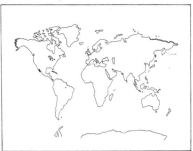

Description The male in breeding plumage has nape, back of head, crown, lores and forehead of pale greyish-green plush-like feathers, these shading to pale buff around the bill. There is a large patch of silvery-white feathers around the eye bordered by a black line, this being less distinct below. Within the patch the eye is set forward, not centrally positioned. Below the eye is an area of pale yellowish-green which extends behind and above it. There is a continuation of the black line downwards behind the cheeks. The chin, throat, neck, mantle, scapulars and tertiaries are white; there is also a white oval patch on each side of the rump. Rest of plumage is more or less of a uniform blackish-grey, somewhat browner on the back, rump and tail. Bill dusky orange. Legs and feet drab yellow, shaded with olive-brown. In eclipse plumage, head and neck are brownish-olive with buff and grey variegations, the spectacle is still evident but now grey. Rest of plumage a mixture of dark brown and grey-black. The female is tawny-brown heavily barred with dark sepia, the barring on head and breast much subdued. The spectacle is pale buff but quite distinct. Bill bluish-grey, legs and feet yellowish. Length 50 to 56 cm. Immatures similar to females but duller and barring less pronounced.

Characteristics and Behaviour Considered to be the most beautiful of the Eiders, it is of medium size and smaller than the King and Common Eiders. The back of head does not have the smooth contour as in the King Eider, it being somewhat irregular. Outside the breeding season much of its life is spent out at sea, well away from the shore. During the latter part of August and early September they leave their inland haunts and move to sheltered coastal waters, where they prepare for their departure out to sea. Occasionally, they are seen flying in compact flocks of up to fifty birds, but more often are met with singly or in pairs and small groups; seen quite often in the company of other wildfowl, in particular the King Eider.

Habitat Out of breeding season it appears to be very much a maritime species. When breeding frequents low-lying coastal areas, deltas, etc. When found inland chooses areas that have countless ponds and lakes, at all times favouring those places where water and land are about equally proportioned, with sedge, moss and lichen growth, and grassy hummocks.

Distribution During the breeding season from Baird Inlet (Alaska) to Colville Delta on the Beaufort Sea coast, also Siberia along the eastern coast, west to the Yana River and including the New Siberian Islands. The main breeding areas are the coastal plain of the Yukon Delta, and very occasionally on St Lawrence Island. In Siberia along the north coast of the Chuckchee Peninsula, the deltas of the Kolyma and the Indigirka, occasionally the deltas of both the Yana and the Lena. Nowhere would it appear to be other than locally common. It is thought to winter in the Bering Sea.

Food When at sea, chiefly molluscs; at other times insects and crustaceans supplemented with vegetable matter, including berries.

Voice Little seems to have been recorded, but males kept in captivity do utter a low 'hoo-hoo'.

Display Probably similar to the Common Eider, but this is only supposition.

Breeding This is governed by the thaw. In the Yukon Delta it is believed that most birds arrive on territory about the third week of May. It is possible that birds in Siberia and those on the arctic coast of Alaska may not be on territory until the first half of June or even later. The nest site is close to the edge of a pond or lake, often on islets or peninsulas, and usually constructed on a slightly elevated position in grass or sedges, with no concealment from above. Substantial quantities of grasses and the like are used to line the nest and later down is added. An average clutch is five to six olive-buff eggs measuring 66 × 44 mm. The female sits very close and has an incubation period of 24 days, after which the ducklings are led to fresh water and closely tended by the female.

Male Spectacled Eider in eclipse plumage

King Eider

Somateria spectabilis

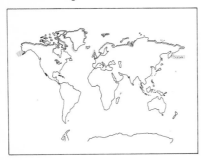

Description The drake is unmistakable, with his very high forehead, the frontal lobe being highly developed and forming a large vivid orange knob in spring. This knob is bordered with black feathers. Nape, crown and forehead are a pearly bluish-grey; slightly paler on crown and forehead. A narrow white band borders the pale grey to above the eye; beneath the eye is a small area of black. Sides of face and cheeks are pale green; chin and throat are white with a V-shaped mark on the latter. The neck and upper back are white, the wing coverts partly white, and the secondaries are tipped with white, wings are black. Rest of back, along with rump and tail, are black. The pinkish buff of breast extends to sides of mantle. Remainder of underparts are black with the exception of a large white patch on either side of the rump. The bill is short and scarlet with a white nail. Iris black though often described as yellow. In spring the legs are bright yellow with dusky webs and black nails. The eclipse plumage is rather mottled overall and very like the Common Eider but somewhat darker with scapulars black. The female's plumage resembles that of the Common Eider but brighter and of a tawny brown with dark brown barring. Bill pale greenish-grey, or yellowish, with dusky webs. Length 60–63 cm. Immatures very similar to those of the Common Eider but bill greyish-pink.

Characteristics and Behaviour From autumn until the following summer, the drake King Eider is mostly black, but with the front third of the body white or whitish; whereas the drakes of both Common and Spectacled Eiders are almost entirely white on the back. This feature is apparent when swimming and even at long distances. In flight the black back is evident, and black also occurs between the white of the rear body and the white area on the wings. In both Common and Spectacled Eiders, the white of back and wing is not broken by the intervention of black. This feature is clearly noticeable even at a distance. The short stubby bill and more rounded head of the female should help distinguish her from females of other Eiders. Slightly smaller than the Common Eider, but similar in that they spend their lives at sea during the autumn and winter, resorting to fresh water when the breeding season approaches. Swift in flight, with a rapid wing beat and appears to be more capable of manoeuvre than the Common Eider.

Habitat Out of the breeding season very much a bird of the open seas, where it rests on floating ice. When breeding occurs it is to be found from high to sub-arctic regions, but usually close to fresh-water ponds and lakes, the availability of which determines to what extent it shall penetrate inland.

Distribution Breeds in Spitsbergen, Novaya Zemlya and the northern peninsulas of both the Russian and Siberian coasts, northern Greenland, the coast of arctic Canada and the islands to the north, also arctic Alaska. Winters south to the Aleutians. If open water remains, then it will winter in the Bering Sea, the Anadyr Gulf, and around St Lawrence Island. Large numbers occur in the waters off west Greenland. and the west Atlantic off

south-west Greenland. May also winter in Barent's Sea, the north White Sea and along the Norwegian coast from Vardø to Harstad. Sizeable numbers winter in the Atlantic south of Newfoundland. During 1964, large rafts of birds were reported in the Pacific–Bering area, these include 50,000 on March 31 in Ugashik Bay, and 100,000 on April 8 in Nelson Lagoon.

Food Chiefly animal matter with a small proportion of vegetable supplement, in the approximate ratio 95:5. Molluscs, crustaceans and the larvae of aquatic insects, also beetles, etc. Eel grass, wigeon grass, algae and other items are among the vegetable intake.

Voice When on migratory flights the females utter a sort of murmuring growl. Notes of the drake are described as a wavering 'hooooooooooo'; also 'kroo-kroo-kroooo' and 'gug gug guggaggug groooooooooo'.

Display Inciting by the duck occurs as in the Common Eider. Head turning by the drake so that each side is presented in turn to the female, and many other postures similar to the drake Common Eider.

Breeding Along with the Long-tailed Duck, the King Eider may be found breeding farther north than any other species of duck. Does not nest in loose colonies as do other Eiders. A preference is shown for those sites that are the first to become free of snow and which are dry but not too far from water; this may be in a well-vegetated area, or ground with a moss and lichen growth, a bare stretch of gravel or sand, or amongst loose stones. Even before down is added to the nest the eggs may be scantily covered with quantities of loose vegetation. Clutches are completed by mid-June in a normal season, but this varies depending on the severity of the weather. Often the same area is used for nesting in successive years. In some instances eggs are laid within a week of the birds arriving on territory. An average clutch would be four to six olive-buff eggs, but the shade may vary from clutch to clutch. They measure 64 × 43 mm, being smaller than those of the Common Eider.

Steller's Eider
(Siberian or Little Eider)

Polysticta stelleri

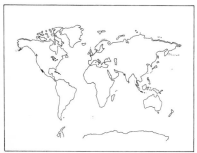

Description The breeding male has white head and upper neck, there is a black ring around the eye, and a greenish patch between base of bill and eye. An area of paler green extends backwards from the eye; the feathers at back of head form a short dark greyish-green crest with a black spot on either side of the nape. Chin and throat are a dull black; lower neck, back, secondaries, and the pointed tail are black with a purple sheen. The black tertiaries are tipped with white; primaries dull black, and wing coverts white. Upper breast is cinnamon with a black spot on either side, underparts shading to a darker cinnamon, sides and flanks paler. Bill very dark grey with paler nail. Legs and feet dark bluish-grey with webs almost black. In eclipse, the plumage is barred blackish and brown. The wing coverts and tertiaries are white. The female is barred almost entirely with light and dark brown, much as the drake in eclipse, but wing coverts not white. Bill and legs are dusky green. Length 42–47 cm. Immatures of both sexes are very similar to female.

Characteristics and Behaviour A good deal smaller than other Eiders, much paler, and by far the most agile. The bill is thin and straight; and when swimming the tail may be angled more or less upwards. Only when extended does the drake's black neck become conspicuous. Should he rear himself from the water, it is then that the cinnamon underparts are apparent, and on flapping the wings large areas of white become prominent. Flocks of Steller's Eiders tend to fly somewhat higher above the sea than other Eiders, their flight is swift and the wings produce a loud whistling sound. At times other than when packed closely in a raft, they tend to occur in smaller groups of between fifteen and forty individuals. Flocks wintering along the Norwegian coast appear to be quite tame and are regularly seen close into shore. One of the most social of all wildfowl when not nesting.

Habitat When breeding, usually on flat tundra some distance inland, away from salt water. Outside the breeding season, much of the time is spent at sea where they prefer the shallow waters along rocky shorelines, also lagoons and inlets. Often seen resting on beaches and sandbars, also flatish seaweed-covered rocks exposed by falling tide.

Distribution The principal breeding range is the high arctic in eastern Siberia, the Bering Sea coast of Alaska, especially between the Kuskokwim and Yukon deltas, also several suitable localities along the arctic coast of Alaska. Most wintering birds frequent waters adjacent to their summer haunts, along the coasts of the Bering Sea wherever open water is available. Around Kodiak Island and Shumagins to the west, also Commander Island, along the Kamchatka coast and the Kurils – Schumschu, Paramushir, and Onekotan. At the approach of spring, large assemblies gather at the outer end of the Alaska Peninsula, with total numbers estimated at 200,000 for Bechevin Bay, Izembek Bay and Nelson Lagoon. Prior to breeding, numbers are often seen in Varanger Fiord, northern Norway.

Food Steller's Eider acquires food by

diving, but will dabble and also up-end in the more shallow waters. Its diet consists principally of animal matter such as crustaceans, molluscs, and the larvae of aquatic insects; but pondweeds and eel grass are also taken.

Voice   During display the drake has a soft cooing or a 'crooing' note, not so loud as the males of other Eiders. The female incites with a loud 'cooay'. She also utters a harsh, guttural growl 'a-a-a-a-rr', similar to the growl of a young dog.

Display   During pair formation it is usual for three to seven drakes to display and chase one another within close proximity of a duck. This includes short flights of up to a few hundred yards, also

fighting takes place occasionally between drakes. Displays by the drake include rearing rapidly whilst swimming; tossing the bill upwards and backwards; also head turning and bill dipping.

Breeding   Nests are in areas of tundra where ponds and small lakes are plentiful, a dry mossy site or a depression between grassy hummocks is selected. Dry grasses usually form the nest and this is thickly lined with dark sooty brown down. Laying is from early June onwards, with seven to eight pale olive-buff eggs being a usual clutch, average size 60 × 41 mm. Incubation period has not been recorded. The males remain on the breeding ground until incubation has commenced.

Red-crested Pochard

Netta rufina

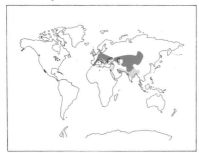

Description The drake in breeding plumage has a bright vermilion head with the feathers of the crest slightly paler towards the back of the head. The nape, upper mantle, breast and underparts are black, contrasting sharply with the white flanks. The upperparts are greyish-brown with a white band across the base of the scapulars, rump and upper tail coverts are black with a greenish gloss, tail grey. The wings have a broad white band across the flight feathers, running right across the trailing edge of the wing. Axillaries and under wing are white. The bill is bright red, iris red, legs and feet orange red. The female has dark brown head and nape, with whitish cheeks and foreneck. Upperparts light brown, underparts brown barred with pale buff. Bill dark grey with pinkish edges and tip, iris brown becoming red in spring. Legs and feet are pinkish with dark webs. Length 55 cm. Immatures resemble female, but are darker and with more mottled underparts.

Characteristics and Behaviour Swims more buoyantly than other diving ducks, but is often content to feed by up-ending in shallow water, or even grazing on land, where it walks easily with little waddling. The flight is typical of most diving ducks, strong with rapid wing beats and an extended take-off run. Not very numerous as a breeding species in Europe, where numbers tend to fluctuate; the bulk of the breeding population being in southern and central USSR.

Habitat Fresh-water lakes with extensive reedbeds and a plentiful supply of submerged vegetation. Also in some areas brackish and salt-water lagoons, extensive marshes and river deltas.

Distribution In the breeding season small numbers in Denmark, Germany, the Netherlands, Czechoslovakia, Rumania, rather more in France and Spain. USSR from the Black Sea across Asia to western Siberia. South to Iran, the Pamirs and Chinese Turkestan. In winter south to the Mediterranean, Black and Caspian Seas, Iraq, Iran, India and Burma.

Food Mainly leaves, stems and roots of submerged plants. Also seeds, occasionally insects and larvae, various small aquatic animals.

Voice Normally silent, but the male has a quiet 'geng', usually repeated and used as an anxiety call, also a harsh 'wheezing' note used in display. The female has a hoarse grating call in addition to a soft quack.

Display Pair formation usually occurs in winter flocks. During courtship the drake's crest is erected and a number of drakes often swim round one female, dipping bills in the water then swimming with head and bill pointing downwards and uttering the harsh wheezy call.

Breeding The season is May to June. Nest is made on islands or in dense vegetation close to water's edge and with a tunnel approach. It is constructed from grasses, leaves, or aquatic vegetation, and lined with down and feathers. Clutch size varies from six to fourteen, but is usually eight to ten. The eggs are pale buff, sometimes with a greenish tinge, average size 58 × 42 mm. Incubation by the female for 26 to 28

days. The downy young are light brown above, with pale markings on body and wings, underparts pale buff, face creamy with a dark line through the eye. They are cared for by the female alone and fledge in 6 or 7 weeks.

Rosy-billed Pochard
(Rosy-bill)

Netta peposaca

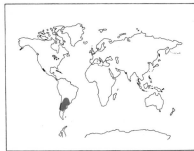

Description   The head and neck of an adult male are purplish-black, the sides of which are highly glossed. Its black upperparts bear minute pale grey or white spots. The breast is black; the abdomen and flanks appear grey as a result of black and white vermiculations. Under tail coverts and under wing are white. The wing coverts are very dark brown and the white secondaries and primaries are tipped with black. Bill bright pink with a black nail; there is a large crimson knob close to the forehead. Legs are yellow. No eclipse plumage. The female is of a uniform rufous brown. Darker on the head and neck, paler on breast and abdomen. Bill bluish grey and only a slight nasal caruncle. Legs are yellow grey. Length 55 cm.

Characteristics and Behaviour   A large dark coloured duck. Although resembling the true Pochards (*Aythya*) in shape and behaviour, it is intermediate between them and the Dabbling Ducks. Rosybills, because of their weight and relatively short wings, are slow to become airborne but once in flight they are fast and proficient. They show a preference for shallow water where they regularly obtain food from the surface. Prior to diving, which the Rosybill does well, it will be seen to make a short but positive jump before entering the water.

Quite a tame species if not persecuted too freely. During the winter months when making flights of any length, during their limited northerly migration, are seen to congregate in sizeable flocks of up to 100, at such times their flight is high and a rough V-shaped formation is assumed.

Habitat   Shallow pools and lakes or lagoons bordered by rushes and other aquatic vegetation.

Distribution   Central Chile (where it is not common), from Valdiva to Atacana. Also in southern Brazil, Paraguay, Uruguay; and Argentina from Mendoza and Buenos Aires south to Rio Negro. Particularly abundant in the province of Buenos Aires.

Food   A diet predominantly of vegetable matter.

Voice   Usually regarded as a silent bird, but in spring the male does utter a soft whining 'coo', the female a harsh 'kraa'; both calls typical of the other Pochards.

Display   That of the male is very basic, consisting of throwing back the head; stretching up the neck with head held high and bill pointing to the sky, this being followed by resting the head on the shoulders.

Breeding   The nest is on the ground and well hidden amongst reeds and rushes, a dry position being chosen. It is well constructed from fresh herbaceous materials and amply lined with down, the latter used to cover the eggs whenever the bird should leave the nest. Breeding occurs from October to December, when up to fourteen greeny-grey eggs are laid, averaging in size 55 × 42 mm, with an incubation period of 23 to 25 days. It would seem that the male may not assist in caring for the ducklings, but this point still requires verification.

[208]

South American Pochard

(Red-eyed Pochard or Southern Pochard)

Netta erythrophthalma erythrophthalma

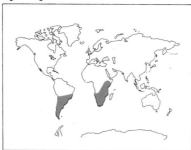

Description The black head, neck and breast of the male are highly glossed with purple; mantle and back are also black but with fine brown vermiculations. The sides and flanks are of a richer and somewhat darker brown than the abdomen. White wing mirror, Bill bluish-grey. Legs grey. Length 50 cm. The female is light buff below and altogether much paler than her mate. A white line through the eye broadens and extends backwards behind the ear coverts, then curves forwards to form a ring around the throat. An irregular whitish patch also occurs around the grey bill. Legs are grey as in the male. Immature birds resemble the female.

Characteristics and Behaviour Closely related to the Rosybill, but smaller and lacking the swollen base to the bill. It sits fairly low in the water with its tail submerged. A timid bird, diving or swimming away if approached. When alarmed it takes to the air, but requires a run across the water to achieve this. Its flight is swift and its thin neck and high forehead are characteristic. Usually occurs in pairs or small flocks.

Habitat A fresh-water species frequenting open flooded marshes, shallow ponds and large rivers particularly those with floating vegetation.

Distribution The northern half of South America, from Venezuela and Colombia through Peru and into Chile in the west; extending eastwards across Bolivia and throughout Brazil north of Rio de Janeiro. Not very numerous in many parts of their range.

Food In the main they feed on vegetable matter such as seeds, the roots and shoots of water plants, with a small intake of crustacea and the larvae of aquatic insects.

Voice The male's call has been described as a nasal 'whrreeooorr' or 'par-ah-ah' particularly when in flight; the female has a short 'quack' or 'quarrrk'.

Display This is simple, the male occasionally throwing the head back but not pointing the bill upwards as is common with many other species of pochard.

Breeding The nest is well constructed of reeds and rushes and built above water in a dryish situation amongst the reeds. Little or no down being used. The five to nine creamy-white eggs average 55 × 41 mm and require an incubation period of 23–25 days.

South African Pochard

Netta erythrophthalma brunnea

Description Similar to the American sub-species but generally lighter and tending to be somewhat browner. The female is readily distinguished from the female Maccoa *Oxyura maccoa* by the ringlike effect around the throat.

Distribution Widely distributed throughout South Africa and extending into Ethiopia. Although it usually occurs in small flocks up to 300 individuals have been recorded at one time.

Breeding In the Cape from August to December and during May; whilst in the Transvaal during February and from July to August. Clutch size six to thirteen creamy-buff eggs, 56 × 44 mm.

Canvas Back

Aythya valisineria

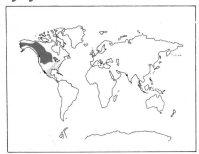

Description Head and neck of breeding male reddish-brown, with front of face and crown shading to a very dark brown. Upper breast and upper back are black; mantle and scapulars pale grey with numerous fine vermiculations of blackish-brown. The lower back is greyish-brown and both speckled and finely lined with pale grey. Rump and vent blackish-brown. The belly and sides are whitish. Bill black, legs greyish-blue. The male in eclipse is altogether duller, with upper and lower parts tinged brown. The head, neck, upper back and breast of female are brown with a mottled appearance. Chin, face and the line through eye much paler. The pale grey mantle has fine black vermiculations, wings are of a much darker grey, tail and rump dark brown. The belly is white, becoming darker towards rear of abdomen. Bill and legs as in male. Length 55 cm.

Characteristics and Behaviour The largest of the Pochards and although quite a colourful bird, because of its unelegant build, it cannot be described as handsome. With its long tapering bill and sloping forehead the head has a wedge-shaped profile. It associates on shallow waters with both Scaup and Redhead; the Canvas Back appears to ride higher than the scaup, and all three have noticeable differences in back colour, the Redhead much the darkest.

It is one of the fastest flying ducks, with rapid wing beat and a direct flight; on migration the Canvas Backs fly in large V-shaped flocks at high altitude.

Habitat In spring and early summer, marshes with shallow waters, and flooded farmland. During mid-summer females congregate on larger marshes and the drakes have favoured moulting lakes. In winter months most move to brackish and alkaline waters near the coast; such as estuaries and shallow bays, rather than take to the open sea. In particular the estuaries in Virginia and North Carolina where large numbers gather.

Distribution During spring and early summer from central Alaska south to central Oregon and northern Utah, New Mexico, and southern Nebraska. There is an overlap in the breeding and wintering range, where adequate shelter and food are available. The Chesapeake Bay and San Francisco Bay areas maintain large winter populations, as does the Detroit area and the central plateau of Mexico, with many also visiting the east Great Lake to upper Mississippi district.

Food Mainly vegetable with a significantly smaller intake of animal matter, in the ratio of about 70:30. A variety of grasses, aquatic plants and seeds, also molluscs and insects including caddis fly and midge larvae, dragonflies, etc.

Voice Except for the cooing call used during display, the drake is usually a silent bird. The female has a whining call heard when pursued in flight by a male or males. Another call is the 'kuk-kuk-kuk' uttered repeatedly when tending the ducklings.

Display The drakes assume various postures such as drawing back the neck and lowering the head, with the bill remaining parallel to the water surface, during which time a bulge appears in

the upper part of the throat; also neck stretching and throwing back the head. The duck incites by stretching her neck and with head held high, pointing her bill towards the drake of her choice. This is followed by pulling at the drake's flank feathers.

Breeding A bulky but well-concealed nest is constructed and this usually amongst reeds or rushes and over shallow water. Full clutches may be found from about the second week of May in the southern regions, to early June in Alaska and north Yukon. It is not until several eggs have been laid that down is added to the nest. An average clutch would consist of seven to ten greyish-olive eggs which may vary in tone from nest to nest, these measure 63 × 45 mm with an incubation period of 23 to 29 days. The Crow (*Corvus brachyrhynchus*) is a constant predator during the nesting period, so also is the Raccoon (*Procyon lotor*) in some areas.

Male Canvas Back

European Pochard
(Common Pochard)

Aythya ferina

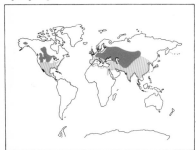

Description The male has reddish-brown head and upper part of neck; breast and rear are black. Fine blackish-brown vermiculations on a whitish ground give the body and wings an overall appearance of medium grey. Belly varies from white to pale buff, even silvery-grey, and with vermiculations of a slightly deeper shade. The bill is dark with a broad central band of slate grey. Legs and feet are greyish-yellow with dusky grey webs. In eclipse the male is a browner version of the above and duller. The female is a brownish coloured bird and similar to the Canvas Back Duck which is described. Length 45 cm.

Characteristics and Behaviour A gregarious species except during the breeding season. In Europe the pale grey of the hind wing is a means of identification. But in North America, where there are two other grey-backed Pochard, it resembles the Canvas Back (*Aythya valisineria*) in colour, but the Redhead (*Aythya americana*) in general body-shape; morphologically it is intermediate between the two. Most of their time is spent on water where they dive for food in the shallows, or occasionally acquire it by upending or dabbling. Time is spent ashore resting and when on land they walk with some difficulty. On the wing their flight is swift.

Habitat When breeding they frequent shallow inland waters such as thickly vegetated lakes, ponds and slow-flowing streams. Similar habitats are also frequented at other times, but now they are also found at the coast in sheltered bays, river estuaries and deltas. For instance, some years over 300,000 are known to winter in the Danube delta; whilst in Europe, those frequenting fresh-water habitats approach 250,000.

Distribution Breeds in the British Isles, France, Germany, Belgium, the Netherlands, Denmark, Norway, central Sweden, Finland and Russia to western central Siberia, south of latitude 60° N, also Roumania, Austria and Hungary. Winters in Britain, Ireland and whole of Western Europe, North Africa and east across India to Burma, China and Japan. Accidental elsewhere. The main moulting lakes are in Russia and central Europe, but Abberton Reservoir in south-east England regularly has a flock of up to 3,000 birds.

Food Largely a vegetarian, feeding in fresh waters on the seeds of pondweeds, and the leaves of aquatic plants. However, during the breeding season substantial quantities of aquatic insects are taken, particularly the larvae of midges. When feeding in salt-water areas, very small mussels and crustaceans are often eaten.

Voice The male is mainly a silent bird but does produce a kind of breathing sound. The female's harsh 'kurr' is heard during display procedure.

Display A number of males will turn in circles around a female, this is followed by bill dipping and holding their outstretched neck parallel to the water surface. Inflating the neck with air; throwing their head backwards and bringing it sharply forwards is all part of the display.

Breeding Nests can be found in late April and May, these built in thick veg-

etation of ponds and lakes, both in the water or some little way from it. A regular clutch would consist of six to nine greenish-grey eggs, measuring 61 × 44 mm. Incubation period is 24 to 26 days. It is quite common for two ducks to lay in one nest, and not necessarily of the same species; Tufted Duck in particular deposit their eggs in the nest of a Pochard. It is the female alone who tends for the young; in early June moulting flocks of drakes have already gathered.

Red-head

Aythya americana

Smaller than the Canvas Back but slightly larger than the European Pochard. It also has a yellow iris where the other two have a red one. Very like the plumage of *Aythya ferina* but the grey vermiculations of the body are coarser and much darker, the general appearance is of a much darker bird. Also of similar habits and behaviour.

Distribution Breeds chiefly southwards from central British Columbia to northern New Mexico and east to Wisconsin. Winters as far south as central Mexico and eastwards to the Gulf Coast and north to Connecticut.

Top Male Pochard
Bottom Male Redhead

[215]

Australian White-eye
(Hardhead)

Aythya australis australis

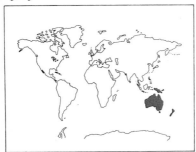

Description The male has crown, nape, back, rump and tail of rich sepia, with side of face, neck and breast chestnut brown. Lower breast feathers are brownish, some with a white tip, this giving a rather mottled effect. The abdomen is dark brown, and under tail coverts white. Wings are brown but tinged with chestnut on upper coverts, outer primaries are brown the rest white tipped with brown; there is a prominent white band across the otherwise brown secondaries. Bill is greyish-black with a broad pale blue-grey band at tip, nail black. Legs are grey. The female is generally paler in colour, and the bill band is narrower. Immatures are as female but duller and the white underside is more mottled in appearance. Length of male 49 cm, female 47 cm.

Characteristics and Behaviour A bird which frequents not only the deep fresh water of lakes and swamps, but also the turbulent waters of inland rivers in full spate and is quite able to swim against the current. It is extremely difficult to approach this shy and wary bird, which if disturbed rises almost vertically from the water and with rapid flight quickly disappears from view. In flight, it is swift and direct with a wing beat that produces a distinctive sound, it is now the white wing bar becomes noticeable. On water it floats rather low, but may be distinguished from the Black Duck by the absence of an eye stripe. The neck is long and thin, but the bill is broad and typical of the genus *Aythya*. There is a slight and gradual increase in size from the northern to southern limits of its range. It is also noticed that individuals show a considerable variation in colour. A favourite game bird and good to eat.

Habitat As already mentioned, the Australian White-eye shows a preference for large expanses of deep water, preferably with dense vegetation, even so, from time to time it may be encountered in most kinds of habitat. With a policy in recent years for draining deep water swamps and the increased usage of such waters for irrigation purposes, this species is in greater danger than other wildfowl in southern Australia.

Distribution Australia, Tasmania, New Zealand, eastern Java, New Guinea, New Caledonia, the Celebes and the New Hebrides. The stronghold in Australia being the Murray–Darling basin. In Western Australia the principal breeding area is in the south-west.

Food Acquired by diving in deep water and by dabbling in the shallows, or stripping aquatic plants of their seeds. Rarely, if ever, do they leave the water to feed on dry land. In the main it is a vegetarian with the seeds of flowers of sedges, aquatic grasses and the like forming the bulk of its intake. Of the animal matter taken this is composed largely of aquatic insects and molluscs.

Voice The Australian White-eye is basically a silent bird, the male with his soft whistle and the female a soft croaking call.

Breeding The months of breeding are determined by rainfall which greatly affects the habitats. With a predominantly winter rainfall clutches are completed in October and November. When the main rainfall comes in

summer then egg-laying is at a peak during January and February. Nests are usually constructed from woven reeds or sedges and built in dense reedbeds growing in several feet of water, but may also be found in bushes at the edge of deep water channels in lignum swamps. A substantial quantity of down is added when the eggs have been laid. An average clutch would be nine to twelve creamy-white eggs measuring 57 × 42 mm, with an incubation period of about 25 days.

Banks Islands White-eye

Aythya australis extima

Smaller than *A. a. australis* but similar in all other respects. Probably confined to the Banks Islands but the scarce populations of the New Hebrides and New Caledonia may well be *A. a. extima*.

Madagascan White-eye

Aythya innotota

Description Resembles the Red-head in shape and build, with rounded forehead and crown but in other respects closely resembles the Ferruginous White-eye.

Distribution Confined to eastern Madagascar from Lake Alaotra, where it is common, south to Antsirabe, at an altitude of 3,000 to 4,000 feet.

Voice and Display As the Red-head.

Breeding Extends from October through to January. The 6 to 8 buffy grey eggs measure 55 × 40 mm and have an incubation period of 26 to 28 days.

Ferruginous White-eye
(Ferruginous Duck or White-eyed Pochard)

Aythya nyroca

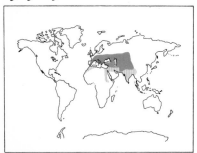

Description The drake in breeding plumage has head, neck and breast deep chestnut with a white spot on the chin, and a dark collar round the base of the neck. Upper mantle chestnut, remainder of upperparts dark brown with greenish gloss. The white speculum is often concealed when the bird is at rest but becomes very conspicuous in flight. The flanks are reddish-brown, underparts white, shading to grey on the abdomen; with the white under tail coverts a diagnostic field mark. Bill slate grey, iris white, legs and feet dark grey. The female is generally similar to the male but duller and browner, with a brown iris, and can be confused with female Tufted (*A. fuligula*) at a distance, when white undertail coverts are best recognition feature. Male in eclipse and immatures resemble female, but immatures have under tail coverts greyish with brown markings. Length 40 cm.

Characteristics and Behaviour The Ferruginous Duck has suffered a marked decline in western and central Europe during this century, and now breeds in any numbers only in Roumania, Russia and western Asia. It is secretive by nature, skulking amongst dense vegetation and not easily put to flight, often avoiding danger by diving in preference to flight. It swims well and dives frequently, although prefers shallow water. Large flocks are unusual, birds are often seen singly or in pairs, occasionally small groups, and seldom associated with other species. Feeding takes place mainly at dusk and during the night.

Habitat Shallow, fresh-water pools, quiet marshes, lagoons with dense marginal vegetation and a plentiful supply of submerged aquatic plants. Does not require such extensive areas of open water as the Pochard (*A. ferina*).

Distribution In the breeding season, small numbers in France, Spain, Germany, Czechoslovakia and Hungary. Also Roumania, southern Russia and Asia Minor east to Kazakhstan and Tibet. Winters in the southern part of breeding range, especially Black and Caspian Seas and Sea of Azov, south to Iraq, Iran, Sudan, Nigeria, Arabia, India, Burma, north-west Thailand and south-west China.

Food Mainly vegetable matter, seeds and roots of aquatic plants, including *Potamogeton*, *Carex*, *Polygonium*, *Lemna*, etc. Also at times small fish, amphibia, molluscs, crustaceans, worms and aquatic insects.

Voice Not very vocal outside the breeding season, the male has calls variously rendered as 'gek', 'kek', 'wuk', etc. in addition to whistling notes. Voice of female similar to Pochard, but quieter.

Display Displaying drakes swim close to the female jerking back the head whilst calling, and occasionally swim with inflated neck extended on the surface of the water.

Breeding From early May to mid-June. The nest is placed on or close to water in dense reed-beds, waterside vegetation, grass tussocks or sedges, always in wet surroundings. It is sometimes constructed from trampled and woven reed stems, with a cup of dry

grasses and leaves, mosses, etc. and lined with down and feathers. Usually well concealed. Eggs normally eight to ten, pale buff in colour, average size 52 × 38 mm. Incubation period about 26 days. The downy young have crown and upperparts dark brown, sides of head and breast bright yellow, underparts paler. They are guarded by the female but obtain their own food and become independent after about 8 weeks.

Baer's Pochard
(Eastern White-eyed Pochard)

Aythya baeri

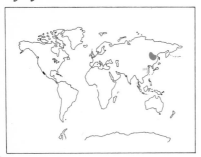

Description The head and neck of a breeding male are almost black, but with a strong greenish sheen; there is also a small white chin spot. Mantle is dark brown with cinnamon tinge; the feathers of sides and flanks are sepia with white tips, shading to a rich chestnut on the breast. Belly is white, under tail coverts are mostly white, tail blackish-brown. Wings very dark brown with white mirror tipped black, inner margin of primaries is pale smoke grey. Bill slaty grey but black at tip and base. Legs are grey. Length 47 cm. In eclipse much duller, with head and neck matt browny-black. The female is similar to male but with head and neck of very dark brown, and there is a dark rufous patch on side of head near the bill. Immatures are like the female, but somewhat browner.

Characteristics and Behaviour A smallish diving duck which superficially resembles the Ferruginous White-eye *Aythya nyroca*, but the head and neck are blackish; the head is also much larger and the neck substantially longer. Baer's Pochard is a species about which little is known, it is timid and less approachable than the Ferruginous, has a stronger and faster flight, and is more adept when out of water. Nowhere is it abundant, and in most of its range may be considered rare; probably less so in north-eastern Asia. Reports suggest they occur in small groups.

Habitat A bird of the more swiftly flowing rivers, also occurring on jungle pools.

Distribution Its principal breeding area is the Amur Basin in Manchuria and adjoining areas both to the north and the west. In winter it occurs locally from Korea and the eastern parts of China, to Thailand, Burma, Assam and Bengal.

Food In spring said to eat frogs, which it catches in ponds and meadows. Birds taken whilst wintering in India are considered inedible because of their fishy flavour, which would suggest that fish are also included in the diet.

Voice Not on record.

Display When threatening another drake, or during moments of excitement, the pupils of the eyes contract to such an extent that only the straw colour of the iris is apparent. The drakes also have a 'head-throw' display when the head and neck are thrown upwards and backwards; the neck is also extended fully, with the head held horizontally and puffed out with air.

Breeding Very little known, but reports say that nests have been located on the ground along the banks of streams and on the shores of lakes. The eggs are pale brown and measure 53 × 38 mm.

Ring-necked Duck

Aythya collaris

Description Head and neck of male black with a purple sheen, the long feathers on the crown forming a short crest. The narrow chestnut collar around the lower neck is not conspicuous, nor is the white on the chin always clearly defined. Upperparts and breast are black and sharply defined from the white belly, the white extending triangularly upwards and forward of the folded wing. The dark vermiculations of lower belly and sides produce shades of light and medium grey. Scapulars and wing are glossed with green, there is a silver-grey mirror. The bluish-grey bill is tipped with black and has two white bands, one at the base and another before the black tip. Legs are yellowish-grey. In eclipse plumage resembles a dark version of the female but with less white on the face. The female has head greyish-brown, darker on the crown, lighter and mottled with white on the cheeks. Whitish on chin, throat and the area around base of bill; a white line extends backwards and downwards from the eye. Remainder of plumage is brown, this being mottled on the breast and sides; the lower breast is white. Length 43 cm.

Characteristics and Behaviour A small Pochard with a body size similar to the Lesser Scaup; it rides high on the water when at rest, just like the Scaups and Tufted Duck. From its name

Ring-necked Duck, one would expect the dark chestnut ring to be a field character, this is not so, but the white bands of the bill are sufficient to distinguish it from the Tufted Duck which it so closely resembles. A gregarious species at all times, even during the nesting period. Although a diving duck it has many characteristics one would expect of a surface feeder; for instance it rides high on the water, often swimming with tail clear of the surface; it is capable of springing at a steep angle from either the water or its nest, and is often seen to fly at heights more typical of the Mallard or the Black Duck. Essentially a daytime feeder but has been observed feeding occasionally on moonlit nights. Relatively tame until the hunting season opens, when it soon becomes gun-shy and very wary.

Habitat Very fond of fresh inland waters, preferring marshes and small ponds, and seen less often than other Pochards on large open waters. Uncommon along both the east and west coasts of North America.

Distribution The main breeding range extends in a band from west to east of North America and spreads north from the Great Lakes to Hudson Bay; east to Nova Scotia and north-east to Newfoundland and into Labrador. West to North and South Dakota, then north-west to British Columbia and the Great Slave Lake. It winters along the entire west coast with the exception of Southern California; throughout Mexico; north-east including Mississippi, Alabama, Georgia, Florida, North and South Carolina and northwards along the coast to New England. Also Cuba, Haiti, Puerto Rico and Jamaica

Food Mainly vegetable (about 80 per cent), such as seeds, pondweeds, sedges, grasses and tender parts of water-lilies. The remainder (about 20 per cent) consists of aquatic insects and molluscs.

Voice The drake produces a hissing, low-pitched whistle, uttered during display or during off-duty periods from the nest when he is joined by the female. At most other times a rather silent bird. The female has a low-pitched purr-like growl, this becoming higher pitched when alarmed or under stress.

Display The male, with tail lifted and crest raised, holds up his head and moves it quickly backwards until almost touching the rump; it is then brought slowly forward. The courtship is that typical of the Pochards.

Breeding Nests are usually constructed on floating islands or other dryish foundations amongst hummocks or tussocks in open marshes; seldom built over water. The selection of a nest site is by the female but she is accompanied by the male. It is not until three or four eggs have been laid that the nest begins to take shape and down is gradually added after the fifth egg is laid. Peak laying is usually during the second and third weeks of May, a normal clutch is six to fourteen creamy-buff eggs measuring 55 × 41 mm. The female usually starts to incubate on laying the last egg and most hatch on the twenty-sixth or twenty-seventh day. The young are brooded in the nest for 12 to 24 hours before being led away to nearby water, but during the first 4 or 5 days they are brooded for lengthy periods, spending only a few hours each day on the water.

Tufted Duck

Aythya fuligula

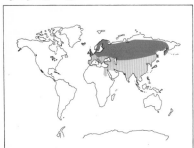

Description The adult male has head, crest, neck, and upper breast black with a purplish gloss. The upperparts, vent and tail are also black but with a greenish gloss; the mantle being ever so slightly freckled with creamy-white; mirror on secondaries white; underwing mostly white. Sides and flanks are also white but sometimes duskily spotted, especially so on the flanks. Abdomen white, shading to dusky white towards vent. Bill slaty blue with subterminal white line and black tip. Legs and feet slaty blue with dark joints and webs. In eclipse, upperparts and breast are brownish-black, the feathers of throat and chin showing white at bases; breast feathers are edged with white; sides and flanks pale brown with whitish vermiculations. The female is generally dark brown, the light edges of feathers producing a mottled effect. Her crest is much shorter than the long hanging crest of the male. The undersides are of a paler brown; belly, centre of breast, and feathers around base of bill are white; there is also a whitish spot on the chin. Bill and legs are slightly duller than those of the male. The female's plumage is subject to considerable variation of tone. Length 43 cm.

Characteristics and Behaviour The Tufted Duck is the most widespread in Europe, and is the only Pochard with a long pendant crest. Throughout most of the year the drake's plumage pattern is very contrasty with the areas of black and white sharply defined. It frequents fresh waters and except during periods of hard frost is rarely seen at sea. Outside the breeding season it occurs in flocks on ponds, lakes and reservoirs, where it obtains its food entirely by diving.

Habitat Occurs on fresh waters of varying size but especially those with reed beds or other aquatic vegetation that offers good cover. It resorts to the more open waters during winter months. Its regular occurrence on lakes and ponds in parks has made it the most familiar of our inland diving ducks.

Distribution Breeds in Iceland (particularly Lake Myvatn with an estimated 5,000 pairs), Great Britain and most of Europe from 50° N to the Arctic Circle, but even farther north in Sweden, Finland, Russia and Siberia; east to Japan, Sakhalin, Kamchatka and Commander Island. Also Syria, Cyprus, Caspian Steppe, Pamirs, Altai and north-west Mongolia. In winter, the Black Sea and the Mediterranean coasts, Africa as far south as Liberia and Kenya; Arabia, India, Burma, Malaysia and the Philippines. The Tufted Duck of north-west Europe winter mainly on inland waters with the exception of some 200,000 birds which frequent the shallow waters of the western Baltic, particularly around the coasts of Denmark.

Food Most of the Tufted Duck's food is acquired by diving, and when feeding on inland fresh waters this consists chiefly of molluscs, the larvae of aquatic insects and various plant seeds. Baltic feeders however, take mussels and other bivalves, also snails and crustacea.

Voice The male has a soft repeated whistle; the female a harsh 'kurr kurr'.

Display On water, raising-up with breast clear of the surface and bill up-

pointed. Short pursuit flights occur in between periods of diving.

Breeding Nests are commonly placed on islands in lakes or lochs, also along the banks of pools and ponds. Usually well hidden amongst reeds or grasses and close to water; consists of a depression lined with grasses and dark down. The greenish-grey eggs number eight to ten and measure 59 × 41 mm; most clutches are laid during May and June. Incubation period 24 days.

Lesser Scaup
(Little Blue-bill)

Aythya affinis

Description The male in breeding plumage has head and neck black shot with violet; upper back, breast and rump are also black; tail brownish-black. Mantle and scapulars are white with rather coarse blackish-brown vermiculations. Lower breast and belly are white; sides and flanks white with varying degrees of vermiculation. The under tail is blackish; primaries buffish brown, darker at tips; outermost secondaries are white with a narrow black border and broad black ends often flecked with white; innermost secondaries are black. Bill pale blue with black nail. Legs and feet usually a dusky grey-green. Some drakes also have a small white spot on the chin. In eclipse, the male has brownish-black head and neck, often with whitish feathering around base of bill. Rest of plumage a mixture of browns; but belly whitish. The female usually has head, front of neck and breast in some shade of dark chestnut; with a whitish area on face around the bill. Upperparts dark brown flecked with buff. Underparts somewhat lighter due to pale edges of feathers. Lower breast and belly are white. Length 44 cm.

Characteristics and Behaviour The most numerous diving duck in North America; an inland species usually only visiting the sea coast during winter months. Rather a shy bird with rafts keeping well out from the shoreline on open waters. In the USA it is far more widespread than the Greater Scaup (*Aythya m. mariloides*). In flight the white patch on the secondaries can be seen in both sexes; where with the Greater Scaup this patch extends into the primaries. Their flight does not appear very purposeful, when in compact but irregular formation they dart about in twists and turns. On non-tidal waters, feeding activities are at a peak during the early morning; but on tidal waters the timing may be governed somewhat by the state of tide, feeding as they do, close in to shore at high tide.

Habitat In summer near inland ponds and lakes, river deltas, also marshy areas. During the winter months, sheltered bays, estuaries, coastal marshes and unfrozen stretches of water near to the coast.

Distribution Breeds in the MacKenzie delta, the Alaskan interior, Churchill (Hudson Bay), then south to Oregon, Utah, Colorado and Iowa. Wintering south of latitude 50° N to Colombia and Venezuela.

Food Both animal and vegetable matter are taken; including pondweeds, grasses and sedges; also aquatic insects and molluscs. The percentage of animal/vegetable intake varies considerably from region to region.

Voice The drake is usually silent except for a 'whew' or 'whee-ooo' uttered during displays. A rather harsh 'kerr-urr' is the inciting call of the female.

Display During the formation of pairs, both male and female will preen behind the wing. Head-throwing, by the drakes, occurs as they approach a female.

Breeding A late breeder with peak laying about mid-May in the south of its range, to mid-June in the extreme north.

[226]

The nest consists of a slight depression, made by the duck, in amongst vegetation and lined with dry grasses and the like; down not being added until several eggs have been laid and continued during the early stages of incubation. There is a tendency for nests to be in loose colonies rather than scattered widely over an area. The nest site may be near the water's edge and quite often on islands in lakes. Usually a clutch would consist of nine to eleven olive-buff eggs, averaging 57 × 40 mm. Incubation period is 21 to 22 days.

European Scaup
(Greater Scaup)

Aythya marila marila

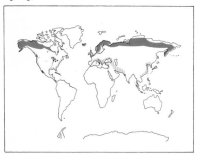

Description The male in breeding dress resembles the Lesser Scaup very closely with no trace of a crest, but is larger and the bill less spatulate. Head black with a greenish gloss; neck, breast, upper back and rump are black. Upperparts pale grey with black vermiculations, these do not extend to the sides of the body as in the Lesser Scaup. Belly, sides and flanks are white. The wing mirror is large and white. Bill pale blue tinged turquoise with black nail. Legs and feet greyish-blue with dusky webs. Female differs from female Lesser Scaup in being of somewhat brighter plumage. The white patch at base of bill is more extensive, and the mantle has a silvery cast. In eclipse, the male resembles the female. Length 48 cm.

Characteristics and Behaviour Being so similar to the Lesser Scaup it is often not possible to distinguish the two species at any distance. If the white wing stripe can be seen, then this is a useful guide, as it extends well on to the primaries, where it only reaches the primaries in the Lesser. It has a more northerly breeding range occupying the entire holarctic region. Being such proficient swimmers, even in rough conditions out at sea, is capable of maintaining steady progress. A very gregarious species during the autumn and winter months, when extensive rafts may be seen on larger expanses of water and these most difficult to approach closely. However, very much a saltwater bird, with the females spending little time ashore except during the breeding period. Dives well, preferring depths of water up to 6 m, may remain submerged for up to 30 seconds, will swim away at great speed under water.

Habitat In the breeding season occurs in exposed coastal areas, also open terrain and low scrubby tundra. Moulting takes place on inland waters and to a lesser extent out at sea. During winter months seeks the shelter of coastal bays and estuaries, also large expanses of unfrozen fresh water in coastal regions.

Distribution Breeds in Iceland, northern Europe and western Asia. Winters in western Europe, British Isles, Mediterranean and Black Sea coasts, Persia, northern India and Indo-China, also China, Korea and Japan.

Food The diet consists almost equally of animal and vegetable matter. At sea feeds mainly on molluscs such as mussels and cockles, etc. On inland waters, pondweeds, sedges and a considerable intake of seeds.

Voice More or less silent in flight. Apart from the male's soft courtship whistle, he has a display call resembling 'pa-whoo' or 'wa-hooo'. The female's call is described as 'krrr' or 'karr karr'.

Display When approaching a female the drake extends neck and holds head high with his bill raised at an angle of 50° or thereabouts. The female in response lifts her neck and utters 'tuk-tuk, turra, tuk'.

Breeding Often nests in colonies and egg-laying usually commences about mid-June. A slightly elevated position may be chosen for the nest and generally the site is quite close to water. Very little material is employed, the eggs laid in a depression on the ground, under cover

of a small bush or sometimes amongst large stones. Grassy sites along the shores of lakes and ponds or the banks of channels are much favoured. The seven to nine olive-buff eggs measuring 62 × 44 mm and take 23 to 27 days to incubate.

Pacific Scaup
(Blue-bill)

Aythya marila mariloides

Description Similar to the European Scaup but with upperparts more coarsely vermiculated.

Distribution In the breeding season, north-west North America, the vast majority nesting in Alaska and most abundant from Kotzebue Sound to Bristol Bay; also common in the interior. Plentiful in the Aleutians particularly on Amchitka and Unalaska. Winters in the coastal areas of western North America and the Aleutian Islands, south to the Mexican border. Also in the southern USA and northwards along the Atlantic coast to Nova Scotia including Lake Erie and Lake Ontario.

[229]

Greater Brazilian Teal

Amazonetta brasiliensis ipecutiri

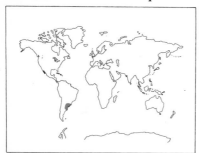

Description   The adult male has front of the head and crown dark brown, back of the head and nape black, with a grey patch on the side of the head behind the eye. The neck is ringed with dark spots. Mantle brown, greater wing coverts and outer secondaries are brilliant metallic green, tinged with purple on the secondaries which have a black bar and broad white tips. Primaries are black tinged with green. The back, rump and tail are black; tail coverts brown. The rufous breast is darkly barred and spotted, the abdomen and under tail coverts are grey. Bill orange-red, iris brown, legs and feet orange. The female has a white spot in front of the eye, and a larger one at the base of the bill; no spots round the neck, and a greyish bill. Immatures similar to females but duller. Two sub-species are recognized, the Lesser Brazilian Teal (*A. b. brasiliensis*), and Greater Brazilian Teal (*A. b. ipecutiri*). The former has a light and a dark phase, the latter is a noticeably larger bird. Length of *A. b. ipecutiri* 45 cm; *A. b. brasiliensis* 37–39 cm.

Characteristics and Behaviour   A small perching duck with a fairly long tail and rounded wings which have a completely glossy appearance apart from the white on the secondaries. Although very numerous in Brazil, little is known of its habits. It flies swiftly and easily through the trees where it often perches. Non-migratory in the north, but the larger southern sub-species probably moves north in the austral winter.

Habitat   Open lagoons in tropical forest areas, swamps and river marshes.

Distribution   *A. b. ipecutiri* is found in the extreme south of Brazil, Uruguay, and north-eastern Argentina. *A. b. brasiliensis* occurs in eastern Venezuela, Colombia east of the Andes, Guyana, Brazil south to São Paulo, Paraguay, north and eastern Bolivia.

Food   Mainly vegetable matter.

Voice   The male has a strident whistle, the female a loud quack.

Display   Very simple. Consists of head and neck movements only.

Breeding   Nests on the ground amongst vegetation, or in old tree nests of other species. Clutch size six to eight white eggs, average size 49 × 35 mm. Incubation period about 25 days. The downy young are brown above, yellow below, with a dark line through the eye. They are cared for by both adults.

Brazilian Teal female head markings

Maned Wood Duck
(Australian Wood Duck)

Chenonetta jubata

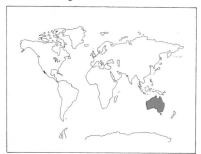

Description The male's mane or crest consists of longish black feathers extending from the crown down the nape. Head and neck are dark brown. Back, rump, tail and belly are black; whilst the breast feathers are mottled in a mixture of greys, black and off-white. Scapulars are grey and black; upper wing coverts grey; the bright green wing mirror is edged with white. Sides of body and flanks have a general appearance of grey, but are very finely marked with wavy lines of black. Bill blackish. Legs and feet olive-black. Length 48 cm.

The female's head and neck are of pale brown with buffish-white bands above and below the eye. Above, the general appearance is grey-brown; breast and flanks are brown mottled with grey and white. Belly and undertail white. Immature birds are similar to the female but a lighter colour version.

Characteristics and Behaviour A shy and very wary species that spends most of its time on land and looks very much like a small Andean Goose. It frequents the edges of swamps and sparsely timbered river banks. Seldom seen on water when it swims slowly and rather awkwardly; is much better adapted for running which it does quite swiftly. When disturbed its slow and usually low flight is accompanied by a sorrowful cry. If alarmed does not adopt the usual duck-like posture with head raised, but remains motionless with head and neck outstretched and quite often slips away quietly and undetected. Flocks of over 2,000 are on record, but up to 100 is the rule.

Habitat Sparsely timbered countryside with short grass and in association with water is the Maned Wood Duck's preference, seldom encountered in the dense vegetation of swamps. Avoids brackish and salt water, and only infrequently met with in thickly forested areas.

Distribution Australia and Tasmania. Most numerous in eastern Australia where there are large agricultural areas, which provide the type of grazing required by this duck.

Food Essentially a grazing bird; a selected area is visited and grazed nightly until the food supply is exhausted; at such a time the flock will seek out new pastures. Where wheat is grown, so the stubble fields offer suitable grazing. Its diet consists almost entirely of vegetable matter but includes very few seeds and less than 1 per cent animal matter.

Voice The mournful 'new' of the female is most characteristic, this is long and drawn out. The male's call is much shorter and higher pitched.

Display The calling females swing their heads from side to side until incited males respond by giving chase, their heads bobbing and breasts puffed.

Breeding After mating the choice of nest site is decided by both birds, and suitable tree holes are carefully inspected. Eggs are laid on the base of the hole without lining but are later covered with down. Whilst the female is incubating the male stands guard in readiness to defend the nest. In north-eastern New South Wales, where a summer rainfall is usual, peak breeding occurs from January to March, but nests

may be found at any time of year. Inland, where the rainfall is unpredictable, the breeding season is erratic as would be expected, but generally speaking it occurs during the months of August and September. The clutch consists of nine to eleven creamy-white eggs averaging in size 57 × 42 mm. Incubation period is 28 days.

Heads of Maned Wood duck
male (*top*) female (*bottom*)

Carolina Wood Duck
(North American Wood Duck)

Aix sponsa

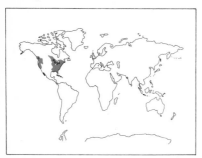

Description The head and long crest of a breeding male are a mixture of metallic greens, blues and violets; the feathers on sides of head are short and velvety. A white line extends backwards from base of bill over the eye and through the crest; another extends from behind the eye through to base of crest. White lines also occur on chin to middle of cheek and up the side of head to junction with neck. Chin and throat are white, mantle iridescent blue. Wings are of metallic blues, greens and blacks, outer webs of primaries are grey shading to silvery-grey distally, the secondaries and tertiaries are tipped with white. Tail is black with a bronzy sheen. Upper breasts purplish chestnut with triangular white spots, lower breast and abdomen are white. Sides are of yellowish buff finely streaked with black, and uppermost feathers tipped alternately with black and white crescents. Sides of rump are reddish-violet, some of the feathers lanceolate and with reddish-orange shaft stripes. Bill, yellow band at base, then scarlet shading through yellow to white; nail and patch between nostrils are black. Legs and feet bright orange-yellow with dusky webs. Male in eclipse resembles female which is various shades of olive-greens or greys above, with sheens that vary from bronze to violet; white below. Chin, throat, also lines around eye and culmen, white. Head, crown, nape and crest, darkish grey with bronzy and purplish sheens. Breast and sides boldly mottled and streaked with greys and medium browns. Bill greyish; legs and feet yellowish with blackish webs. Length 47 cm. Immatures similar to female.

Characteristics and Behaviour The Carolina Wood Duck really is a woodland dweller, where it may be encountered perching on stumps and tree branches. Most commonly met with in pairs, single birds or small groups; its flight through the tops of trees or even lower under a closed canopy of leaves is accomplished quite readily. On forest pools and lakes it tends to keep to shaded areas rather than frequent the more open stretches. When in flight the bill is set at a downward angle, and its white belly, and square tipped tail are apparent. Other ducks with white bellies would have either smaller tails or pointed tails, and would fly with forward pointing bill. An unwary bird and reasonably tame where unmolested.

Habitat Prefers the shallow waters of deciduous and mixed woodlands, particularly those that offer the least disturbance. Uncommon on salt water, but does occur in brackish waters such as the upper reaches of tidal streams and estuaries.

Distribution Breeds in the eastern half of North America, from Nova Scotia westwards to Lake Superior, then north to Lake Winnipeg, and south down to San Antonio in Texas. Also Cuba, southern British Columbia, northern Idaho, throughout Washington; Oregon west from the Cascade Range, and Nevada west of the Sierra Nevada. Winters in the southern half of its eastern breeding range, also within its breeding range in Oregon, Nevada and Cuba.

Food May be described for the most

part as a surface feeder, where it takes the seeds of aquatic plants, also other edible vegetation; is often seen with head and neck immersed in its search for food. Has a liking for acorns and berries. Vegetable matter accounts for 90 per cent of its diet, the remaining 10 per cent comprising such items as insects (taken both on land and in the water), also crustaceans.

Voice The drake, when swimming before his mate: 'ji-ihb, ji-ihb, ji-ihb'. Also a very soft and squeaky 'jeeb'. The female in flight 'oo-eek, oo-eek'. When nest hunting, a low but rapid 'tetetetetetet'.

Display The female incites with rapid pointing movements of the bill in the direction of preferred male. The drake preens behind wing with primaries and secondaries spread very briefly in full view of female. Also swims alongside with back of his head turned towards her.

Breeding A natural tree hole, or the old nest sites of Pileated and other

Woodpeckers are used; nest boxes are also utilized. Will return in successive years to a favourite nesting area, often using the very same site. There is no defence of the breeding area by the Wood Duck, but a male will defend his mate against intruding drakes. The first eggs to be laid are buried in the accumulation of litter in the nesting cavity, nest down being added continually after about the fourth egg. Usually the clutch consists of nine to fourteen ivory white eggs measuring 51 × 39 mm. Incubation continues for 31 to 35 days and is by the female alone; the drake usually follows her back to the nest after feeding but generally does not stay near the nest for anything but a brief period before flying back to his waiting place. This procedure continues until well into incubation before departing to moult. The ducklings usually leave the nest early the day after hatching, and are enticed to do so by the soft 'kuc-kuc-kuc' of the female, immediately they vacate the nest falling to the ground or water below whilst uttering their 'peep peep' call.

[235]

Mandarin

Aix galericulata

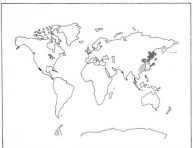

Description The drake in breeding plumage has probably the most elaborate and ornamental appearance of all wildfowl. The forehead and crown are black with metallic green gloss, the longer feathers at the back of the head tinged with purple and bronze. The brown eye is surrounded by a white patch which extends back down the side of the crest. Cheeks are tawny buff, deepening into chestnut on the long feathers forming the ruff at the front and sides of the neck. Upperparts olive glossed with green. The orange chestnut 'sails' are formed by enlarged central tertials. The breast is maroon with a dark gloss, bordered at the rear by black and white stripes. Flanks are orange brown, abdomen and under tail coverts white. Bill red with flesh-coloured nail, legs and feet are yellow. The female has a grey head with white ring round the eye extending back towards the nape, dark brown upperparts, breast and flanks streaked and spotted pale buff. The bill is grey, legs and feet browny yellow. Drake in eclipse similar to female but with a red bill. Length 45 cm. Immatures very similar to females.

Characteristics and Behaviour The Mandarin is a small, long-tailed perching duck with a natural range restricted to eastern Asia. During the last 50 years a feral population has established itself in Britain which now numbers 300 or 400 pairs. This population is centred on Windsor Great Park and nearby areas of Surrey and Berkshire, close to the location of the original release. Other scattered breeding groups are nearly all close to sites of permanent collections. The status of the Mandarin is such that it was formally admitted to the British list in 1971. Flight is strong, usually low down below tree-top level, where it manoeuvres expertly to avoid obstructions. It can also rise easily and acutely from confined surroundings. It feeds both on water, usually on the surface, and on land where it walks easily and frequently perches on low branches. Normally shy and retiring, it prefers to remain close to the cover of trees and bushes where it can take refuge, generally avoiding open ground or extensive sheets of water.

Habitat Mature deciduous woodland or parkland with quiet pools and streams. Prefers woodland with dense secondary growth, especially rhododendron.

Distribution Breeds in Ussuriland, Sakhalin, Manchuria, north-eastern China and Japan. Some populations are sedentary, particularly in Japan, but in China the wintering area is mainly south of the Yangtze. Sedentary in Britain where breeding is recorded in Buckinghamshire, Berkshire, Surrey, Sussex, Kent, Hampshire, Isle of Wight, Hertfordshire, Gloucestershire, Norfolk, Cheshire and Perthshire.

Food Varied; seeds, nuts, snails, insects, rice and fish. In winter in Britain mostly acorns, sweet chestnuts and beechmast. In the East, feeds in rice fields during August and September and consumes quantities of land snails in autumn.

Voice The drake has a weak whistle, the duck a soft quack.

Display During communal courtship the drake erects his crest and orna-

mental sails, he also engages with other drakes in darting wildly side by side, performing threatening gestures such as bill jerking. During pair formation and in defence of territory, drakes will threaten intruders of either sex that may approach too closely. Communal courtship begins in September and continues through the winter months, with peaks in February and March; mainly takes place at times of poor light, such as dusk and dawn.

Breeding April and May in Britain. The nest site is chosen by the female, usually a hole in a tree, and up to 10 m above the ground, occasionally higher. No nest material is collected but the natural hollow is lined with down. Nests are difficult to find in woodland as the birds are very secretive in the vicinity. Clutch size is usually nine to twelve eggs, white and averaging 51 × 37 mm. Incubation is by female alone with the male on guard near by, period 28 to 30 days. The ducklings are very active and secure their own food, mainly insects and larvae, with some small fish and vegetable matter. Young are tended by the female alone, becoming independent after 6 or 7 weeks.

Female Mandarin

[237]

African Pygmy Goose
(Dwarf Goose)

Nettapus auritus

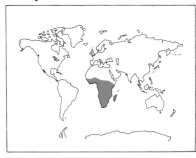

Description The male is a strikingly colourful bird with sides and front of head along with throat and collar, of pure white. A large pea green patch on the side of its neck is bounded by a broad black line. Dark glossy green extends from the crown, down behind the neck, across the back, rump and wings. A large white wing bar occurs across the secondaries. The breast, lower neck and flanks are chestnut, as is the upper back but this is also streaked with dark green. Tail and vent are black, and the remaining under parts are white. The deep yellow bill has a black nail. Legs are black. No eclipse. The female is very similar to her mate but somewhat duller, with the white of head and neck mottled grey. She does not have the large pale green patch on the side of her neck, as in the male. Immature birds are very much like the female but with less-distinctive markings. Length 32 cm.

Characteristics   and   Behaviour Because of its small size it cannot be confused with any other species of goose or duck; seldom leaving the water but when in flight the wing is seen to have a conspicuous central line. The flight is swift and very low over the water surface, and usually only for short distances. A comparatively tame and confiding bird, where it is not hunted, occurring on all suitable waters, especially the quiet backwaters of streams and rivers, etc. where they may be seen swimming around in small groups or pairs. May choose to perch or even roost in trees.

Habitat A resident species on open waters and sluggish rivers, preferably where the water is deep and overgrown with such floating vegetation as water-lilies among which it feeds. May also be encountered in swamps or even estuaries.

Distribution In West Africa, as far north as Senegal and Mauritania; and in East Africa as far north as Ethiopia; also in Madagascar.

Food Aquatic vegetation which is either collected from the surface or they may dive to acquire it; water insects are also taken.

Voice The male has a soft whistle which has been described as 'choo-choo, pee-wee'. The female a weak quack.

Display The male swims close to his intended, with a turning movement of the head, thus displaying the lovely green patches to best advantage.

Breeding Holes in trees are much used but will also utilize similar sites in cliffs or on the ground, even the old bulky tree nests of other birds may be adapted. The nest which is made of grasses may be lined with a variety of materials such as leaves and the like, but no down is added. Breeding occurs at all times of the year, but October to December is the norm in South Africa. The clutch consists of six to seven creamy-white eggs of 43 × 33 mm. The incubation period does not appear to be on record.

Indian Pygmy Goose

(Australian Pygmy Goose or Cotton Teal)

Nettapus coromandelianus coromandelianus

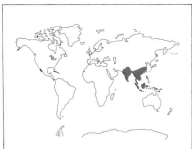

Description The male in breeding dress has a blackish crown and forehead, a thin black line around the eye and a black band running from low behind the neck around the middle of the breast, this contrasting sharply with the otherwise white plumage of head and neck. Both back and mantle are of glossy dark green. Sides of body are white freckled and shaded with grey, underparts are white. The black tail has under coverts mottled brown and white. A large sub-terminal band of white occurs across the brown primaries. Bill and legs are black. Length 33 cm. In the female the crown is black-brown and there is a distinct stripe through the eye. The back is brownish rather than green and both neck and breast are mottled and barred with fine brown marks, rest of body is brownish mottled. Immatures are similar to the females, with no green gloss and a more distinct eye stripe.

Characteristics and Behaviour The Indian Pygmy Goose is not really a goose at all but the smallest of all ducks. It is entirely aquatic spending the daytime in pairs or numerous small groups, floating and swimming with quick jerky movements, often amongst water-lilies or other vegetation; sometimes leaving the water, only to rest on fallen branches

and logs or some muddy bank. Although they rise awkwardly from the water their flight is rapid and they have the ability to twist and turn in and out the trees that might otherwise impede their flight path, in much the same manner as Carolinas or Mandarins. On water the white neck and almost entirely white face of the male readily distinguishes it from the Green Pygmy Goose *N. pulchellus*; the females are much more difficult to differentiate. In flight the males of the two species are also separated, not only by the white neck of *N. c. coromandelianus* but also by the white near the wing tip; in *N. pulchellus* the white is near the wing base. If not molested they become very tame; this is apparent on the ponds in close proximity to human habitation.

Habitat Pygmy Geese show a preference for ponds and isolated creeks where pondweeds and water-lilies grow in profusion. Sluggish rivers and bays with similar vegetative growth are also much frequented.

Distribution India (especially Bengal), Ceylon, Burma, Thailand, Vietnam, China (breeding commonly in the Yangtze valley and has been recorded as far north as Peking), and those islands to the north and north-east of Australia, including the northern part of New Guinea.

Food This is mainly vegetable and acquired by dabbling, but tender leaves and seeds are also taken from plants such as pondweeds, sedges and aquatic grasses. The intake of insects is in the region of 10 per cent. Their feeding action has been likened to that of the Coot (*Fulica atra*).

Voice The continuous rattling cackle of the male is mostly heard when in flight; the female is silent but for the occasional weak squeaky quack.

Breeding The nest site, as with most of the Perching Ducks, is a tree hole –

more often a hole in the trunk and in a tree close to water – but nesting under the eaves of a building and in the walls of ruins, etc. are on record. Little or no attempt is made to construct a nest but a small quantity of down is usually added. The clutch size is variable; from eight up to fifteen eggs have been recorded and these are described as creamy or pearly-white, with no details of incubation. The period of breeding is June to September with a peak during the wet season (July to August).

Australian Pygmy Goose
(Cotton Teal)

Nettapus coromandelianus albipennis

Description Similar to, but somewhat larger than *N. c. coromandelianus*. Length 37 cm.

Distribution Not numerous and restricted to the northern half of Australia's east coast, particularly from Rockhampton to Ingham, with greatest densities in the districts of Ayr, Townsville and Charter Towers. Local numbers tending to reach a peak during the dry seasons (February to March), falling to none during the wet season.

African White-backed Duck

Thalassornis leuconotus leuconotus

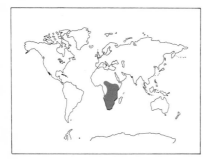

Description The plumage of both sexes is similar, with crown, nape, back of neck, cheeks, chin and throat black, but somewhat speckled yellowy buff. Front and sides of neck and head are a warm buff colour, but the head is heavily spotted black; upperparts, sides and breast are barred with buff on very dark brown; lower back is white. The wings are brown with secondaries and coverts barred buff; underparts are flecked and barred with grey-brown and rufous. The black rump and upper tail coverts have bars of pale buff; under tail coverts have white tips, and the black tail is spotted with buff. The yellow bill is mottled with black and has a light spot at the base. Legs are a light greyish green. Length 43 cm. Immature birds are more uniformly marked with much less pronounced barring.

Characteristics and Behaviour Unlike the Stiff-tails it has a very short tail, but equally stiff and with short coverts. A bird which is uncommon to locally common, and readily distinguished by the light patch at base of bill. It sits low in the water, moving little when encountered but usually remaining on the surface with neck and head held high. If disturbed, is more inclined to flatten itself on the water surface than dive for safety; swims but slowly. Requires a long run across the water in order to take flight, at such time the conspicuous white bar down its back is sufficient to identify it from the Maccoa Duck *Oxyura maccoa*. On land the White-backed Duck appears very awkward indeed. Has been described as Grebe-like in its habits and general appearance; although much of its food is obtained from the water surface, it is a capable diver. Usually met with in small groups of up to six or seven individuals. Quite quarrelsome, but generally of sluggish behaviour.

Habitat Frequents ponds, bays in lakes and other open sheets of water; particularly those where the floating vegetation is not too dense but can be used for cover.

Food Mainly seeds of aquatic plants, but little information has been recorded.

Voice Said to be a soft musical chuckle or a short high-pitched squeaky whistle 'curwee curwee'.

Display Except for an upward stretching of the neck there is no other display on record.

Breeding Breeds in most months of the year except April, August and September; but with peaks in November and December; in the Transvaal these peaks are somewhat earlier. The nest is built among reeds and floats above the water resembling that of a Coot, no down is added. Eggs usually number six to ten, they are yellow-brown and measure 62 × 49 mm. Incubation period not recorded.

Madagascar White-backed Duck

Thalassornis leuconotus insularis

Description Of smaller build and generally more vividly marked than *T. l. leuconotus*, with abdomen darker and crown of denser black.

Distribution Confined to the lowlands of Madagascar up to 760 m.

[242]

Old World Comb Duck
(Knob-billed Duck)

Sarkidiornis melanotos melanotos

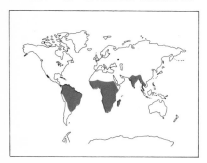

Description The male has white head and neck with varying degrees of black spotting; nape and back of neck are heavily spotted and in the breeding season may have a tinge of golden yellow. The white lower parts and the light grey flanks contrast sharply with the bright metallic blue-green of the upper parts. The overall effect is that of a conspicuous black and white bird with bronze coloured secondaries. When in full breeding dress the under tail coverts are of orange-yellow in front of which is a black band; sometimes a row of black-tipped feathers form an incomplete bar across the otherwise white breast. Bill and knob (or comb) black, the latter varies in size being at its largest during the breeding season. Legs are dark grey. Length 77 cm. The female is considerably smaller and duller, lightly mottled below with brown, does not possess the black band on breast and near tail, nor the knob or comb on her bill. Otherwise similar to the male. Immatures are light buffy brown; with darker brown crown, eye stripe, mantle, wings and tail. The flanks are spotted dark brown on a pale buffy brown ground.

Characteristics and Behaviour
Comb Ducks are, by reputation, silent birds. They are also somewhat shy by nature and spend much of the daytime resting on sandbanks or islets; feeding early morning or late evening. Their slow wing beat is deceptive and wrongly suggests that they are slow in flight. They perch quite readily and their strong claws enable them to cling to trees. Numbers are subject to considerable fluctuations, moving with the rains as they search for food; otherwise mainly sedentary. Flocks of 100 are on record but usually seen singly or in small groups.

Habitat Flat open areas with an abundance of clean water and marshes, and an adequate choice of trees large enough to provide nest sites.

Distribution Throughout Africa south of the Sahara, Madagascar and southern Asia, particularly Ceylon, India, Burma and Thailand. Whilst it is very rare south of the Orange River and in north-eastern South Africa, it is nevertheless regularly recorded in Basutoland.

Food It shows a preference for the seeds of water-lilies and grasses, and is occasionally regarded as a pest on agricultural land. The diet also includes locusts and the larvae of aquatic insects.

Voice Generally regarded as a silent bird, but when in flight has been heard to utter a rather hoarse whistling sound.

Display At the approach of the breeding season, male birds are seen to confront each other with head and neck held high and wings slightly lifted. For several minutes they will strike each other with their wings until one or other admits defeat by taking flight. A courting male will approach a female and display to her by lifting his chest, and then with wings slightly raised and neck curved, the head is moved gently from side to side and regularly dipped downwards.

Breeding Although nests have been recorded on the ground in long grass and amongst stones, they are more usually located in the holes of dead or dying trees. The same site is often used in successive years. No down is included in the nest and the five to eight pale yellow eggs measure 63 × 44 mm. Incubation requires 30 days.

American Comb Duck

Sarkidiornis melanotos sylvatica

Description Very similar to *S. m. melanotos* but smaller, and the male has sides and flanks of black not pale grey.

Distribution Found in Tropical South America, very roughly north and east of a line drawn from the equator on the north-west coast, to Rio de la Plata.

Muscovy Duck

Cairina moschata

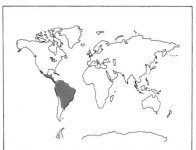

Description　In the wild, both sexes are of similar plumage, mainly glossy black with both a greenish and purplish gloss. The upper and under wing coverts are of pure white, as are the axillaries. In the drake the feathers of forehead and upper neck are quite long, and combined form both a crest and mane; these being much reduced in the female. The skin round eyes and bill (of the drake) is bare and blackish with pinkish, purplish or blackish wart-like caruncles; these becoming most enlarged coinciding with breeding. Bill is dusky with a pink tip, and also a narrow pink band in the drake. Legs and feet are black. Length of male 82 cm, of female 65 cm. Immatures are less glossy than adults, also browner and with little or no white on wing coverts. No eclipse plumage according to some authorities, but this is questioned by others.

The domesticated Muscovy is much heavier, and has larger caruncles; it occurs in a variety of colour forms, ranging from all white (occasionally), black streaked with white, some shade of buffy brown, and not uncommonly, even to bluish.

Characteristics and Behaviour　The truly wild Muscovy is a beautiful and well-proportioned bird, large although not heavy, but with short legs and large feet that tend to mar its overall appearance. At night-time it roosts on large branches, and also spends part of the daytime perched in trees. Usually seen in small groups only, but on occasions flocks of up to fifty or so have been recorded. A wary bird, but has been much persecuted in parts of its range, and here the numbers have greatly diminished. A sedentary species, moving only in search of food. Outside the breeding season the sexes tend to remain apart, living in separate groups.

Habitat　Shows a preference for forest streams, or ponds and marshes in forested regions; except during the rainy season when the savannas are flooded, the Muscovy is rarely encountered far from its woodland habitat.

Distribution　Its natural range is Mexico (from Sinaloa, Nuevo Leon and Tamaulipas), south to the Peruvian coast in the west; and the River Plate estuary, Argentina in the east.

Food　Mainly vegetable items are taken, including seeds of aquatic plants; but the diet also includes crabs, fish and insects. Are known to break open the nests of termites with their powerful bills.

Voice　The male is silent except when threatened or during display, at such times a 'hissing' note is uttered. The female has a soft quack, which is used when afraid or excited, also whilst tending her young.

Display　During the breeding season, males are very aggressive and violent fights occur between individuals; at such times the wings, hooked bills, and sharp-clawed feet are used effectively. In display the male will engage in a rhythmic bobbing of the head forwards and backwards, and with neck outstretched and crest raised, the wings are partially raised and the long tail vibrated.

Breeding　The male Muscovy appears to be polygamous, with one

male controlling a number of females. Nests are built by the female in hollow trees, or between branches, and at heights varying from 3 to 20 m; although ground nests are on record, these are far from common. Down is used to line the nest and the usual clutch size is eight to fifteen white eggs with a greenish tinge averaging 67 × 46 mm. Incubation continues for about 35 days, after which the female takes the responsibility of caring for the young.

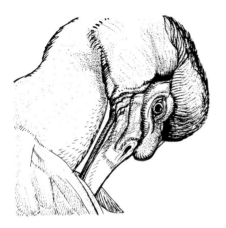

Muscovy drake showing facial warts around the eye

Hartlaub's Duck

Cairina hartlaubi

Description The adult male has the head and part of the neck black, with a white patch on the forehead. The body plumage, including the lower neck, is chestnut shading to olive-brown on the rump, tail and scapulars. The primaries are also olive-brown, and the upper wing coverts china blue. Bill black with a greyish band near the tip, and a black nail; becoming swollen at the base during the breeding season. Iris reddish-brown, legs and feet pale olive to dark brown, sometimes with black markings. Individuals occur with more variable white on the head, extending from the base of the bill to the crown, and below the eye. Females resemble males but are smaller and have browner heads. Length 55 to 60 cm. Immatures are much like the female but with buffish tips to feathers of underparts.

Characteristics   and   Behaviour Smaller than the White-winged Wood Duck, approximately Mallard size, with rounded wings and a long tail. The fairly uniform plumage appears black at a distance. A true forest duck, it spends much of the day perching in tall trees, feeding mainly in the evening close to the roost. It is not particularly wary, but if approached too closely will often seek cover at the edge of the water rather than fly. Flight is not rapid. It is non-migratory and usually encountered singly, in pairs, or small family parties, occasionally groups of up to twenty. Not often seen on open stretches of water.

Habitat Tropical rain forest with pools and streams that are densely vegetated at the edges. Mangrove swamps, etc.

Distribution West and equatorial Africa from Sierra Leone and Liberia, east to southern Sudan, Cameroun, Gabon and Zaire; south to northern Angola.

Food Both vegetable and animal matter including aquatic insects and larvae, fresh-water snails and shrimps, worms, spiders, etc.

Voice Not normally very vocal, but various calls have been described. When taking flight a quick repeated quacking is sometimes used. Other notes include a harsh 'karr-karr' and a softer 'whit-whit' from feeding birds.

Display Male and female face each other, bowing heads and touching bills; the male whistling wheezily and the female making clucking sounds.

Breeding Little is known about the breeding behaviour of this species in the wild, where most nests are probably in holes in trees. In captivity the clutch size is normally eight to twelve, average size of the eggs 53 × 40 mm. Incubation by the female takes about 32 days. The downy young are dark brown above; with sides of head, underparts, and patches on wing and side of rump, yellowish. There is a dark line through the eye. Bill, legs and feet are black. Sharp claws enable the ducklings to climb easily in their early stages. Fledging period is about 8 weeks.

Hartlaub's ducks (male on right). Courtship pair facing one another touching bills

White-winged Wood Duck

Cairina scutulata

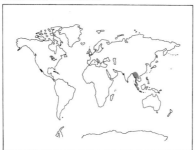

Description Adults have the head and neck white, densely spotted with black. The extent of white is variable, some birds from the southern part of the range have had completely white heads and necks, and others with white extending to the breast and mantle have been recorded. Mantle, rump, and upper tail coverts are black glossed with green. Primaries are brown, secondaries blue-grey, and upper coverts white. Upper breast black glossed with green. Underparts deep reddish-brown. The bill is orange with dark markings; iris orange-red; legs and feet orange. Females are much like males, but duller and smaller. Length 60–70 cm. Immatures are browner than the adults.

Characteristics and Behaviour A large perching duck with broad wings, short legs, and feet equipped with strong sharp claws. It is sedentary throughout its range. Habitually seeks shaded areas, perching during the daytime in dense rain forest, where it can be very difficult to see. It feeds within the forest on shady pools and streams, but during the dry season has to resort to open swamps. On such occasions, it usually flights just before dusk, returning to the forest as dawn approaches, although it will remain longer if undisturbed. It is a good diver and can rise easily from the water. Flight is usually low, over open country or amongst trees, often calling as it goes. The decline in numbers which started in the first half of the century has continued and accelerated in the second half, making the White-winged Wood Duck currently one of the most threatened species of wildfowl. The present situation is due mainly to loss of suitable habitat, through felling of the forest for timber production and agricultural purposes. This has resulted in increased human disturbances and increased accessibility of the remaining suitable areas. These are now highly fragmented with resultant isolation of small populations.

Habitat Dense tropical rain forest with sluggish streams and weedy ponds, ideally with open swamp marshes near by for alternative feeding in dry season, when it will also visit wet stubbles and rice fields. Seldom on open water.

Distribution Bangladesh, north-eastern Assam, Sumatra. Probably northern Burma. Former haunts in Thailand, Malaysia and Indo-China are apparently unoccupied.

Food Varies according to season but includes a lot of animal matter. Molluscs, amphibians, worms, small fish and insects. Also seeds and some aquatic vegetation.

Voice The flight call is a long bugling note, but whistles, hisses and grunts are also recorded.

Display Not elaborate. Male swims with neck outstretched and making pumping movements.

Breeding Season variable according to location. In Assam eggs are laid in April or May, but much earlier in Indonesia in the southern part of the range. Nests of wild birds have been little studied but are stated to be in holes in trees, or placed on thick branches. In captivity the clutch size varies from six to thirteen, the eggs are white with a

greenish tinge, average size 67 × 49 mm. The incubation period is about 35 days. Downy young are brown above with yellowish face and underparts, and yellow patches on the wings and sides. There is a dark stripe behind the eye and another slightly below. Growth rate is slow, the fledging period being about 14 weeks.

White-winged Wood duckling showing characteristic extra eye-stripe

Gambian Spur-winged Goose

Plectropterus gambensis gambensis

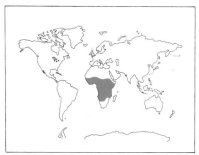

Description The adult male has a patch of bare, dull red skin on the front of the head and face. The back of the head, nape, mantle, scapulars and wings are black heavily glossed with metallic green and bronze. There is a red patch of bare skin on each side of the neck. The front of the breast, abdomen, and under tail coverts are white; tail black. The bill is pinkish, frontal knob reddish, legs and feet pink. The female is smaller, has less-extensive patches of bare skin, and a smaller frontal knob. Both sexes have a sharp spur projecting forward from the bend of the wing which shows clearly in flight. Length 90–100 cm. Immatures are brown above, buffish and brown below, and have no bare patches on the head. The more northerly sub-species (*P. g. gambensis*) has much more white in the plumage than (*P. g. niger*), which has a completely black neck and breast, also less-extensive bare patches, and frontal knob absent.

Characteristics and Behaviour A large, powerful, goose-like perching duck with broad wings, long legs and neck, and generally unattractive appearance. One of the largest species of wildfowl with males weighing 6 or 7 kg, and up to 10 kg being recorded. Feeding takes place mostly in the evening or early morning, but on moonlight nights may continue through until dawn; causing considerable damage to crops. Regular flighting takes place to good feeding areas, the birds returning to roost on open water in swamps, or to perch in trees. The flight is strong but not very fast. Often occurs in very large flocks, but is shy and wary. Non-migratory, but local movements determined by the rains and food supply.

Habitat Swamps, lakes, flooded meadows, grassy plains, farmland and cultivated regions, large rivers especially with sandbanks and marginal vegetation. Avoids dense forest.

Distribution Africa south of the Sahara, from Gambia, east to the Sudan and Ethiopia, south to Angola in the west, and the Zambezi River in the east. South of the Zambezi *P. g. gambensis* is replaced by *P. g. niger*, but the species is absent from the arid south-west.

Food Mainly vegetable. Young shoots, and grasses, seeds, fruit; cultivated crops including sweet potatoes and ground nuts.

Voice The male has a squeaky, whistling voice used in display, the female is normally silent.

Display Very simple, only ruffling of feathers on neck and scapulars, recorded.

Breeding Season very variable. February to July in Zambia, January to May in Rhodesia, and September to April in South Africa. The nest is usually on the ground amongst thick grasses, or in reedbeds, but has also been found among rocks in mountainous country, in holes in termite nests, in old tree nests, and very occasionally in holes in trees. It is a large structure of reeds, grasses and roots, etc. lined with down. Clutch size varies from seven to twelve, sometimes more; the

eggs are glossy ivory, average size 73 × 56 mm. Incubation is by the female alone, the period is unrecorded. The downy young are creamy-yellow, darker above, with paler marks on wings and rump. On hatching they are led to a suitable stretch of water for better protection from predators.

European Black Scoter
(Common Scoter)

Melanitta nigra nigra

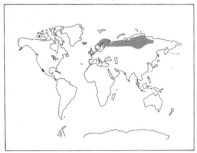

Description The drake is entirely black with a metallic gloss. There is a black knob at base of bill; between this and the bill tip there is a yellow patch. Legs and feet dusky with blackish webs and joints. In the American Black Scoter (*M. n. americana*) the bright orange-yellow of the knob extends forward to beyond the nostrils, the edges and tip of upper mandible being black. The female is sooty brown with a paler area, below the eye to mid-way down the neck, being sharply defined. Bill black without knob or yellow patch. Length 47 cm. Immature males similar to female but paler on lower breast.

Characteristics and Behaviour Readily distinguishable from both Velvet Scoter (*M. fusca fusca*) and Surf Scoter (*M. perspicillata*) by the complete absence of white in plumage, even more so when in flight. The duck's dark cap on an otherwise pale head is quite noticeable when in flight even at a distance. A bird which seems to prefer the less-sheltered areas and may be seen out on open waters in scattered groups or strung out as individuals swimming swiftly or diving. In flight they occur as a string of birds or as scattered groups, and will frequently change formation. They fly with more apparent ease than the Velvet or Surf Scoter, on wings that produce a whistling sound. Except during times of breeding, they are seldom seen on land.

Habitat During the breeding season Black Scoters may be found on high ground and usually in close proximity of water, ponds and lakes, etc. especially in the forest-tundra zone. At other times, on lakes and estuaries, but chiefly in coastal waters. It is very vulnerable to oil pollution. Between 1969 and 1971, spillages occurring in the Baltic accounted for the deaths of over 7,000 birds.

Distribution During the breeding season, Scotland, Shetlands and Orkneys (Northern Ireland occasionally), Iceland (Spitsbergen occasionally); also northern Sweden, Finland, Russia, most of Siberia both above and below the Arctic Circle. Winters in the coastal waters around the British Isles, and along the coasts of western Europe (up to 250,000 in the Baltic), and the coast of West Africa. The American Black Scoter breeds along the west coast of Alaska and in north-east Asia, east from the River Lena to include Anadyrland, Kamchatka Peninsula and north Kuriles. Wintering on both the Atlantic and the Pacific coasts, with the majority of birds in the Bering–Pacific area, especially the coastal waters of southeast Alaska, and British Columbia.

Food In winter, predominantly molluscs (Blue Mussels and Periwinkles), also crustaceans. During the summer months, midge larvae, frogs, fish spawn, and tadpoles. Animal matter accounting for 90 per cent of its food, the remaining 10 per cent being principally algae and the roots of pondweeds.

Voice Noisier than the other Scoters, the drake with his musical call 'wheeuu', also a prolonged and plaintive 'cour-cour-cour-loo, courlou', the duck a low growling 'krrr-r-r-r-r' as is usual with diving ducks.

Display Head-shaking by the drake,

this usually preceded the 'rush'; when with head lowered he paddles furiously across the water surface for 4 feet or so churning up spray in all directions.

Breeding Full clutches may be found from the end of May onwards, but mostly early to mid-June. The nest site may be the edge of a pond or large lake, often an island in a lake and usually in a dryish place amongst grasses, sedges, under cover of willows or dwarf birches. The eight to nine creamy or ivory coloured eggs measure 65 × 45 mm and are incubated by the duck alone for a period of 27 to 28 days. Males leave the sitting females and journey to their moulting areas off the coasts of Britain or the Netherlands, also off the Danish coast where the number of moulting birds often reaches 200,000.

Black (*top*) and Surf Scoter (*bottom*)

Eastern Harlequin Duck

Histrionicus histrionicus histrionicus

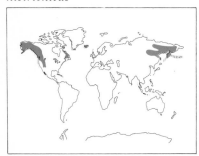

Description The male in breeding plumage has head and neck of medium greyish-blue with a glossy black band extending from base of bill over the crown and down the nape. Front part of cheek is white and this continues as a band upward and over the eye, where it becomes reddish chestnut as it passes downward on each side of the nape. There is a large white spot on the ears and a further one on the sides of the neck. The chin, throat, and front of neck are black; there is a narrow white band at base of neck and a wider band on sides of the breast; both of these white areas are bordered black. Upperback, mantle, and breast are of slaty grey. The white scapulars are narrowly bordered with grey on outer webs and form a broad white band; rump and tail are black. Most of the sides, and the flanks are rich chestnut; abdomen dark brownish-grey. Innermost secondaries have white webs bordered black; the coverts are dark brown but tipped with black and white. There is a small white spot on each side of the black rump. Bill bluish-grey, legs and feet grey with dark webs. Female dusky brown with whitish ear patch and paler areas on each side at base of bill and in front of eyes. Underparts are mottled brown and white. The male in eclipse is similar to female but darker,

and the whitish patches on head are more distinct, also has white markings on wings and side of breast. Length 43 cm.

Characteristics and Behaviour When swimming or flying, quite often encountered in small compact groups, more so than any other species of duck. The flight is rapid and usually low over the water. Often seen standing in shallow waters, or sitting on rocks in midstream. Even though so conspicuously marked, the effect is such that the bird's outline is broken against the turbulent waters of a fast flowing and rocky stream or river. They are expert swimmers and most adept divers, being the only duck in the Northern Hemisphere capable of feeding in fast-flowing rivers. Quite a tame bird, especially so in Iceland.

Habitat In summer, requires an inland habitat that offers shallow fast-flowing rivers, with an adequate supply of aquatic insect larvae; and sufficient scrub or grass cover for nesting purposes. Harlequins usually move to the nearest coastal waters during the winter months and do not have long migratory flights.

Distribution There are two races, the Eastern Harlequin (*H. h. histrionicus*) breeds in Iceland and southern Greenland, south-eastern Baffin Island and Labrador. Whilst the Pacific Harlequin (*H. h. pacificus*), which has a somewhat larger bill, breeds in eastern Siberia, the mountainous regions west of Lake Baikal, the Anadyr basin and Chukchi Peninsulas, Kamchatka, Sakhalin and the Kurile Islands, Alaska, Yukon, British Columbia, the mountainous regions of south-western Alberta, the north-eastern half of Washington, the north-east corner of Oregon, northern half of Idaho and into Montana and Wyoming, also California east of Sacramento.

Food Almost entirely animal, any vegetable intake probably accidental.

When at sea mainly crustaceans and molluscs; on inland water in summer, the larvae and pupae of Diptera, especially black flies, but also midges. The larvae of caddis flies are often collected from underneath stones on the river beds.

Voice A high-pitched squeak uttered by both sexes, but mainly during display.

Display Inciting by female, when head is first lowered with chin touching or almost touching water, then rotated from one side to the other. Drakes, often in small groups, will rotate on the water so that all parts of the plumage are dis-played to the females. Also the head may be thrown back with the bill held pointing upwards and open wide. Wing flapping with body reared out of the water, or whilst standing out of water; the wings being flapped twice rapidly.

Breeding Harlequins are late nesters, from the last week of May in Iceland, or to late June in more arctic conditions. The nest consists of grasses, etc. down being added as the five to six eggs are laid. They are creamy-yellow when fresh and measure 58 × 41 mm. Incubation is by the female alone and continues for 28 to 30 days. When incubation has commenced the drakes leave for the coast, where they gather in flocks prior to moulting.

Long-tailed Duck
(Oldsquaw)

Clangula hyemalis

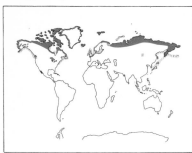

Description   The drake has three distinct plumages, but is most handsome in winter dress (November–April), for it is then that courtship and pair formation take place. During this period he appears as a mainly black and white bird. Crown white with an area of yellowish-orange; nape, back of neck, and upper breast, white; sides of head pale grey but with a white ring around the eyes, and a large sooty brown patch on rear of cheek. The lower breast is blackish-brown, as are the backs of the wings and the tail (the streamers being extremely long and on occasions reach 24 cm). Sides are pearly grey, underparts white. Bill slaty blue with a broad pink band and a blackish nail. Legs and feet pale bluish-grey with dusky webs. In spring/summer plumage (April–July), the drake has head (apart from an oval area of pale grey around the eyes), neck, breast and back, dark chocolate brown; but feathers on the back have chestnut borders. Rest of plumage as in winter. In eclipse (August–October), similar to summer plumage, but breast appears somewhat barred, and there is a slightly larger area of grey on the face, the crown and upper nape are whitish. The female in summer is similar to the male in summer, but head and neck are paler, and grey area around the eyes extends backwards as a line down the neck, also breast and sides are barred and mottled in pale brown and whitish. No tail streamer, and bill slaty blue. Length 53 cm. Immatures are similar to female in summer plumage.

Characteristics and Behaviour   The Long-tailed Duck is the only member of its genus and bears no close relation to any other duck, an added distinction being its three very different plumage changes annually. The flight is swift during which there is a tendency to roll from side to side, thereby showing the belly and the back alternately. Of all the sea ducks this is the most accomplished diver, reaching depths of over 20 m and staying submerged for up to a full minute, with average dives of 40 seconds duration. They seldom come to land outside the breeding season, but are none the less capable of an erect and easy walk. Gregarious, may be seen flying in flocks of 50–100 birds which tend to split into smaller groups after alighting on water. Very much a bird of the open seas where they are noisy and very active, feeding by day in small groups and usually closer to shore.

Habitat   A tundra breeding species throughout most of its range, but also occurs in the semi-tundra of Iceland and parts of Scandanavia. Seems to be absent from large areas that are void of lakes and rivers. In the winter months occurs in northern coastal waters, particularly those remaining open at high latitudes.

Distribution   Is said to breed farther north than any other duck, and may be found throughout the Northern Hemisphere's tundra and tundra–forest zones (740,000 breeding pairs in western Siberia). Most of Europe's 100,000 wintering birds occur in the Baltic. Also the Caspian Sea, Kamchatka, the Kuriles, northern Japan, the Sea of Okhotsk, and the north Bering Sea. In America from the Aleutians down the Pacific coast to Oregon, on the Atlantic

coast from Newfoundland south to Chesapeake Bay. Also the Great Lakes (excluding Lake Erie) and the south-west coast of Greenland.

Food About 90 per cent animal matter such as crustaceans: amphipods, mud crabs, shrimps and crayfish; a large number of molluscs: mussels, periwinkles and whelks; also insects and fish. The remaining 10 per cent including the seeds of grasses and pondweeds.

Voice Very noisy, especially during the period late winter to spring. During display a musical 'a-oo, ah-oo, a-oo-ah' the last syllable being emphasized. Also a loud resonant 'ow owooolee' which is the duck's commonest call and heard mostly at sea, very impressive when many birds call together.

Display This occurs from winter through to spring. Many drakes, with their tail streamers held straight up, will congregate around a female; the neck is then extended fully and lowered towards the duck. This may be followed by turning the back of the head towards her. The female will display by a rapid chin-lifting movement while keeping the head well down on the shoulders.

Breeding Pairs usually nest in isolation but in some areas Long-tailed Duck's nests may occur comparatively close together. One such place is Lake Myvatn in Iceland, where there are known to be in the order of 700 breeding pairs. A dry site, but not too far from fresh water, is desirable, a thick cover of grasses or sedges is chosen, often concealed by dwarf willows or under the low growth of a birch or spruce. An accumulation of dry grasses may be added if available, with down being included later. A late nester with full clutches from mid-May in the warmer regions; beginning of June in Iceland and north-west Alaska; on to early July in the Canadian high-arctic, north-west Greenland and Siberia. A normal clutch would be five to seven eggs in some shade of buffish or greyish-olive, average size 54 × 38 mm. Incubation by female alone for 24 to 26 days. The drake stays near by on some tundra pool during the early stages of incubation before leaving to moult.

[259]

European Goldeneye
(Common Goldeneye)

Bucephala clangula clangula

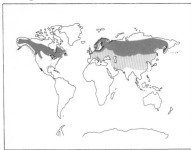

Description The drake in breeding plumage has back and head black, but glossed with metallic green. A roundish white cheek spot and a white neck. The white elongated scapulars have wide black borders on both webs; wing coverts and secondaries are white; primaries and tertiaries are black. There is a broad black border on outer webs of feathers on upper limits of the sides and flanks. The thighs and vent have brownish-grey feathers with white tips. Bill almost black; legs and feet orange-yellow with dusky webs. Female has head of dark chocolate-brown; most of neck, and region from lower breast to vent, white; the medium grey feathers from vent to tail are pale at tips. Upper-parts are mottled blackish-brown and slate grey, many of the feathers having white edges. Bill blackish with a narrow band of dusky orange near the black nail. Legs and feet are yellow with dusky webs. The male in eclipse is more or less a bright version of female, but with a black bill. Length of male 47 cm, female 43 cm. Immature males similar to male in eclipse and do not acquire the white face spot until their second year. The American Goldeneye (*B. c. americana*) is a sub-species, slightly larger than *B. c. clangula* and with a heavier bill.

Characteristics and Behaviour For most of the year the drake's plumage is of a very distinct black and white pattern. When on water it will be noticed that no dark areas extend down to the water line, except at the rear. May be distinguished from Barrow's Goldeneye (*B. islandica*) at distance, as they exhibit a larger area of white and have no black extending down the forward sides. At closer range the white crescent face patch and the white spotted scapulars of Barrow's are apparent. There is, however, no way to distinguish the females at distance. Goldeneyes are swift in flight, and usually occur in small compact groups, the loud whistling sound produced by their wings is characteristic, and by it, experienced wildfowlers can identify flying Goldeneye on the darkest nights. They are daytime feeders and dive, not only for food, but find underwater travel easier than swimming on the surface.

Habitat During spring and summer when breeding, lakes, ponds, shallow rivers and slow-running streams, especially those with vegetative marginal growth, and within close proximity of mature woodlands; although the latter is not necessarily essential as some birds prove. At other times, on inland waters to moult; also shallow coastal bays and estuaries.

Distribution Breeds in the forest taiga zone of Scandinavia and the USSR, west to Kamchatka, also south to Germany, Poland, British Isles, Switzerland, Yugoslavia, Bulgaria and Roumania. Winters in the southern Baltic (up to 100,000), south to the Black and Caspian Seas (50,000), the northeast coasts of the Mediterranean, Asia Minor, Persia, northern India and Burma. Also China, Korea, Formosa and Japan. The American sub-species (*B. c. americana*) breeds across North America from Newfoundland and Labrador in the east, to British Columbia and Alaska in the west, but excluding the north-eastern half of Mackenzie,

Keewatin, and northern Quebec. Nowhere is it a common nester. Winters in the Atlantic coastal waters from the Gulf of St Lawrence to South Carolina. Also along the Mississippi and Ohio Rivers, and inland along the north coast of the Gulf of Mexico. On the Pacific coast, from the Aleutians south to mid-California.

Food In winter, mainly mussels and crustaceans such as shrimps and small crabs. During the summer months, feeds on midge and caddis-fly larvae taken from pools in its woodland habitat. Also fresh-water mussels, frogs and tadpoles. The vegetable items include pondweeds, etc.

Voice For most of the year a silent bird. The male utters a piercing 'speer speer', also a rasping 'quee-reek'; the female a harsh croak-like call common to most diving ducks.

Display This is very elaborate and cannot be dealt with in full. It includes such movements by the drake as 'head flicking'. This consists of holding the bill downwards at an angle of 35° and turn-ing head once to the right and once to the left. This usually follows one of the many other movements, such as the 'head-throw' where with bill held horizontal the head is thrust straight forward then lowered backwards on to the rump; performed slowly or quickly, and on occasions ending with a kick which produces an upward spray of water.

Breeding The preference is for a natural cavity in a tree, but the disused nest-holes of larger Woodpeckers are often used. Nowhere is there an abundance of natural sites and this results in strong competition between females. Nest-boxes in trees, or attached to poles, are readily accepted; in treeless areas burrows or crevices between rocks are used. Laying commences about the first week of May, much later and into early June at the northern limits of its range. The eggs are bluish-green, an average clutch containing nine to ten eggs, measuring 59 × 42 mm (61 × 44 mm in *B. c. americana*). Incubation is by female alone for a period of 28 days, the drake staying in the vicinity at least during part of this period.

[261]

Barrow's Goldeneye

Bucephala islandica

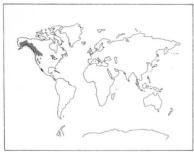

Description The male's breeding plumage is very similar to that of the Common Goldeneye, but the black head has a sheen of metallic bluish-violet, and the white facial spot between side of bill base and eye is crescent-shaped. Upperparts are mostly black and with a similar sheen as the head, the black extending down the sides forward of the wing. (There is a row of white spots on each wing, these being a good aid to field identification.) The neck and most of underparts are white. Bill black; legs and feet pale yellow. The female is brownish above with white underparts and cannot be distinguished from that of the Common Goldeneye. Bill orange-yellow flecked with brown at base (is the most common in North America); elsewhere, blackish with a narrow band of dusky orange near black nail. Legs yellowish with dusky webs. Males in eclipse, and immatures, very similar to those of *B. c. clangula*. Length 52 cm.

Characteristics and Behaviour Distinguished from Common Goldeneye, by crescent-shaped spot on face, and row of white spots on wing, as already mentioned. In parts of their range, they roost at night on fresh-water lakes, or in sheltered bays, dispersing at daybreak to feed in small groups or pairs. A strong flier once airborne, but on windless days may have to run over water surface for some distance to achieve this. As with the Common Goldeneye a whistling sound is produced by the beating wings, but perhaps not quite so pronounced. On short journeys the flight may be as low as 1 m above the water, but at much higher altitudes when travelling some distance overland.

Habitat Open water is essential, and lakes with thick aquatic vegetation and having a depth of 2–5 m are particularly favoured during the summer, even to altitudes of 10,000 feet as in the Rockies. During spring and autumn, lakes and ponds at lower elevations are frequented. In winter the majority of birds are to be found in sheltered bays and inlets of coastal waters, where they can find adequate supplies of food in the shallow waters amid the rocky reefs and ledges.

Distribution Breeds in north-west Iceland (about 1,000 pairs at Lake Mývatn and along the River Laxá), and winters along the southern coast. Also breeds and winters in south-western Greenland, in the Godthaab and Frederikshaab districts. In North America, breeds in north-west Labrador and north-east Quebec, the principal breeding area being British Columbia and into western Alberta, also in southern parts of the Yukon and Alaska. In western USA it breeds locally in Washington, Montana, Wyoming, Oregon and California. Wintering from the eastern Aleutians down the west coast to Los Angeles. Down the east coast from the Gulf of St Lawrence to Long Island.

Food This is obtained solely by diving, and the diet is very similar to that of the Common Goldeneye, with perhaps a larger intake of insects. About 80 per cent animal matter including the nymphs of dragonflies and other Odonata, the larvae of caddis flies, and various water-beetles. Also molluscs and an assortment of crustaceans. The 20 per cent vegetable matter includes

[262]

seeds of pondweeds and the leaves of underwater plants.

Voice The drake is silent except during display when he makes a grunting noise described as 'e-eng'; the duck has a grating croak or growl.

Display Similar, in some instances, to that described for Common Goldeneye. Drakes will defend their territory against other drakes of the species; less frequently so the duck, which will occasionally threaten other females who venture too close to her mate.

Breeding Usually nests in natural holes of dead or dying trees, often in the disused nest-hole of a Pileated Woodpecker. In treeless areas, crevices amongst rocks, holes in lava rock, under large stones, or in thick scrub cover. Early clutches are completed by the beginning of May, but most by the third week of that month. An average clutch would contain eight to ten bluish-green eggs, measuring 62 × 44 mm. Incubation is by the female alone, begins with the last egg and continues for 30 days. Most drakes leave during the early stages of incubation, gathering in small groups of up to fifteen by late May or early June, for the purpose of moulting.

Buffle-head

Bucephala albeola

Description The breeding male has head and upper neck black with sheens of bluish, greenish and violet. Two broad bands of white extend from behind the eye to meet at back of head; lower neck is white. Black above with secondaries and coverts white; rump black; upper tail coverts light grey. Breast, sides and flanks white; abdomen off-white. Bill bluish-grey; legs and feet pinkish. Female has head and neck sooty brown, with a broad white patch on side of head behind the eye (but much narrower than that on male, and not meeting behind the head). Upperparts blackish-brown many of the feathers with greyish tips, there is a white area on some of the secondaries and on several of the greater coverts. Underparts greyish-white. Bill blackish, legs and feet fawny pink. Male in eclipse similar to female but head blackish and white patch larger. Length of male 39 cm, female 36 cm. Immatures very similar to female, adult plumage is acquired in second year.

Characteristics and Behaviour About Teal size, very much smaller than other Goldeneyes. Short necked with a head that is often puffed out to almost twice its natural size, and a smallish somewhat stubby bill. A very active, restless and beautiful duck that takes to the wing easily, when its flight over water is usually low with 'whirring' wings, and often in the company of one or a few others of its kind. There is no audible 'whistling' of the wings as with the Common and Barrow's Goldeneye. During daytime will rest on the water as if asleep; seems not to care for rough waters, diving to escape the crest of an oncoming wave, and during such conditions it is doubtful if they attempt to feed.

Habitat During the breeding season, fresh-water habitats associated with mixed woodlands. The larger lakes with extensive marginal vegetation are not particularly favoured, and even less at higher altitudes. In winter the Buffle-head is found in sheltered coastal waters; also on inland waters of varying size that remain unfrozen.

Distribution Restricted to North America, from central Alaska through the Yukon and central southern Mackenzie, most of British Columbia and Alberta, Saskatchewan except the southern and north-eastern extremes, the southern half of Manitoba, Ontario except inland along Hudson Bay, also central southern Quebec. Breeds sparingly in extreme north of Washington, central western half of Oregon, eastern California north of Sacramento, also Idaho/Montana/Wyoming at the junction of the state boundaries. Winters, very approximately, in the western, southern and eastern states of the USA.

Food During spring and summer when feeding in fresh-water habitats, mainly insects but also seeds, in the approximate ratio of 75:25. At other times when at sea, mostly crustaceans and molluscs, with very few insects.

Voice Not a very vocal species. The drake utters a growling call in winter and spring. During display when the duck is following a drake, she will be heard to utter a growling oft repeated 'grrrk' or 'ik-ik-ik-ik-ik'.

Display The duck's main response to

the drake is 'following'. This she does quite energetically, paddling at great speed from some distance behind until close-in behind his tail. With the drakes, 'head bobbing' is that most frequently employed. It starts from a rather crouched position with the head lowered, which is then thrust rapidly upwards until neck is fully extended, then lowered with equal rapidity until bill is almost touching water. This is usually followed by 'head shaking' and raising the crest. Display flights are often preceded by a bout of 'wing lifting'.

Breeding The nest site is chosen by the female and often used again in consecutive years. Like the Goldeneyes a natural tree-hole is sought, but the disused nesting-hole of a Flicker is also a favourite choice. Often Starlings or Squirrels will take possession of a nest cavity by eviction. The most common clutch size is nine eggs with the usual range being six to eleven, the first few being laid on alternate days and the completion on consecutive days. They vary in colour from cream to pale olive

buff and measure 52 × 37 mm. Clutches in southern British Columbia are complete from early May, but a month later in the Alaskan interior. The duck alone incubates for a period of 29 to 31 days; the drakes leaving the breeding area half-way through incubation, when they gather in small groups before leaving for a moulting location.

Female Buffle-head looking out from nest hole made by a North American species of Woodpecker

[265]

Hooded Merganser

Mergus cucullatus

Description The male in breeding dress has large white crest with black border, remainder of head black. Neck and mantle, black with greenish sheen, extensions of mantle continue as two bars down each side; the front one being the broader which on occasions continues across the white breast. Back blackish-brown; rump and tail greyish-brown; lesser wing coverts buffy grey; secondaries and their coverts are black and white; primaries and their coverts sepia. Underparts are mainly white; sides reddish-brown with fine black vermiculations; the white under tail coverts are darkly spotted. Bill black; legs and feet vary with season and with the individual, yellow, pale olive or pale brown, webs dark. The female has head and neck dull brown; crest dusky cinnamon and paling to whitish buff on top. Upperparts brownish grey, the feather tips of a paler shade; rump and upper tail coverts blackish; wing as in male but duller. Upper breast greyish, sides and flanks brownish-grey, lower breast and belly white. Bill greenish-black with orange edges, legs and feet dusky. Male in eclipse similar to female but brighter and with more white on wings. Length of male 45 cm, female 42 cm. Immatures as female but less white in wing, smaller crest, and of a lighter shade overall.

Characteristics and Behaviour A small duck with high forehead, large white fan-shaped crest bordered black, white belly, rusty sides, black back and stubby bill. Usually seen in small groups, rarely in large numbers; feeds during the daytime by diving in shallow water, and occasionally in fast flowing, woodland streams or rivers. Does not perch in trees but roosts on logs and rocks in, or near, water. When disturbed takes to the air with apparent ease, and much quicker than the large Mergansers. Fast in flight, with a rapid wing beat, and a diminutive size that tends to exaggerate its obvious speed. Is able to make swift changes of direction, and has the surprising habit of appearing as if from nowhere, and touching down in the open water with a sudden splash then swimming to a more sheltered spot in the shallows. Much of its time is occupied by preening, when the beautiful feathering is so effectively displayed. Deforestation, resulting in the loss of suitable nesting-trees, and the drying up of many small streams, are both contributing against any major increase in its numbers.

Habitat Requires fresh water and is largely dependent on natural tree holes for nesting purposes; much as the Carolina Wood Duck. Frequents woodland streams, ponds and swamps, also fast-flowing streams with pebbly beds. Outside the breeding season visits brackish estuaries and swamps; and, along the Pacific north-west coast, even occurs on salt water which is normally avoided elsewhere.

Distribution Breeds in the southern half of British Columbia and into the extreme western part of south-west Alberta. Throughout Washington, the extreme north of Oregon, northern Idaho, and the north-west corner of Montana. In the east, within a triangular area roughly drawn between Lake Winnipeg, the mouth of the St Lawrence River, and north-west Louisiana. Win-

[266]

tering from Vancouver Island along the coast south to Los Angeles; also throughout Florida and in coastal areas between New York and New Orleans.

Food   The Hooded Merganser's diet consists mainly of animal matter, with fish and crustaceans forming the bulk; also a small intake of aquatic insects. Any vegetable matter eaten is probably accidental.

Voice   The drake during display has a rather throaty purring described as 'crrroooooooooo' which on a still day may be heard over a distance of 800 m. The duck has a hoarse grunt 'croo-croo-crook'; this is sometimes uttered in flight and not unlike that of the Common Merganser, though softer.

Display   The drake's displays include raising his crest, head shaking, turning the back of his head towards a female; also 'upstretching' accompanied by 'wing flapping'. The duck incites by bobbing her head upwards in a rather jerky manner and with bill pointing upwards.

Breeding   A natural tree cavity is preferred, or even the old nest-hole of a woodpecker, provided it is sufficiently large to accommodate the female and her clutch. Nest-boxes are readily taken, especially so if close to water. Height seems to be of little importance, there are nests on record in such unlikely places as fallen hollow logs, and even in a ground cavity under a stump. The same site may be used in successive years and probably by the same bird. Pale grey down is added over a period after laying has commenced. Most clutches are started during March in the southern limits of its range, but can be as late as April or even the beginning of May in colder regions. Usual clutch size is eight to twelve glossy white eggs measuring 54 × 44 mm. Incubation is by the female alone, and for a period of 31 days, the drake quitting the scene during the early stages and journeying to a moulting area.

[267]

Smew
(The White Nun)

Mergus albellus

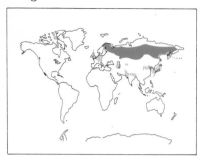

Description The mature drake in breeding plumage is mostly white. There is a black eye patch that extends to the base of the bill, and a similarly coloured one on the crest. Back, rump and wings have greyish-black markings, these continue down the forward sides as two narrow crescents. The sides are pale grey and darkly vermiculated. Bill dark grey, and not obviously serrated; legs and feet dark greenish-grey. Female has upperpart of head and back of neck chestnut brown; lower sides of head and throat are white; upperparts including sides mottled medium grey; belly white. Bill and legs greenish-grey. Male in eclipse is similar to female but darker overall, especially the back. Length 40 cm. Immatures also similar to female.

Characteristics and Behaviour The smallest of all the Mergansers, which unlike its larger relatives, shows a preference for the smaller and more shallow pools. Often seen in small groups as they dive for food. Swims and dives well, and springs from the water with apparent ease; its flight is swift with a rapid but quiet wing beat. On land, it walks easily, and frequently perches in its woodland habitat. A wholly migratory species which is probably on the increase.

Habitat In the breeding season, wooded regions with numerous small lakes or ponds, also rivers with quiet backwaters. Seldom found in regions of open tundra. At other times, lakes, ponds and rivers of less-wooded regions, also estuaries; but only very occasionally at sea.

Distribution Breeds in Scandinavia, Finland, Russia and across Siberia to Kamchatka and Anadyr. Winters in south-east England, along the southern coasts of Sweden, the Baltic, central Europe; the Netherlands being by far the most important wintering area in Europe (in excess of 10,000). Also along the coasts of the Black Sea and Sea of Azov (65,000), Greece, Turkey, Palestine, northern India, China, Korea and Japan. Only very occasionally in North America. A female was seen in the harbour at Buffalo, New York, on several days between mid-February and early April 1960. There are indications that the European populations of Smew may well be increasing.

Food Fish make up a good proportion of the Smew's diet, and prior to diving will locate its prey by submerging the head under water; a habit common to all Mergansers. Crustaceans and molluscs are also taken, as are the larvae of insects (particularly Trichoptera). Food is usually brought to the surface for eating and it is then that marauding gulls challenge for the catch of fish.

Voice Silent except during display, when the drake utters a rattling sound which has been likened to the winding of a pocket watch, or described as a hissing whistle. The duck has a hoarse quack.

Display The drake raises the front feathers of his crest, then slowly draws his head backwards until in contact with his shoulders; on bringing it forward, and with neck outstretched, he surges quickly through the water. The duck has the curious habit of first raising her bill and then pressing it to her breast, fol-

lowed by bobbing her head up and down quite rapidly.

Breeding Tree holes are used for nesting purposes, both natural cavities and the disused nest-holes of woodpeckers being sought. In particular those of the Black Woodpecker *Dryocopus martius*. The Smew also takes readily to fabricated nest-boxes. The clutch of eight to nine eggs is usually laid during April or May, cream or creamy-buff in colour and measuring 53 × 38 mm. Incubation is 30 days, by the female alone.

Occasionally, a female Smew and female Goldeneye will lay in the same nest-hole and produce a mixed brood. There is even a record of a wild hybrid between these two species.

The Smew could well be described as a link between the Mergansers and the Goldeneye; with its feeding habits and bill-shape intermediate between the two. Further relationships are seen in its black and white plumage and also in the down pattern of the young.

Female Smew

[269]

Common Red-breasted Merganser
(Redhead)

Mergus serrator serrator

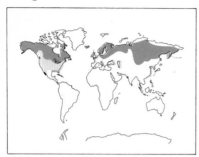

Description The breeding male has long shaggy crest and head, dark bottle green, with a black stripe down the nape; remainder of neck is white. Upper breast brown spotted and flecked with black. Undersides are creamy white, the flanks with fine black bars. At close quarters the white spots on its black shoulders become apparent. Outer scapulars and wing coverts are white edged with black, remainder of wing black except for white patches on secondaries. Bill ruby red with a black central stripe from base to nail. Legs and feet some shade of red. Female has sepia head with a crest that is held horizontally (in the female Goosander the chestnut crest tends to droop). The body is mainly barred and mottled medium grey with brown. Bill and legs as male. In eclipse the male is very similar to female. Length of male 65 cm, female 58 cm. The Greenland Merganser *M. s. schioleri* is identical to *M. s. serrator*, but is a little larger and with a stronger, broader bill.

Characteristics and Behaviour Not sufficiently smaller than the Goosander for size comparison to be a means of field identification and both species fly with bill, neck and body in one long line, giving an over emphasized impression of the bird's length. The drakes, however, are readily separable even at distance; the Red-breasted Merganser has a dark upper chest, the Goosander's being creamy white. Females of the two species are distinguished by their white chin patch; this being less well defined in the Red-breasted Merganser, also the female Goosander has a more reddy brown head. Outside the breeding season usually seen in pairs or small groups, but counts have been made well in excess of a thousand individuals, but these scattered over an area where food is in abundance. Usually patters across the water to become airborne, and when in flight can travel at 80 m.p.h. (130 k.p.h.) over a short distance is on record, with an average speed of about 50 m.p.h. (80 k.p.h.). Pairs will fly close together, but groups of birds would be in 'line' formation. An expert diver, with serrated mandibles that enhance the ability to grasp its slippery prey.

Habitat In the breeding season, inland waters such as lakes and rivers; also in coastal waters. Occurs both in wooded areas and, farther north, in treeless tundra; also on offshore islands. At other times, although many birds remain on the larger inland waters, it is mainly a bird of the shallow coastal waters with sheltered bays. Far more maritime than the Goosander, which much prefers fresh-water habitat.

Distribution Breeds farther north than the other Mergansers, up to 70° N in Russia. Also Iceland, north-west British Isles, northern Germany, Denmark, Scandinavia, up to 10,000 pairs in Finland, Siberia, Kamchatka, the Aleutians, Alaska and much of Canada. Winters across North America, south to Arizona, New Mexico and north-west Texas. Also British Isles (where there is a resident population), the coastal regions of Norway, southern Sweden, the Baltic (up to 20,000 birds), Denmark, the Netherlands, France, Spain and North Africa. Also the Black

Sea, Sea of Azov, Caspian Sea, the coast of Iran, China, Korea and Japan. *M. s. schioleri* is confined to Greenland, where it breeds along the west coast to Nugssuak Peninsula, beyond which it breeds locally to the Upernavik District. Along the east coast it is a local breeder to Scoresby Sound.

Food When in search of food, often swims with head submerged, or explores underwater terrain probing bill in crevices or between loose stones to disturb fish. Fish forms the major part of the diet, young salmon and young trout are taken in quantity from fresh-water rivers and lakes, other items include Lampreys, Eels and Minnows, crustaceans and insects. In winter months when in salt-water habitat, Sticklebacks and Gobies form the major part of the diet.

Voice The drake is usually silent except during display, when a low 'yeoww' or some similar mewing sound is uttered. Both sexes have a call described as 'wark' used only in flight. The female has a harsh croaking 'krrrr'.

Display Drakes will make sudden spurts across the water towards groups of females. Also the head is at times brought suddenly forwards, then with neck outstretched the head is given a slight downward jerk, at this time the purring 'yeoww' can be heard.

Breeding Unlike the other Mergansers, the Red-breasted does not seek tree cavities, but chooses to nest at ground level in dense scrub, heather, or dwarf scrub, even amongst rocks, by the banks of streams, rivers, lakes and ponds, often on small islands; usually no great distance from water. Early eggs from the beginning of May, continuing until late June or early July, depending on latitude. Down is added when about half the clutch has been laid. An average clutch would be eight to ten greyish or greenish-buff eggs measuring 65 × 44 mm. The drake stays in the vicinity while the eggs are being laid, and the female joins him when not laying and in 'off duty' periods during early incubation; soon afterwards small parties of drakes begin to gather in the broad vicinity, before leaving the area entirely.

[271]

European Goosander
(Common Goosander or Red-head)

Mergus merganser merganser

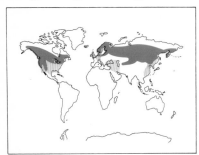

Description The male in breeding plumage has head and upper neck black with a greenish gloss; crown being somewhat greener, and no crest, but the long feathers of crown and nape give the head an exaggerated size. Mantle glossy black; centre of back grey, shading darker towards tail. Wings black with white coverts and all but the innermost secondaries are white with a narrow black edge on outer web. Upper back, lower neck, breast, sides and belly, are pale salmon pink. Area on side of tail finely lined with grey. The long red bill has a dark line running from base to tip and is strongly hooked. Legs and feet reddish-orange. Female has rich chestnut brown head, crown, neck and drooping crest; the chin and upper throat are white, which unlike the Red-breasted Merganser are sharply defined. The bluish-grey upperparts are faintly mottled with brown. Primaries and outer secondaries are black; inner secondaries and coverts are mainly white. Underparts are creamy white; sides and flanks grey, the white edges of feathers giving a mottled effect. Bill, legs and feet as male. Drake in eclipse resembles female but with white wing coverts, face paler, and crest much shorter. Length of male 67 cm, female 63 cm. Immatures also resemble female but with paler head, and faint streak of buff through eyes. Two other races are recognized: the American Goosander (*M. m. americanus*), which shows a black wing bar and has bill less strongly hooked; the Central Asian Goosander (*M. m. orientalis*), smaller with a more slender bill.

Characteristics and Behaviour In flight, the length is exaggerated by the manner of holding neck outstretched and bill pointing forwards, as is the case with other Mergansers. They often fly in single file, low over the water; when seen from behind the drakes are not readily distinguished from the Red-breasted Merganser at a distance. At other times, the white neck and body are adequate field characters. A social bird out of breeding season, when groups may be seen ranging in size from a few birds to fifteen or twenty. At all times very wary and difficult to approach, if alarmed while ashore will immediately run to the nearest water, which it does quite well and with an upright stance. Well able to perch in trees; in fact, the female is very capable and may be seen inspecting tree cavities when selecting a suitable site.

Habitat When breeding prefers wooded areas with fresh-water rivers, lakes and pools that are not overgrown with reeds or in anyway muddy. Will also breed in treeless areas but the availability of clear fresh water is essential. Winters on large unfrozen inland waters and fast-flowing rivers; although estuaries and shallow coastal bays are visited, its preference is fresh water. Even on migration flights the Goosander keeps close in to shore and takes advantage of any fresh or brackish waters that are available.

Distribution Breeds in Iceland, Scotland, Scandinavia, Finland (about 4,000 pairs), Russia, Novaya Zemlya and Siberia to 71° N. Also Denmark, Germany, Austria, Switzerland, Yugoslavia, Roumania, and east to Mongolia

[272]

and Kamchatka. Winters in the British Isles, Iceland, southern Scandinavia, the Baltic (with up to 30,000 along the Danish coast), the Netherlands, Germany, the Mediterranean, Black Sea, Sea of Azov, Caspian Sea, Aral Sea, Asia Minor, Iraq and Iran. The American Goosander (*M. m. americanus*) breeds in south Alaska, the southern halves of the Yukon and Mackenzie, throughout British Columbia, all but the south-east corner of Alberta, southern half of Saskatchewan, across central Manitoba, most of Ontario, the southern halves of Quebec and Labrador, Newfoundland, New Brunswick, Nova Scotia. Throughout Washington and into Idaho, Montana, Wyoming, Colorado and New Mexico. Also western parts of Oregon and California. Winters south to about the Tropic of Cancer. The Central Asia Goosander (*M. m. orientalis*) breeds in Afghanistan, the Himalayas, Tibet and Altai. Winters in India, Burma and western China.

Food Almost entirely fish, which it locates with head submerged, and dives to catch. Also searches underwater, probing in rock crevices and amongst stones. Salmon fry, Trout, Eels, Minnows and Perch. In coastal waters, Sticklebacks, Blennies and Gobies; also shrimps, small crabs and mussels.

Voice Both sexes utter low quack-like calls in winter. During display the male has several notes or calls, such as purring and croaking; the latter, when uttered repeatedly, becomes high pitched and sounds almost bell-like. Female warning call is a harsh 'karrrr'.

Display The female makes a sideways pointing movement towards males other than the one of her choice, then rushes forward with outstretched neck and open crest. A drake will swim rapidly near to or around a female.

Breeding Egg-laying is from early April to early June in the more northerly latitudes. The female usually chooses a natural cavity in a tree, although nestboxes are readily taken, and ground nesting does occur in treeless regions such as Iceland. An average clutch would consist of ten to eleven creamy-white eggs measuring 67 × 46 mm. Incubation is by the female for 30 days.

[273]

North American Ruddy Duck

Oxyura jamaicensis rubida

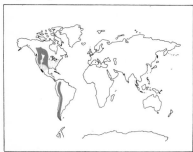

Description The male in breeding plumage has forehead, crown and nape black; with some feathers on each side of crown that become erect during display to form two small 'horns'. The cheeks are white and this extends narrowly under the chin. Upperparts, flanks and upper breast are deep chestnut, but the shade varies with individuals; tail dusky brown. Underparts silvery white but finely mottled and barred with brown. Legs and feet bluish-grey with dusky webs. Bill greyish-blue with brownish nail. Female, the black feathers of forehead, crown and nape, have brown tips; side of head and chin buffish white with a dark stripe extending from ear coverts to gape. Upperparts dark brown but speckled and barred with paler shade of brown, and often lightly tinged chestnut. Sides and upper breast barred with medium and pale browns, and tinged with yellowish-red. Lower breast and underparts are silvery white, but lightly barred and mottled with brown; tail sooty brown. Legs, feet and bill slate grey. Male in eclipse is similar to female but head darker, and sides of head white. Length 36–40 cm. Immatures very like female, but lighter overall. *O. j. jamaicensis* of the West Indies is considered by some authorities to be no different from *O. j. rubida*. The Peruvian Ruddy Duck *O. j. ferruginea* is much

darker overall, the drake having no white on face. The Colombian Ruddy Duck *O. j. andina* is very similar to *O. j. rubida* but the drake's white facial patch is heavily spotted and mottled black.

Characteristics and Behaviour A small stocky duck with a short thick neck. Often seen on water in groups of thirty to fifty, evenly spaced and with a tendency to dive in concert – which they do if danger threatens rather than take flight. To become airborne the Ruddy Duck patters across the water for a considerable distance, its short wings beating rapidly. When on dry land it walks awkwardly and with an upright stance because the legs are set well back on the body. The feet are large, but the pointed wings very small when compared with the body size; all in all the Ruddy Duck is very Grebe-like. A daytime feeder, usually diving to acquire seeds that have settled to the bottom, but on occasions will feed by dabbling.

Habitat Fresh-water marshes during the breeding season, but on migration larger expanses of shallow water with dense aquatic vegetation. In winter, coastal areas with sheltered brackish and salt waters, but also common on inland waters that stay free of ice.

Distribution Main breeding areas are the eastern half of British Columbia, throughout Alberta, Saskatchewan except the north-west, south and south-west Manitoba. Then south from Winnipeg to the River Grande de Norte; also from Seattle south to Los Angeles, but absent in the central regions between these two areas (see map). Winters south of a line from Vancouver Island in the west, curving down to Nebraska in the central states, and up towards Boston in the east. *O. j. jamaicensis* is resident in the Bahamas and the Greater and Lesser Antilles. The Colombian Ruddy Duck occurs in the marshes and lakes of central and eastern Colombia. The Peruvian Ruddy Duck

occurs from southern Colombia to Tierra del Fuego. The Ruddy Duck's introduction in southern England during the 1950s and 1960s is a result of escapes from wildfowl collections. Chew Valley Lake in Somerset and waters in Staffordshire account for the bulk of the British population.

Food   Roughly 70 per cent vegetable matter, 30 per cent animal matter. Mainly pondweeds and sedges including tubers and seeds. The animal intake is chiefly of midges and caddis flies, also various water-beetles, molluscs and crustaceans.

Voice   The drake is silent except for a peculiar call described as 'raa-anh' which is heard during the 'bubble' display. The duck has a low nasal call 'raanh'.

Display   The duck assumes aggressive postures, when she swims with head held low and forward, bill gaping. The drake in his 'bubble' display first cocks his tail and then causes the two tufts of feathers on his head to raise like small horns. The neck is then inflated and the bill begins to beat rapidly on his chest, producing a very hollow tapping sound and causing numerous bubbles to form on the water surface because of the bill's dipping action.

Breeding   Dense vegetation is the preferred site, and the duck constructs a floating platform from available plant material, this she securely anchors before laying her eggs. Down is subsequently added during the early stages of incubation. Early clutches may be found in late April, or the first week of May in the southern states, but farther north up to 5 weeks later. The eight to ten white eggs measure 62 × 46 mm. Incubation commences with the last egg and is by the female alone for a period of 23 days. The ducklings leave the nest when almost 2 days old and take their first flight at about 6 weeks.

[275]

White-headed Duck

Oxyura leucocephala

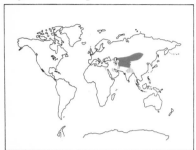

Description The drake in breeding plumage has forehead, sides of the head, and chin white; the crown and sometimes the nape are black, with a black collar round the neck. Upperparts are grey and reddish brown, upper tail coverts chestnut, and tail black. The breast is deep chestnut, shading to greyish-brown on the abdomen and the under tail coverts. The bill is bright blue and swollen at the base, legs and feet are grey with dark webs. The drake in eclipse has more black on the crown and nape, less chestnut on the body, and a slate grey bill. The female has body plumage similar to the male, but more greyish-brown, dark brown crown and nape, buff cheeks with a brown line across, and a dark grey bill also swollen at the base. Length 45 cm. Immatures are much like females but duller.

Characteristics and Behaviour The only representative of the *Oxyurini*, or stiff-tails native to the palaearctic region. The very large head and bill are unmistakable; and the stiff pointed tail feathers, whether held erect or trailing on the surface of the water, are a characteristic shared only by feral Ruddy Duck amongst European birds. Leads a highly aquatic life and avoids flying whenever possible. Take-off is very laborious with rapid wing beats and a long pattering run, the flight is usually low and somewhat resembles that of the Coot. Often secretive in behaviour and usually seeks the shelter of waterside vegetation when disturbed. Rather scarce and decreasing dramatically in Europe where there are an estimated thirty breeding pairs at most, and a world population in the region of 15,000. Half that number have been recorded in winter on a single lake in Turkey.

Habitat Shallow inland pools and lakes with dense vegetation for cover, and profuse growth of submerged plants for food; preferably fresh water in the breeding season, but brackish and saline lagoons in winter.

Distribution Highly disintegrated, resembling that of the Red-crested Pochard, and suggesting a relic of a former widespread distribution. In the breeding season, very small numbers in Spain. In North Africa, only Algeria, Tunisia and probably Morocco. Also Turkey and the southern USSR, with main concentrations in Kazakhstan. Winters in the Mediterranean, Turkey, USSR, and south to Afghanistan and Pakistan.

Food Leaves of underwater plants, including pondweeds, eel grass, wigeon grass, etc. seeds, molluscs, crustaceans, aquatic insects and dipterous larvae. Food obtained mostly by diving.

Voice Almost silent, but male has a soft rattling note and a high-pitched piping call; the female a quiet 'gek'.

Display Courtship display commences with flocks of birds swimming in formation, the leading bird with neck erect and tail horizontal or raised to 45°. In later movements, the drake assumes hunched attitudes with head lowered and tail horizontal. Tail may also be twisted sideways and rapidly vibrated.

Breeding Late May to June. The nest is usually a floating platform of dead reeds or, alternatively, old nests of Coot, Grebe or Tufted Duck may be used. Clutch size is five to ten dull white eggs

with a rough surface, average size 67 ×
51 mm. The eggs are exceptionally large
and weigh more than those of the Shelduck or even the Brent Goose. Incubation is by the female, 25 to 26 days in
captivity. The ducklings are able to dive
within minutes of leaving the nest, and
by the third day can remain submerged
for up to 15 seconds and obtain most of
their food under water.

Australian Musk Duck

Biziura lobata

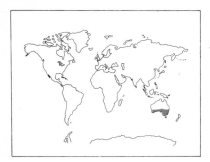

Description Crown, nape and back of neck are black. Feathers on sides of head, throat and remainder of neck are blackish-brown with a white tip giving a somewhat mottled effect. The general colour of upperparts and upper breast is browny-black finely barred with lines of light brown. Primaries and tail are blackish, lower parts of breast are white with a brownish mottle. There is a large pendulous lobe on the underside of the black bill. Legs and feet are dark leaden grey. Length of average male is 66 cm and female 55 cm. Sexes are alike but the lobe on the female's bill is only rudimentary. Immatures resemble female.

Characteristics and Behaviour The Musk Duck is entirely aquatic, seldom if ever coming on land but occasionally will crawl on to clumps of vegetation to rest. If placed on land, will slither about as would a seal and it is only with great difficulty that a half-erect posture is assumed. Their habit of sinking slowly under the water leaving only nostrils and eyes above the surface is typical, and in this way they escape detection. Usually seen floating far out from the bank when the black profile of heavy head, large hanging lobe and stiff erect tail prevents confusion with other species of duck. The males also have the peculiar habit of splashing the water noisily behind them.

Habitat Unlike the Pink-eared Duck, the Musk prefers deep permanent water with vegetation that is not too dense to permit the presence of open pools amongst the reeds. The tea-tree swamps of coastal regions and the cumbungi swamps inland are ideal as breeding areas. Out of breeding season they are to be found on open water such as inland lakes at varying altitudes, also lagoons and rivers.

Distribution Found only throughout southern Australia and Tasmania, avoiding the arid areas for the large swampy regions. In New Zealand, the fossil remains of an extinct species *Biziura deloutouri* indicates that they were more widespread in days gone by.

Food They acquire food by diving and their diet is mainly one of animal matter, such as water-boatmen, water-beetles and the larvae of dragonflies, etc. with just a small percentage of vegetable matter, including a variety of seeds.

Voice The male's shrill whistle can be heard throughout the year, but during the breeding season a deep 'plonk' will also be evident, this may be caused by the action of their feet against the water. The only sound made by the female is a soft quack.

Display Musk Ducks display from autumn through winter. The male swims out from the reeds very deliberately, kicking with both feet so strongly as to cause large quantities of water to be ejected; this kicking of the water is continued at length even when the bird has assumed a stationary position. Then with neck and cheeks inflated, head raised high and lobe quite taut, the tail is raised and held fanned over its back. Now gyrating and with water still splashing the resonant 'plonk, plonk, plonk' will be evident. Should a female approach, then copulation will soon follow.

[278]

Breeding At the height of the breeding season the pendant pouch or lobe under the male's bill assumes its greatest proportions, from a normal diameter of 5·5 cm during March to 7·75 cm in November. At this time too, the musky odour issuing from the male's uropygian gland is most intense. The purpose of this musky smell is not known, but the bird derives its name from this characteristic feature. The nest is usually well concealed within a clump of rushes, where the stems are woven loosely together and a sparse lining of leaves and down are added. One to three pale greenish-white eggs are laid, these are soon stained brown by the wet vegetation. On average, each egg measures 80 × 55 mm. The incubation period has not yet been established.

Flying Steamer Duck

Tachyeres patachonicus

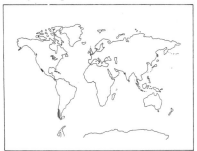

Description By far the smallest of the Steamer Ducks. Both sexes are pretty similar, with bluish-grey crown, remainder of head and neck being mottled white and pale grey. A white stripe extends backwards from the eye. The throat is tinged with red, more so than *T. pteneres*. Except for the breast, the underparts are white; the remainder of the plumage mottled grey and reddish-grey. Bill is orange-yellow shading to bluish near the nostrils and becoming almost white towards the tip. Legs are yellow with black claws. The female's head and neck are of a somewhat darker grey tinged reddish-brown on the sides, and the area of reddish-brown on the throat is larger. Bill greenish. Length 65–70 cm. Young males resemble the female.

Characteristics and Behaviour Is often mistaken for one of the flightless species of steamer duck, this because of its sometimes seeming reluctance to take to the air. Even when swimming out at sea it will dive or steam away rather than fly. When in flight, it is a graceful bird, even though the flight is somewhat laboured and has been likened to that of the Eider Duck. In summer they have been seen to take what can only be described as 'joy-rides'. At such times, two or more individuals will leave the sea together and make a semi-circular flight inland or even a complete and very large circle may be described. During these flights they periodically and simultaneously check the fast movement of the wings stooping downwards, with a moments pause after each wing beat.

Habitat During the summer months, may be encountered along the shoreline or on lakes and lagoons of brackish or fresh water, from sea level to the more mountainous regions. In winter, flies less often and can be found resting or sleeping on frozen inland waters, but in Isla Grande (Tierra del Fuego) it is restricted to the coast during winter months.

Distribution Southern South America including the Falkland Islands. From Valdivia in Chile south to Tierra del Fuego; also Patagonia.

Food Crabs and other crustaceans, prawns, etc. that occur in salt or fresh water. Only a small percentage of the more thicker shelled molluscs are taken.

Voice No record.

Display No record.

Breeding The breeding season is from November to January. Nests are to be found in bushes or swamps, even amongst forest debris and often far from water. An average clutch would be seven eggs of 76 × 52 mm. Incubation period not recorded. The fledglings, just like those of the flightless species, acquire their wing quills very slowly. Even when the down has disappeared entirely, there is a considerable period of time during which the primaries have only barely sprouted.

Magellanic Flightless Steamer Duck

Tachyeres pteneres

Length 73–83 cm. The largest and heaviest of the three species, which because of its very short wings is incapable of flight. Sexes are almost identical, and plumage-wise are similar to, but paler than, *T. patachonicus*. Distributed along the coasts and islands of western South America from Concepçion in Chile, south to Cape Horn. An average clutch would be six to twelve ivory-white eggs, 85 × 67 mm.

Falkland Flightless Steamer Duck

Tachyeres brachypterus

Smaller than *T. pteneres* and incapable of flight. The sexes do have plumage differences. The male has a paler head, redder throat and more yellow round the neck than *T. pteneres*. The female is much redder overall, with the head and sides of the neck reddish-brown; the breast tinged with pale brown and the yellow neck collar more pronounced.

Confined to the Falkland Islands.

The Wildfowl Trust's Reserves and Refuges in Britain

Slimbridge

(The Trust's headquarters), open daily 9.30 a.m. to dusk (except 24 and 25 December). Between Bristol and Gloucester, 5 miles from the M5 motorway.

The world's largest and most varied collection of wildfowl, almost 3,000 birds of some 170 different kinds are on view to the public at all seasons of the year. During summer months cygnets, goslings and ducklings of all descriptions are to be seen. Winter months are particularly exciting when Bewick's Swans and White-fronted Geese arrive from their breeding quarters in Siberia; members can watch the Bewick's Swans from the comfort of the Swan Observatory.

Welney

Open daily from 10.00 a.m. (except 24 and 25 December). Situated near Wisbech in Cambridgeshire.

From the many hides and a spacious observatory excellent views of the birds are possible. Tens of thousands of Wigeon, Mallard, Teal and Shoveler visit the refuge each winter, but the special feature must be the 1,000 plus wild Bewick's Swans that return annually.

Martin Mere

Open daily 9.30 a.m. to dusk (except 24 and 25 December). Situated near Burscough in Lancashire, 5 miles from Southport, 14 miles from Preston and 17 miles from Liverpool.

Covers 360 acres of marsh land on the site of what was once Lancashire's largest mere. Visited by thousands of wild geese and ducks; the collection contains over 1,000 wildfowl and is rapidly increasing. Spacious hides have been constructed to give visitors excellent views over the wild refuge. Tens of thousands of Pink-footed Geese visit the area each winter.

Peakirk

Open daily 9.30 a.m. to dusk (except 24 and 25 December). Situated 5 miles from Peterborough in Northamptonshire.

The Waterfowl Gardens are on the site of an old osier bed through which passes the ancient Car Dyke. Special attractions are the Black-necked and Coscoroba Swans, also the Andean Geese. Altogether some 600 wildfowl of over eighty kinds are on display.

Washington

Open daily 9.30 a.m. to dusk (9.00 a.m. during June, July and August, closed 24 and 25 December). Situated 3 miles from Sunderland in Tyne and Wear.

The Refuge is on the side of a hill sloping down to the River Wear, covering 103 delightfully landscaped acres on the north bank of the river. Over 1,000 birds of some 100 different kinds are on show and a special feature is being made of those from North America.

Arundel

Open daily 9.30 a.m. to dusk (except 25 December). In Sussex, 10½ miles from Bognor Regis and 10½ miles from Chichester.

This is the Wildfowl Trust's latest centre, situated less than a mile from the town of Arundel, between Swanbourne Lake and the River Arun, and set against Arundel Castle and the wooded hillside of Offham Hanger. The reserve extends over 55 acres of attractively landscaped pens, lakes and paddocks, and will ultimately consist of almost 1,500 wildfowl from many parts of the world. The central attraction is Swan

Lake and special attractions include the colony of Australian Black Swans, and many Diving and Sea Ducks.

Caerlaverock

Open daily from 1 September to 15 May. Situated on the Solway Firth, 7 miles from Dumfries.

This Refuge covers 1,000 acres including a part of the Caerlaverock National Nature Reserve which lies on the north Solway shore. A comfortable observatory, two towers and strategically positioned hides provide superb close views of many wildfowl and waders which roost or feed here. Huge flocks of Barnacle Geese (over 7,000 in 1976/7), Pink-footed Geese (over 3,000), and Golden Plover (over 5,000) spend a large part of the period September to March in the Refuge. Other visitors include Bewick's and Whooper Swans.

Wildfowl Collections around the World

Afghanistan
Kabul Zoological Gardens, Barikot Park, Kabul.

Argentina
Jardin Zoologico de Buenos Aires, Republica de la India 2900, Buenos Aires.

Jardin Zoologica de la Plata, Avda. 52 y 118, La Plata.

Australia
Adelaide Zoological Gardens, Frome Road, Adelaide, South Australia.

Sir Colin Mackenzie Sanctuary, Healesville, Victoria.

Melbourne Zoological Gardens, Royal Park, Parkville, Melbourne, Victoria

Perth Zoological Gardens, Labouchere Road, Perth, Western Australia.

Taronga Zoo and Aquarium, Mosman, Sydney, New South Wales.

Westbury Zoo, 10 Mary Street, Westbury, Tasmania.

Austria
Tiergarten Schönbrunn, 1130 Vienna XIII.

Belgium
Société Royale de Zoologie d'Anvers (Koninklijke Maatschappj Voor Dierkunde Van Antwerpen), Koningin Astridplein 26, Antwerp.

Brazil
Fundação Parque Zoologico de São Paulo, Avda. Agua Funda, São Paulo.

Jardin Zoologico do Rio de Janeiro, Quinta Boa Vista, Rio de Janeiro.

Parque Zoologico do Rio Grande do Sul, Caixa Postal 36, São Leopoldo.

Bulgaria
Zoological Gardens, Boul. Tolbouhin 15, Sofia.

Burma
Rangoon Zoological Gardens, Lake Road, Rangoon.

Canada
Calgary Zoo and Natural History Park, St George's Island, Calgary, Alberta.

Alberta Game Farm, RR1, Androssan, Edmonton, Alberta.

Jardin Zoologique de Québec, 8191 Avenue du Zoo, Orsainville, Québec, Québec.

Provincial Wildlife Park, Shubenacadie, Nova Scotia.

Assiniboine Park Zoo, Winnipeg, Manitoba.

Ceylon
Zoological Gardens of Ceylon, Anagarika Dharmapala Mawatha, Colombo.

China
Peking Zoological Garden, Si Shin Men, Peking.

Shanghai Zoological Gardens, 2381 Hong Qiao Road, Xi Jiao Park, Shanghai.

Congo Republic (Kinshasa)
Jardin Zoologique de Lumumbashi, Lumumbashi.

Cuba
Jardin Zoologico de la Habana, Ave 26 y 47, Nuevo Vedado, Havana.

Czechoslovakia
Zoologicka Zahrada Mesta Brna, Brno-Bystrc, Brno.

Vychodeceska Zoologicka Zahrada ve Dvore Kralove n.L., Dvur Kralove.

Zoopark a Zamek Lesna, p.

Kostelec-Stipa, okr. Gottwaldov,
Lesna.

Zoologicka Zahrada
Ostrava-Stromovka, Ostrava.

Zoologicka Zahrada, Prague.

Denmark
København's Zoologiske Have,
Roskildevej 32, Copenhagen.

Dominican Republic
Jardin Zoologico, Santa Domingo.

Finland
Korkeasaaren Elaintarha/Helsinki
Zoo.

France
Parc Zoologique de Clères, S.-M.,
Cleres.

Parc Zoologique de Branféré, 56 Le
Guerno, Morbihan, Le Guerno.

Parc Zoologique Henri de Lunaret,
Bois de Lavalette, Montpellier.

Parc Zoologique et Botanique de la
Ville de Mulhouse, 1 Avenue de la 9°
DIC, 68 Mulhouse.

Parc Zoologique de Paris, 53 Avenue
de St Maurice, Paris.

Germany
Augsburger Tiergarten, Parkstr 25a,
89 Augsburg.

Aktien-Verein des Zoologischen
Gartens zu Berlin, Hardenbergplatz 8,
1 Berlin 30.

Tierpark Berlin, Friedrichsfelde, Am
Tierpark 125, DDR-1136 Berlin.

Bremer Tierpark George Munro,
Achterdiek, 28 Bremen 33.

Tiergrotten u. Nordseeaquarium,
Bremerhaven.

Aktiengesellschaft Zoologischer
Garten Köln, 5 Köln Riehl, Riehlerstr
173, Cologne.

Tierpark Dortmund, 46
Dortmund-Brünninghausen,
Mergelteichstr 80, Dortmund.

Zoologischer Garten Dresden,
Tiergartenstr. 1, 8020 Dresden.

Zoo Duisburg, Mulheimerstr. 273, 41
Duisburg.

Zoologischer Garten Frankfurt/Main,
Alfred Brehm Platz 16, 6 Frankfurt
am Main 1.

Ruhr-Zoo Gelsenkirchen, Bleckstr 64,
Gelsenkirchen.

Zoologischer Garten Halle, 402 Halle
(Saale), Fasanenstr. 5a, Halle.

Carl Hagenbeck's Tierpark,
Hamburg-Stellingen 54, Hamburg.

Zoologischer Garten Hanover,
Hindenburgstr. 53, 3 Hanover.

Tiergarten Heidelberg, Gemeinn.
GmbH, Tiergartenstr. 8, 69
Heidelberg 1.

Krefelder Tierpark, Uerdingerstr. 377,
415 Krefeld.

Zoologischer Garten Leipzig, Dr Kurt
Fischerstr. 29, Leipzig C1.

Zoologischer Garten Magdeburg, Am
Vogelgesand 12, Magdeburg.

Münchener Tierpark Hellabrunn Ag,
Siebenbrunnerstr 6, Munich.

Tiergarten der Stadt Nürnberg, Am
Tiergarten 30, 85 Nürnberg.

Tierpark Rheine, Tiergartenverein
Rheine e.V., 444 Rheine/Westfalia.

Zoologischer Garten Rostock,
Tiergartenallee 10, 25 Rostock.

Vogelpark Walsrode KG, Am
Rieselbach, 303 Walsrode/Hannover.

Zoologischer Garten Wuppertal, 56
Wuppertal-Elberfeld, Hubertusallee
30, Wuppertal.

Great Britain

Zoological Garden, Hazlehead Park, Aberdeen.

Curraghs Wildlife Park, Ballaugh, Isle of Man.

Bristol, Clifton and West of England Zoological Society, Clifton, Bristol 8.

Wild Life Park, Cricket St Thomas, Chard, Somerset.

Zoological Gardens, Upton-by-Chester, Chester.

Scottish National Zoological Park, Murrayfield, Edinburgh.

Norfolk Wildlife Park and Pheasant Trust, Great Witchingham, Norfolk.

The Bentley Wildfowl Collection, Halland, Lewes, Sussex.

The Sladmore Gardens, Cryers Hill, near High Wycombe, Bucks.

Jersey Zoological Park, Les Augres Manor, Trinity, Jersey, Channel Islands.

Harewood Bird Garden, Harewood Estate, Leeds, Yorkshire.

Zoological Society of London, Regent's Park, London.

Penscynor Bird Gardens, Neath, Glamorgan. (closed winter)

Flamingo Gardens and Tropical Bird Zoo, Weston Underwood, Olney, Bucks.

Padstow Bird Garden, Fentonluna Lane, Padstow, Cornwall.

The Herbert Whitely Trust, Zoological and Botanical Gardens, Paignton, Devon.

The Tropical Bird Gardens, Rode, near Bath.

Stagsden Bird Gardens, Bedford.

Whipsnade Park, Bedfordshire.

Mole Hall Wildlife Park, Widdington, near Saffron Walden, Essex.

Hong Kong

Botanic Gardens, Garden Road, Hong Kong.

Hungary

Föváros-Állat-és Növénykertje, Budapest.

India

Municipal Hill Garden Zoo, Kankaria, Ahmedabad 22.

Zoological Garden, Alipore, Calcutta 27.

Delhi Zoological Park, New Delhi.

Assam State Zoo and Botanical Gardens, Gauhati, Assam.

Nehru Zoological Park, Hyderabad, Andhra Pradesh.

Sri Chamarajendra Zoological Gardens, Mysore.

Indonesia

Kebun Binatang Surabaja, Djalan Setail 1, Wonokromo.

Iran

Teheran Zoological Gardens, Av. Pahlavi, Shemiran, Teheran.

Israel

The Zoological Garden Society, Keren Kayemeth Blvd, Tel Aviv.

Italy

Parco Zoologico di Ville Sirene, Faenza, Prov. Ravenna.

Giardino Zoologico di Napoli, Viale Kennedy, Campi Flegrei, Naples.

Giardino Zoologico e Museo di Zoologia del Comune di Roma, Viale Giardino Zoologico 20, Rome.

Giardino Zoologico della Citta' di Torino, Corso Casale, Turin.

Japan

Kobe Oji Zoo, Ojicho 3-chome, Nada-ku, Kobe.

Kyoto Municipal Zoo, Okazaki, Hoshojicho, Sakyoku, Kyoto.

Nagoya Higashiyama Grand Park (Nagoya Higashiyama Zoo), 2–215 Higashiyamamotomachi, Chikusaku, Nagoya 464.

Maruyama Zoo, 3–1 Miyagaoka Maruyama, Sapporo.

Sendai Yagiyama Zoological Park, 43, 1-chome, Yagiyama Motomachi, Sendai.

Tama Zoological Park, Hodokubo, Hino-Shi, Tokyo.

Ueno Zoological Gardens, Ueno Park, Taitoku, Tokyo.

Nogeyama Zoological Gardens, 63 Oimatsucho, Nishiku, Yokohama.

Korea (North)

Zoological Park, Daesong District, Pyongyang.

Malaysia

Zoo Negara (National Zoological Park), Ulu Klang, Kuala Lumpur.

Mexico

Park Zoologico del Bosque de Chapultepec, Mexico City.

Mozambique

Zoo Trindade, Beira.

Netherlands

Stichting Koninlijk Zoölogisch Genootschap Natura Artis Magistra Plantage Kerklaan 40, Amsterdam.

Burgers' Zoo, Schelmseweg 85, Arnhem.

Stichting Koninklijke Rotterdamse Diergaarde, Van Aerssenlaan 49, Rotterdam.

Dierenpark Wassenaar Zoo, Rijksstraatweg 667, Wassenaar.

New Zealand

Auckland Zoological Park, Grey Lynn, Auckland.

Wellington Zoological Gardens, Newtown Park, Wellington.

Poland

Slaski Ogrod Zoologiczny Katowice-Chorzow, Katowice 2.

Miejski Ogrod Zoologiczny W Lodzi, ul. Konstantynowska 8/10, Lodz.

Municipal Zoological Gardens, ul. Zwierzyniecka 19, Poznon.

Miejski Ogrod Zoologiczny W. Warszawie, ul. Ratuszowa 1/3, Warsaw.

Miejski Ogrod Zoologiczny, ul. Wroblewskiego 1, Wroclaw.

Portugal

Jardin Zoológico e de Aclimação em Portugal, Estrade de Benfica, Lisbon.

Roumania

Gradina Zoologica Bucuresti, Aleea Vadul Moldovei 4, Bucharest.

Singapore

Jurong Bird Park (PTE) Ltd, Jalan Ahmad Ibrahim, Jurong 11.

South Africa

Johannesburg Zoological Gardens, Jan Smuts Avenue, Johannesburg.

Natal Zoological Gardens (Pty) Ltd, Umlaas Road, Pietermaritzburg.

National Zoological Gardens of South Africa, Boom Street, Pretoria.

Spain

Parque Zoologico de Barcelona, Parque de la Ciudadela, Barcelona.

Jardin Zoologico y Botanico 'Alberto Duran', Tempul, Jerezde la Frontera.

Sweden

Stiftelsen Skanes Djurpark, Fostavallen, Hoor.

Zoological Department, Nordiska Museet och Skansen, Stockholm.

Switzerland

Zoologischer Garten Basel, 4000 Basel.

Städtischer Tierpark Dählhölzli, Berne.

Zoologischer Garten Zürich, 8044 Zürich.

Thailand

Dusit Zoological Park, Bangkok.

Trinidad

Emperor Valley Zoo, Royal Botanical Gardens, Port of Spain.

Tunisia

Parc Zoologique, Tunis.

Turkey

Zoo-Külturpark, Izmin.

USSR ﹨

Alma-Atinskii Zoopark, Klevernaya ul. 166, Alma-Ata, Kazakhstan.

Turkmenistan Dovlet Zoologi Bogy, ul. Engelsa 51, Ashkabad, Turkmenistan.

Zoologicheskii Park Askaniya-Nova, Askaniya-Nova, Ukraine.

Bogi Khaivonoti Dushanbe, Putovskii spusk, Dushanbe, Tadzhikstan.

Grodznenski Dzyarzhauny Zaalagichny Park, ul. Timiryazeva 17, Byelorussia Grodno.

Respublikinis Zoologijos Sodas, 16-tos Divijos pl. 21, Kaunas, Lithuania.

Khar'kovskii Zoologicheskii Park, Sumskaya ul. 35, Khar'kov, Ukraine.

Kievskii Zoologicheskii Park, Brest-Litovskii prospekt 80/2, Kiev, Ukraine.

Leningradskii Zoologicheskii Park, Park Lenina 1, Leningrad.

Moskovskii Zoologicheskii Park, Bolshaya Gruzinskaya ul. 1, Moscow.

Odesskii Zoologicheskii Park, Estonskaya pl. 25, Odessa, Ukraine.

Rigas Zoologiskais Darzs, Mežapark prospekt 1, Riga, Latvia.

Tallinna Loomaaed, ul. Mäekalda 45, Tallin, Estonia.

Tashkent Khaivonot Bogi, ul. Khamida Alimdzhana 23, Tashkent, Uzbekistan.

United Arab Republic

Zoological Garden, Alexandria.

Zoological Gardens, Giza.

USA

Baltimore Zoo, Druid Hill Park, Baltimore, Maryland.

Birmingham Zoo, 2630 Cahaba Road, Birmingham, Alabama.

Buffalo Zoological Gardens, Delaware Park, Buffalo, New York.

Chicago Zoological Park (Brookfield Zoo), Brookfield, Chicago, Illinois.

Lincoln Park Zoological Gardens, 100 W. Webster Avenue, Chicago, Illinois.

Cincinnati Zoological Society Inc., 3400 Vine Street, Cincinnati, Ohio.

Cleveland Zoological Park, Brookside Park, Cleveland, Ohio.

Columbus Zoological Gardens, 9990 Riverside Drive, Columbus, Ohio.

Dallas Zoo in Marsalis Park, 621 E. Clarendon Drive, Dallas, Texas.

Denver Zoological Gardens, City Park, Denver, Colorado.

Detroit Zoological Park, 8450 W. 10 Mile Road, Royal Oak, Detroit, Michigan.

Mesker Park Zoo, Bement Avenue, Evansville, Indiana.

Fort Wayne Children's Zoological Gardens, 3411 N. Sherman Street, Fort Wayne, Indiana. (closed winter)

Fort Worth Zoological Park, 2727 Zoological Park Drive, Fort Worth, Texas.

Roeding Park Zoo, 890 W. Belmont Avenue, Fresno, California.

Brit Spaugh Zoo, N. Main Street, Great Bend, Kansas.

Honolulu Zoo, Waikiki Beach, Kapiolani Park, Honolulu, Hawaii.

Houston Zoological Gardens, 509 City Hall, Houston Texas.

Indianapolis Zoological Park, 3120 E. 30 Street, Indianapolis, Indiana.

Jacksonville Zoological Park, 8605 Zoo Road, Jacksonville, Florida.

Kansas City Zoological Gardens, Swope Park, Kansas City, Missouri.

Paddling Ponds, (private, visits by arrangement), Litchfield, Connecticut.

The Los Angeles Zoo, 5333 Zoo Drive, Los Angeles, California.

Louisville Zoological Garden, 1100 Trevilian Way, Louisville, Kentucky.

Crandon Park Zoo, 4000 Crandon Boulevard, Key Biscayne, Miami, Florida.

Milwaukee County Zoological Park, 10001 W. Bluemound Road, Milwaukee, Wisconsin.

Louisiana Purchase Gardens & Zoo, Thomas Street, Monroe, Louisiana.

Audubon Park Zoo, Audubon Park, New Orleans, Louisiana.

New York Zoological Park (Bronx Zoo), 185 Street and Southern Boulevard, New York, New York.

Oklahoma City Zoo, Oklahoma City, Oklahoma.

Duck Puddle Farm (private collection), Berry Hill Road, Oyster Bay, New York.

Philadelphia Zoological Garden, 34 Street and Girard Avenue, Philadelphia, Pennsylvania.

Phoenix Zoo, 60 Street and E. Van Buren, Phoenix, Arizona.

Seneca Park Zoo, 2222 St Paul Street, Rochester, New York.

St Louis Zoological Park, Forest Park, St Louis, Missouri.

Salisbury Zoological Garden, Salisbury, Maryland.

Jean Delacour World Waterfowl and Game Bird Preservation Center, 1155E 4780S, Salt Lake City, Utah.

San Antonio Zoological Garden, 3903 N. St Mary's, San Antonio, Texas.

San Diego Zoological Garden, Balboa Park, San Diego, California.

San Francisco Zoological Gardens, Zoo Road and Skyline Boulevard, San Francisco, California.

Woodland Park Zoological Gardens, 5400 Phinney Avenue, Seattle, Washington.

Great Plains Zoo, 15th and Kiwanis, Sioux Falls, South Dakota.

Walter D. Stone Memorial Zoo, 149 Pond Street, Stoneham, Massachusetts.

Busch Gardens Zoological Park, 3000 Busch Boulevard, Tampa, Florida.

Toledo Zoological Gardens, 2700 Broadway, Toledo, Ohio.

Topeka Zoological Park, 635 Gage Boulevard, Topeka, Kansas.

Randolph Park Zoo, 900 Randolph Way, Tucson, Arizona.

Busch Gardens, 16000 Roscoe Boulevard, Van Nuys, California.

Washington National Zoological Park, Smithsonian Institution, Washington, District of Columbia.

Turtle Back Zoo, 560 Northfield Avenue, West Orange, New Jersey.

Yugoslavia
Zooloski Vrt Grada Zagreba, Zagreb

Bibliography

Ali, S. and Ripley, S. D. *Handbook of the Birds of India and Pakistan*. Volume 1. Oxford University Press, Oxford, 1968.

Atkinson-Willes, G. L. (Ed.). Wildfowl in Great Britain. HMSO, London, 1963.

Bannerman, D. A. *The Birds of West Equatorial Africa* (Two vols). Oliver and Boyd, Edinburgh, 1953.

Bannerman, D. A. and Lodge, G. E. *The Birds of the British Isles*. Vols 6 and 7. Oliver and Boyd, Edinburgh, 1953–63.

Bannerman, D. A. and Vella-Gaffiero, J. A. *Birds of the Maltese Archipelago*. Museums Department, Malta, 1976.

Carp, E. (Ed.) (1972). *Proceedings of International Conference on Conservation of Wetlands and Waterfowl, Ramsar, 1971*. International Wildfowl Research Bureau, Slimbridge.

Coward, T. A. and Barnes, J. A. G. (Eds). *Birds of the British Isles and their Eggs*. Warne, London, 1969.

Cramp, S. and Simmons, K. E. L. (Eds). *The Birds of the Western Palaearctic*. Vol. 1. Oxford University Press, Oxford, 1977.

Delacour, J. *The Waterfowl of the World* (Four vols). Country Life, London, 1954–64.

Etchéopar, R. D. and Hüe, F. *The Birds of North Africa*. Oliver and Boyd, Edinburgh, 1967.

Fisher, J., Simon, N. and Vincent, J. *The Red Book*. Collins, Glasgow, 1969.

Frith, H. J. *Waterfowl in Australia*. Angus and Robertson, Sydney, 1967.

Godfrey, W. E. *The Birds of Canada*. National Museum of Canada, Ottawa, 1966.

Gooders, J. (Ed.). *Birds of the World*. 1. 1969.

Humphrey, P. S., Bridge, D., Reynolds, P. W. and Peterson, R. T. *Birds of Isla Grande (Tierra del Fuego)*. University of Kansas Museum of Natural History for the Smithsonian Institute.

Johnson, A. W. *Birds of Chile and Adjacent Regions* (Two vols and Supplement). Platt Establecimientos Gráficos, Buenos Aires, 1965–72.

Landsborough-Thomson, A. (Ed.). *A New Dictionary of Birds*. Thomas Nelson, London, 1964.

Mackworth-Praed, C. W. and Grant, C. H. B. *African Handbook of Birds*. Longmans, London, 1952.

Ogilvie, M. A. *Ducks of Britain and Europe*. T. and A. D. Poyser, Berkhamsted, 1975.

Olney, P. J. S. (Ed.) (1965). *List of European and North African Wetlands of International Importance*. Project Mar. IUCN Publications. New Series, 5.

Owen, M. *Wildfowl of Europe*. Macmillan, London, 1977.

Palmer, R. S. (Ed.). *Handbook of North American Birds*. Vols 2 and 3. Yale University Press 1976.

Roberts, A. *Birds of South Africa* (Revised edition, 5th impression 1965). The Central News Agency, Capetown, 1940.

Schauensee, R. M. de. *A Guide to the Birds of South America*. Livingston Publishing Co.. Philadelphia. 1970.

Scott. P. and The Wildfowl Trust. *The Swans*. Michael Joseph. London. 1972.

Sharrock, J. T. R. *The Atlas of Breeding Birds of Britain and Ireland*. British Trust for Ornithology, 1976.

Smart, M. (Ed.) (1976). *Proceedings of International Conference on Conservation of Wetlands and Waterfowl, Heiligenhafen, 1974.* International Wildfowl Research Bureau, Slimbridge.

Snow, D. W. (Ed.). *The Status of Birds in Britain and Ireland.* Blackwell Scientific Publications, Oxford, 1971.

Snyder, L. L. *Arctic Birds of Canada.* University of Toronto Press, Toronto, 1957.

Vaurie, C. *The Birds of the Palaearctic Fauna* (Two vols). H. F. and G. Witherby, London, 1959–65.

Voous, K. H. *Atlas of European Birds.* Thomas Nelson, London, 1959.

Wildfowl Trust. *Wildfowl.* Annual Reports, Slimbridge, 1947 to date.

Zoological Society of London. *The International Zoo Year Book.* Vol. 12. Lucas, J. and Duplaix-Hall, N. (Eds). London, 1972.
Zoological Society of London. *The International Zoo Year Book.* Vol. 13. Duplaix-Hall, N. (Ed.). London, 1973.

Index of English Names

For the majority of entries in the indexes, the page numbers refer to the principal description of each bird, and for the 128 species which are illustrated, the colour photograph is located on the facing page.

Species are indexed under their main grouping, i.e. Duck, Goose Swan, Teal, etc., with the individual names as sub-entries. Exceptions to this are the larger groups of ducks, (Wood Ducks, Tree Ducks, Whistling Ducks, etc.) which are indexed as main entries.

[295]

Index of Latin Names

See page 1 for an explanation of the families and genera of wildfowl.

[296]

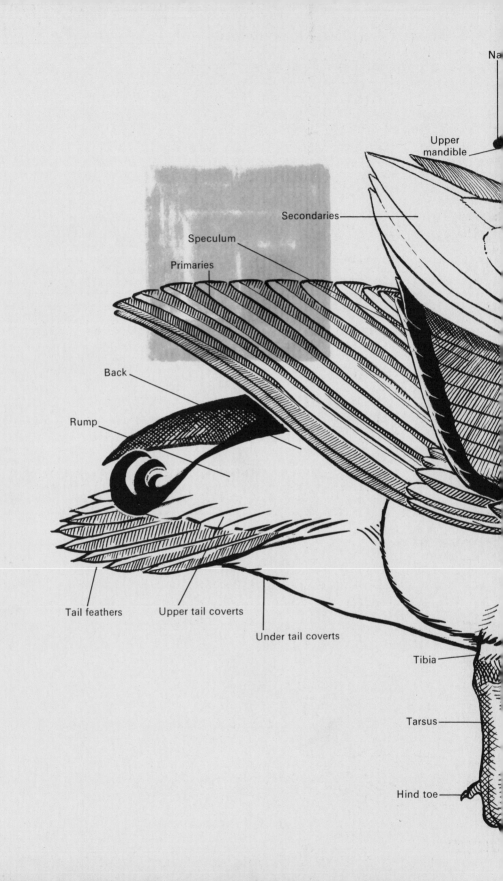

Na

Upper
mandible

Secondaries

Speculum

Primaries

Back

Rump

Tail feathers

Upper tail coverts

Under tail coverts

Tibia

Tarsus

Hind toe